The Encyclopedia of
NORTH
AMERICAN
ANIMALS

The Encyclopedia of
NORTH
AMERICAN
ANIMALS

BRYAN RICHARD

BARNES & NOBLE BOOKS
NEW YORK

This edition published by Barnes & Noble Publishing, Inc.,
by arrangement with Parragon Publishing.

2005 Barnes & Noble Books

M 10 9 8 7 6 5 4 3 2 1

ISBN 0-7607-7275-4

For details of photographs see pages 382/383

Produced by Atlantic Publishing
Designed by Judy Linard

Printed and bound in China

CONTENTS

INTRODUCTION

From the snowy tundra of Alaska to the wetlands of Florida, through the more arid Great Plains, North America's diverse habitats teem with wildlife at every level of the environmental web. Included here are all the most common and the most remarkable of the multiplicity of fauna that inhabit the lands and waters of North America: from the Bald Eagle, that soaring, majestic specimen symbolic of US national identity, to the tiniest, most delicate of insects, the Green Lacewing.

Identification

Virtually every species selected for inclusion is photographically illustrated with a stunning clarity that aids identification of even the smallest animal. The beauty of a Painted Lady butterfly is captured as vividly as the majesty and splendor of the Polar Bear or the fierceness of the tiny orange and black insect, the Bee Assassin, which preys on bees, immobilizing them by injecting a chemical agent and then sucking out their insides.

In addition to visual images, for each creature, information panels specify the scientific name, size, habitat and range, identifying features, and ways to distinguish between similar species. These details are further elaborated through explanations about life styles, life cycles and behavior. We come to understand that the Star-nosed Mole is highly aquatic, eating small fish as well as earthworms and insects, but is also able to live off fat reserves in its tail when frozen ground makes burrowing for food difficult. We learn that the Gray Catbird, which earns its common name from the fact that its normal call sounds like the mewing of a domestic cat, is an excellent mimic, copying the calls of other birds in the vicinity.

Range maps

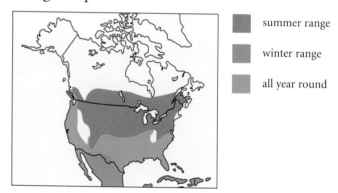

summer range

winter range

all year round

A series of maps inset into the photographs indicates habitat and range for those mammals, reptiles, birds, insects and fish not found across the whole of North America. For migratory creatures such as the Ruddy Duck, maps are color-coded to show winter, summer and all-year-round ranges: green for all-year-round; red for summer; blue for winter. Although some animals do make slight variations in range when the vagaries of weather or a creature's innate positioning system takes it off course, the maps will show the most likely species within a particular area. As such they are useful means of making decisive identification. For example the females of the summer-visiting birds, the Scarlet Tanager and the Summer Tanager, are similar in appearance, and although there is some slight overlap they have quite distinctive ranges; the Summer Tanager is to be found in woods across the whole of the southern United States, while the Scarlet Tanager inhabits the forests of the east to the north of the Carolinas.

Scope and groupings

Although it is not possible to incorporate every single species of creature to be found in North America, included is a vast scope and array which provide insight into the rich and varied wildlife of these lands. There are sections on mammals, reptiles, amphibians, fish, invertebrates and birds. For details on the latter category much gratitude is due to Michael Vanner, author of *The Encyclopedia of North American Birds*. Within each of these large sections individual species are, where possible, grouped according to their taxonomical relationships. The main heading for each entry gives the common name, with the scientific, or Latin, name given in the information box. The scientific name is given in two parts: the genus, which indicates a closely related group, and the species name which identifies a specific creature. Thus, in *Canis lupus*, *Canis* describes a wolf and *lupus* indicates specifically the Gray Wolf, as opposed to *Canis rufus* which is the Red Wolf.

Ethics of wildlife observation

Observing wild animals in their environment is a fascinating and rewarding experience. However, it is important to always be aware that human presence will have an impact upon creature life, behavior and habitat. Although it is impossible to avoid some disturbance, try to minimize it and be aware that actions such as making excessive noise, leaving litter, trampling brush or grass can have seriously detrimental effects. Remember too that while observing one creature you could be causing damage to the habitat of another creature in nature's delicate web! Over the last few hundred years many North American species have become extinct as a result of the destruction of their habitat by human activity. Many more have become endangered; although there have been notable success stories, like that of the Bald Eagle whose numbers dropped perilously low in the 1970s but have since recovered through careful conservation.

MAMMALS

VIRGINIA OPOSSUM

Scientific name:	*Didelphis virginiana*
Identification:	Around the size of a domestic cat, but rat-like in appearance; long, pointed snout and large, hairless ears and tail. Gray, grizzled fur with white face
Length (including tail):	22–40 inches
Weight:	6–14lb
Habitat/range:	Woodland, farmland, suburban and urban areas across most eastern and central states and along the Pacific coast. Currently extending its range northwards
Similar species:	None

The Virginia Opossum is the only marsupial (pouched mammal) to be found in North America. After a gestation period of around only two weeks, the female typically bears up to fourteen young, which she then carries and weans inside her pouch for two months. Following this, the juveniles ride around on their mother's back for a further two to three weeks, transferring to a highly varied diet of carrion, insects, amphibians and reptiles, small mammals, birds and their eggs, as well as various fruits and grains. When threatened by predators or rivals, opossums exhibit various defenses, including loud clicking and hissing, salivating, the baring of their many teeth, and of course, "playing possum", whereby the animal will feign death, sometimes entering a catatonic state for several hours. Solitary, nocturnal and good climbers with their prehensile tails, opossums often escape the attention of man. However their scavenging behavior has seen the species expanding into suburban and urban areas and has unfortunately increased the likelihood of encountering them as road-kill.

NINE-BANDED ARMADILLO

Scientific name:	*Dasypus novemcinctus*
Identification:	Yellowish-brown, with a long snout, erect ears, short legs and a long tail. Bony plates cover top of head, body and tail
Length (including tail):	25–35 inches
Weight:	10–15lb
Habitat/Range:	Sandy woodland or brush areas in south-eastern states from Texas to Florida
Similar species:	None

The Nine-banded Armadillo is unmistakable amongst North American mammals due to its scaly armor plating. It takes its name from the nine or so narrow, jointed plates which cover its midsection and which allow enough flexibility for the armadillo to curl into a ball to protect its soft underside when threatened. More often than not however, a startled armadillo will either bound vertically into the air before running for the safety of its burrow, or attempt to dig one on the spot, both of which it can achieve with surprising speed. Armadillos are not strictly nocturnal but tend to be so in hotter weather, spending their waking hours digging burrows or searching for food underground and amongst leaf litter, rotting logs or vegetation. The armadillo's diet consists mainly of insects, but it will also eat carrion, reptile and bird eggs, amphibians and crayfish, being undeterred by water and able to swim short distances. When breeding, armadillos will form a nest of grass or leaves within their burrows, giving birth to four, identical, same-sex young, which are born able to see and can walk within hours. The hard bony plating is not present initially but slowly forms as the young develop.

EASTERN OR "COMMON MOLE"

Scientific name:	*Scalopus aquaticus*
Identification:	Short, dense, velvety fur, varying from gray in northern range to golden-brown elsewhere. Broad, spade-like forepaws with slightly webbed toes and a short, naked tail
Length (including tail):	5–9 inches
Weight:	3–5oz
Habitat/Range:	Fields, meadows, lawns and woodland with light, well-drained soil, throughout most eastern states
Similar species:	Similar to most other species of mole found in the US, but can be distinguished from those found within its range, such as the Hairy-tailed mole, by its naked tail

The Eastern Mole spends the majority of its life underground and as such is less frequently seen than the evidence of its presence; the mole hills and surface ridges which it forms whilst burrowing its shallow tunnels in search of food. Its diet consists chiefly of worms but the Eastern Mole will eat various subterranean insects and their larvae, feeding most actively after rain, in the early morning or late evening. A solitary and sometimes aggressive species, the Eastern Mole will avoid contact with other individuals until the breeding season in early spring and following mating the female will retreat to a nest chamber in a deeper, more permanent burrow, where some four weeks later she will give birth to a litter of up to five, naked young. The Eastern Mole does not hibernate in winter but it will seek refuge in one of its deeper tunnels.

STAR-NOSED MOLE ▲

Scientific name:	*Condylura cristata*
Identification:	Black, velvety fur, large forepaws typical of moles, with a long, hairy tail and distinctive star-shaped projections around its nose
Length (including tail):	6–8 inches
Weight:	1–2oz
Habitat/Range:	Wet grasslands, woodlands and marshes in eastern states, from the Great Lakes area of Canada, southeast to the Georgia coast
Similar species:	Easily distinguished from other moles by the tendril-like appendages around its nose

The Star-nosed Mole differs from the majority of mole species in a number of ways, most noticeably in appearance, sporting a number of sensitive, fleshy protrusions around the tip of its nose which are used to detect prey. As with other moles the diet of the Star-nosed Mole is mainly made up of earthworms, but it is also highly aquatic and will catch prey such as small fish, particularly when frozen ground in winter may make burrowing for insects more difficult. The Star-nosed Mole also uses its tail as a fat reserve, which thickens in winter to provide energy when breeding in spring or at times when food may be scarce. A litter of up to seven young are born in late spring or summer and develop rapidly, able to leave the shelter of their nest after only three weeks.

MASKED/CINEREUS SHREW

Scientific name:	*Sorex cinereus*
Identification:	A very small, long-tailed shrew with a pointed snout and tiny ears. Gray-brown in color with a more silvery underside. The tail may be nearly half its overall length, is lighter on the underside and has a dark tip, though this may not always be apparent
Length (including tail):	3–4 inches
Weight:	$\frac{1}{16} - \frac{1}{2}$ oz
Habitat/Range:	Found in all kinds of habitat throughout Canada, (except in the far north) and across the northern US, but preferring relatively damp brush, woods, grasslands and marshes
Similar species:	Of the similar species within its range, the Masked Shrew may be distinguished from the Southeastern Shrew, which is smaller and has a shorter tail, and the Vagrant Shrew, which tends to have lighter-colored flanks

Of the thirty or so species of shrew found in North America, the Masked or Cinereus Shrew is amongst the most widely distributed, with the majority of other species being fairly limited in their range. In fact, it is thought to populate a more diverse assortment of habitats than perhaps any other mammal in North America, though it is most likely to be found in moist, vegetated areas. The Masked Shrew, like all species of shrew has an incredibly high metabolism and is almost constantly searching for food, frequently eating its own bodyweight in insects, spiders, slugs, snails and worms in a single day. As with most shrews, this species is active throughout the winter and typically breeds from spring to late summer, producing around six, but sometimes as many as ten young, which are weaned within three weeks of birth.

NORTHERN SHORT-TAILED ▲ SHREW

Scientific name:	*Blarina brevicauda*
Identification:	Large, dark gray shrew with short tail
Length (including tail):	4–5 inches
Weight:	$\frac{1}{2}$ – 1oz
Habitat/Range:	Woodland, grasslands and marshes, throughout southeastern Canada and north-eastern US, south to Kentucky and Alabama
Similar species:	Most similar to the Southern Short-tailed Shrew, but usually larger

LEAST SHREW

Scientific name:	*Cryptotis parva*
Identification:	A very small brown shrew with a pale underside and a tiny tail
Length (including tail):	3–3$\frac{1}{2}$ inches
Weight:	$\frac{1}{8}$ – $\frac{1}{4}$oz
Habitat/Range:	Moist grasslands and woodlands, though less common in marshland than many species. Found throughout the eastern half of the US
Similar species:	Similar to the Short-tailed Shrew, but smaller and brown rather than gray in color

The Northern Short-tailed Shrew is both the largest shrew, and amongst the most common of all mammals to be found in North America. However, as with all shrew species it is secretive and not easily encountered, spending much of its time in underground burrows in which it searches for worms, slugs and various insects. It is also interesting to note that this species and others of the genus *Blarina* are unique amongst mammals, in that they produce venomous saliva which may help them to overcome larger prey such as smaller shrews and young mice. Large nests are made amongst dense vegetation or under tree stumps and logs, where litters of up to eight young are produced, sometimes more than once per year.

Unusual amongst most shrew species, the Least Shrew can be highly sociable, with up to thirty individuals inhabiting a single burrow or nest at any one time, particularly throughout the winter and during breeding. Nests are usually ball-shaped structures formed of grass and leaves and tend to be hidden away beneath logs or tree stumps. Females give birth to litters of four or five young and may produce several litters per year. The Least Shrew is perhaps more nocturnal than most shrew species, but it remains a voracious hunter, feeding on insects and their larvae, worms and spiders. The Least Shrew is also known to enter and even to nest in beehives where it will feed on bees and their young, and hence it is sometimes referred to as the "bee shrew" or "bee mole".

MUSKRAT

Scientific name:	*Ondatra zibethicus*
Identification:	Fairly large aquatic rodent, ruddy-brown with a pale belly, large partly webbed hind feet and a long, narrow, scaly tail
Length (including tail):	18–25 inches
Weight:	2–4lb
Habitat/Range:	Ponds, lakes, slow-flowing rivers and marshland across North America, except for the extreme north, Florida and driest southern states
Similar species:	Smaller than both the Beaver and Nutria, and with a flattened tail which is higher than it is wide

Muskrats are more closely related to voles and lemmings than they are to beavers but they exhibit similar behavior when it comes to building their homes. Although they will occupy burrows in lake or riverbanks, Muskrats also construct lodges in much the same way as beavers, albeit on a smaller scale, utilising grasses and reeds rather than large tree branches. Muskrats are normally solitary but will sometimes share these dwellings, though they will become territorial whilst breeding. Breeding takes place throughout the year, except during the coldest months in the northernmost extent of its range. Litters of up to eleven young are not uncommon and a female may produce several litters each year, with the offspring becoming independent at about one month. Muskrats feed on most aquatic vegetation but will also take crustaceans and amphibians at times.

NUTRIA/COYPU

Scientific name:	*Myocastor coypus*
Identification:	Large aquatic rodent, brown back, usually paler underneath and white around the snout and chin. Large, webbed hind feet, and with a long, rounded, nearly hairless tail
Length (including tail):	$2\frac{1}{2}$ – $4\frac{1}{2}$ feet
Weight:	10–25lbs
Habitat/Range:	Ponds, lakes, marshlands and swamps in scattered populations across the US
Similar species:	Larger than the muskrat, which also has a narrow flattened tail, and smaller than the beaver, whose tail is broad and flat

The Nutria is not a native species and was first introduced to the US from South America for its fur, but it has also been released in certain areas in order to clear waterways of vegetation. As such, the Nutria has been useful to man, but is also considered a pest as it can cause extensive damage to crops, and it breeds prolifically, competing with native muskrats. The Nutria burrows into bank-sides but will occupy existing muskrat or beaver burrows and may also be found on raised feeding platforms above water, amidst rushes or similar vegetation. In warm climates Nutria will breed throughout the year, sometimes producing as many as ten offspring per litter, which are well developed and able to swim and eat plant material within twenty-four hours of birth.

(American) Beaver

Scientific name:	*Castor Canadensis*
Identification:	Large, brown, aquatic rodent with prominent, orange incisors, webbed hind feet and large, scaly, flattened tail
Length (including tail):	3–4½ feet
Weight:	30–60lb+
Habitat/Range:	Various inland waters, from ponds to lakes and rivers, but prefer slow-moving water. Found throughout Canada and the US except in the far northern reaches of Canada, much of Florida, and the deserts of California and Nevada
Similar species:	Similar to the Muskrat and Nutria, but considerably larger with a wide, horizontally flattened tail

Once threatened with extinction across much of the US due to excessive trapping, the Beaver is once more widespread. It is the largest rodent in North America and is highly specialized to lead an aquatic existence, using its large webbed feet and rudder-like tail to swim powerfully through the water. Its ears and nostrils can be closed when diving and beavers can remain submerged for around 15 minutes at a time. Beavers tend to live in bank-side burrows along faster-flowing rivers but in quieter waters they build quite complex dams and lodges. Felling nearby trees with their strong front teeth and floating or carrying branches to their chosen site, beavers construct large dome-like homes up to six feet high, where the female will give birth to around four or five young in early summer, after a gestation period of around four months. The kits will remain with the parents, which usually pair for life, for about two years. Beavers typically feed on leaves, bark and other vegetation and will store food underwater as a winter reserve. Still regarded by some as a pest, beavers are however, increasingly respected as being fundamental to the maintenance of important wetland ecosystems.

Woodchuck/"Groundhog"

Scientific name:	*Marmota monax*
Identification:	Large, stocky rodent with short legs, dark brown or black feet and a short, bushy tail. Usually grizzled brown
Length (including tail):	18–30 inches
Weight:	5–12lb
Habitat/Range:	Meadows, pastures and open woodland from British Columbia, across southern Canada and much of north, central and east of US
Similar species:	Within its range, only likely to be confused with the Hoary Marmot, but this species is silver-gray with distinctive black and white facial markings, or the Yellow-bellied Marmot which tends to occur further south and has a yellowish underside

Legend has it that the Woodchuck emerges from hibernation on February the 2nd each year, that is, "Groundhog Day". However in many areas it will not appear until later in the spring, when it is warmer. The Woodchuck hibernates for some six months of the year in a grass-lined burrow, relying on fat reserves which it will have built up in late summer. Upon waking, the male will immediately seek a mate, who will give birth to a litter of four or five young after a gestation period of 28 days. Woodchucks feed on grass and other green plants such as clover, and although ground-dwelling, may escape from potential predators by climbing trees. They are solitary, diurnal animals and tend to be highly alert, often sitting upright on the lookout for danger, emitting a shrill whistle when threatened, before taking refuge in their burrows.

Yellow-bellied Marmot ▶

Scientific name:	*Marmota flaviventris*
Identification:	Stocky, bushy-tailed rodent, very much like the Woodchuck in overall body-shape. Yellow-brown or gray in color, with yellow underside, a white patch between the eyes and light brown feet
Length (including tail):	18–28 inches
Weight:	5–10lb
Habitat / Range:	Rocky hills and valley slopes from British Columbia, south through western US
Similar species:	Usually smaller and differing in color from the Woodchuck and Hoary Marmot

The Yellow-bellied Marmot is very much like the Woodchuck in appearance and habit, though it tends to be smaller, with yellow coloration and a slightly bushier tail. Like the Woodchuck, this species will hibernate for around six months of the year and when active prefers to graze on grass and other vegetation during the day, though it will take shelter in a burrow when it is extremely warm. The Yellow-bellied Marmot differs from its relative in terms of habitat, however, tending to make its burrows beneath rocky outcrops on alpine slopes rather than in lowland meadows, and it is also a highly sociable animal, living in small colonies of perhaps thirty or more individuals.

BLACK-TAILED PRAIRIE DOG ▶

Scientific name:	*Cynomys ludovicianus*
Identification:	Large ground squirrel, yellowish or buff in color with a pale or white underside and short, black-tipped tail
Length (including tail):	14–16½ inches
Weight:	2–3lb
Habitat / Range:	Prairies, short-grass plains from Montana, south through central US to Arizona, New Mexico and Texas
Similar species:	Only prairie dog which has a black tail tip

Amongst the most sociable of all mammals, at one time Black-tailed Prairie Dog colonies or "towns" extended across many miles of the Great Plains and may have been home to millions of individuals. However, many were culled as ranchers began to see them as competition to grazing cattle herds. Today the animals still remain in significant numbers though, living in large groups divided into families, maintaining social bonds through grooming, touching noses and numerous vocal calls, including the dog-like bark from which they get their name. Their burrows are extensive and the openings are usually marked by large mounds of excavated earth which act as vantage points. Vegetation around burrow entrances is also cropped short. Prairie dogs eat a variety of grasses, but will also eat insects such as grasshoppers. Burrows contain many chambers and females will give birth to around four or five young in an underground nest in spring, where they will remain for about six weeks before beginning to venture outside.

WHITE-TAILED PRAIRIE DOG

Scientific name:	*Cynomys leucurus*
Identification:	Buff with white underside and short, white-tipped tail, black spots above and below eyes
Length (including tail):	13–14½ inches
Weight:	1½–2½ lb
Habitat / Range:	Mountain meadows at high altitude in Wyoming, south into Utah and Colorado
Similar species:	Differs from other prairie dogs due to its white tail-tip and facial markings

Unlike the Black-tailed Prairie Dog, the White-tailed Prairie Dog is active for only half the year, living at higher, colder altitudes and hibernating throughout the long winter months. It is also a less gregarious animal, living in smaller groups and displaying less interactivity, though it remains highly vocal, particularly in warning others of its kind of potential danger, most often from birds of prey. The White-tailed Prairie Dog is also preyed upon by snakes and carnivorous mammals such as the Coyote and Bobcat. White-tailed Prairie Dogs themselves feed on grasses, but also on coarse alpine vegetation, consuming great quantities in preparation for hibernation. In spring females produce a litter of around five young which will emerge from the relative safety of the burrow in early summer.

EASTERN GRAY SQUIRREL

Scientific name:	*Sciurus carolinensis*
Identification:	Gray with red-brown tinged fur on head, shoulders, back, tail and feet. Lighter underside. May occur in black form in north
Length (including tail):	16–20 inches
Weight:	1–1½ lb
Habitat/Range:	Mixed or deciduous forests, urban and suburban parks and gardens, across southern Canada and the eastern US, with introduced populations in the northwest
Similar species:	Smaller than the Eastern Fox Squirrel, whilst Western Gray Squirrel has a whiter belly and is usually more silvery

Probably the most commonly encountered mammal in North America, the Eastern Gray Squirrel is active throughout the year, but especially in the fall when it can be seen eagerly gathering and burying nuts to see it through the winter months. These squirrels are particularly fond of acorns, walnuts and beechnuts, but will eat a wide variety of seeds, bark, buds and fruit depending on that which is most readily available. The Eastern Gray is a tree-dwelling species and makes its home in tree cavities, but also builds nests of twigs and leaves where it will tend to raise its summer litter, the first, in spring, being likely to be born in a more permanent hole or hideaway within a tree. Litters usually average two to three young, and are cared for solely by the female. The similar **Western Gray Squirrel** (*Sciurus griseus*) is found only in forests along the Pacific Coast, is often slightly larger and shuns human attention.

The **Eastern Fox Squirrel** (*Sciurus niger*), exhibits much the same behavior as the Eastern Gray, and is found across a similar range and habitat, but is the largest North American tree squirrel and may be up to twice the size and weight. It also tends to be somewhat more colorful, with a yellow underside and face and a rusty-brown tail. The Fox Squirrel is frequently tamer, but does prefer more open woods or parkland and is thus less at home in many urban areas. In the south of its range the Eastern Fox Squirrel may be found in mangrove swamps. They are considered to be endangered in some locations.

Another gray tree squirrel which occurs in the west is **Abert's Squirrel**, or the "Tassel-eared Squirrel". This squirrel is fairly large, up to around 2lb in weight and inhabits coniferous forests in mountainous areas of Utah, Colorado, New Mexico and Arizona. Abert's Squirrel is dark gray with a reddish back and has distinctive ear tufts. It produces litters of around four young between spring and summer, sometimes reproducing more than once a year.

Opposite: Abert's Squirrel
Above: The Eastern Gray Squirrel

RED SQUIRREL ◄ SOUTHERN FLYING SQUIRREL

Scientific name:	*Tamiasciurus hudsonicus*
Identification:	Small tree squirrel, red or rusty brown with a white belly. Ear tufts in winter
Length (including tail):	10–15 inches
Weight:	5–9oz
Habitat/Range:	Coniferous, deciduous and mixed forests across Canada and northern parts of the US, south through the Rocky Mountains
Similar species:	Douglas' Squirrel is more brown than red, with an orange or gray underside

Scientific name:	*Glaucomys volans*
Identification:	Small tree-dwelling squirrel, gray-brown back, with white underside. Loose folds of skin along each side between front and rear legs, edged with black. Tail is flattened
Length (including tail):	8–10 inches
Weight:	2–3½ oz
Habitat/Range:	Deciduous forests from the Great Lakes in southern Canada throughout eastern US, excluding southern Florida
Similar species:	Northern Flying Squirrel is almost identical but prefers coniferous forests, is slightly larger and the underside is gray and white

All tree squirrels share much in common in terms of behavior; nest building, diet and so on, but the Red Squirrel is particularly striking in appearance and is perhaps more vocal than other tree-dwelling squirrels, chattering and emitting shrill calls at the first sign of any perceived danger. Abundant in coniferous woodland, Red Squirrels are especially fond of pine seeds, and stripped pine cones are a good sign of their presence. They also eat a variety of other seeds, nuts, berries, fungi and sugary sap, and will also eat birds' eggs. In common with other tree squirrels, Red Squirrels will occasionally take nestlings if the opportunity arises. Active at all times of the year, the Red Squirrel stores food, but unlike gray squirrels, will hoard food in caches in the ground or in tree hollows, rather than burying individual nuts or acorns. Typically reproducing twice a year, once in spring and again in summer, litters average four or five young.

Gliding from tree to tree, the Southern Flying Squirrel uses the membranes between its fore and hind legs rather like a parachute, and does not actually fly. Unusual amongst tree squirrels, it is a nocturnal species and also an aggressive hunter, preying on moths, other insects and small vertebrates, though it also eats and hoards seed, nuts and berries in much the same way as other tree squirrels. Like the Red Squirrel, the Southern Flying Squirrel also enjoys the sap from maple trees. It does not hibernate, but in winter may enter a deep sleep, maintaining body temperature by sharing a nest with several other individuals. It makes its home in hollow trees, favoring disused woodpecker holes, but may also make leaf nests in the summer. Females are sexually active for only one day of the year in spring and produce a litter of 2–6 young after a gestation period of around forty days.

ROCK SQUIRREL

Scientific name:	*Spermophilus variegates*
Identification:	Large ground squirrel, mottled gray-brown with lighter underside. Long, bushy tail
Length (including tail):	17–20 inches
Weight:	1–2lb
Habitat/Range:	Rocky canyons and hillsides in southwestern US
Similar species:	Can be distinguished from other ground squirrels in its range due to its large size, also has the bushiest tail amongst ground squirrels

The Rock Squirrel is ground-dwelling, making its burrow beneath rocks in canyons and gorges, though it is a good climber and will scale the juniper bushes and oak trees, which it tends to live close to, in search of food. Generally active throughout the year, except in colder locations where they may hibernate briefly, Rock Squirrels usually gather food in the morning and late afternoon, avoiding the hottest part of the day, though they can often be seen basking on rocks close to their dens. Rock Squirrels feed on nuts, berries, fruit and cacti and will store food within their burrows. Living in small colonies, there are usually main burrows occupied by females and juveniles, with a dominant male and other males living close by in the surrounding territory. Rock Squirrels produce two litters of 4-8 young per year, usually from spring to early summer and again from late summer to fall.

GOLDEN-MANTLED GROUND SQUIRREL

Scientific name:	*Spermophilus lateralis*
Identification:	Gray-brown back, red or copper head and shoulders, light belly. One white stripe on each flank, bordered with black
Length (including tail):	9–12 inches
Weight:	6–10oz
Habitat/Range:	Mountain forests in Canada and western US
Similar species:	Sometimes mistaken for a chipmunk, but larger and lacking stripes on face

Often living in close proximity to the Uinta Chipmunk, the Golden-mantled Ground Squirrel is sometimes mistaken for a chipmunk itself, being similar in coloration. Like chipmunks it is also a burrowing species, but lacks their tree-climbing skills. Its burrow, which can extend for anything up to 100 feet, usually opens amongst the roots of a tree or similar cover and it is here that the squirrel will spend many months of the year dormant, though sometimes waking to feed on hoarded food. The Golden-mantled Ground Squirrel eats a variety of seeds, fruit and nuts and also some insects and fungi. Sometimes hibernating for seven months, they produce only one litter per year of 4-6 young, which are born in May or June.

THIRTEEN-LINED GROUND SQUIRREL

Scientific name:	*Spermophilus tridecemlineatus*
Identification:	Brown or tan with thirteen alternate light and dark stripes on back, partly broken into spots
Length (including tail):	$6\frac{1}{2}$–12 inches
Weight:	4–$9\frac{1}{2}$ oz
Habitat/Range:	Prairies, parks, roadsides and lawns wherever grass is kept short. Range extends from southern Canada and the Great Lakes region, south through central states to New Mexico
Similar species:	Very similar to the Mexican Ground Squirrel, although the latter is larger and lacks solid stripes. Hybrids between the two are not unknown however

This ground squirrel, like many of its kind, hibernates for around six months between October and March, slowing its heart-rate and breathing and living on fat reserves which it builds up throughout the summer months. Active by day, and preferring the sun, the Thirteen-lined Ground Squirrel will tend to remain in its burrow at night and during unsettled weather, venturing from its home in favorable conditions to feed on plants and seeds, sometimes upsetting gardeners in the process. They do however also eat caterpillars, insects such as grasshoppers and occasionally smaller mammals. The burrow is usually quite shallow, but extensive, with deeper nesting and hibernation chambers, and though generally solitary, the Thirteen-lined Ground Squirrel will sometimes hibernate in groups. These squirrels mate in spring following hibernation, producing up to ten young in early summer.

LEAST CHIPMUNK

Scientific name:	*Tamias minimus*
Identification:	Small chipmunk, yellow-gray back with five dark stripes, rust-brown flanks and gray-white underside. Pale facial stripes above and below eyes
Length (including tail):	7-9 inches
Weight:	1-3oz
Habitat/Range:	Extremely varied habitat, from coniferous forests, tundra, cliffs and meadows to sagebrush desert. Found across southern Canada, south through the western US to New Mexico
Similar species:	Of the 22 species of chipmunks found in North America, the Least Chipmunk is the most pale

EASTERN CHIPMUNK ▲

Scientific name:	*Tamias striatus*
Identification:	Red or brown back with central black stripe, white stripe on each side bordered with black. Pale underside and pale facial stripes above and below eyes
Length (including tail):	9–12 inches
Weight:	2½–5 oz
Habitat/Range:	Deciduous forests in southeastern Canada and eastern US
Similar species:	Similar to the Least Chipmunk, but larger, with fewer stripes

Chipmunks are small, highly vocal, ground-dwelling members of the squirrel family and usually live in burrows, but they are good climbers, often feeding and sometimes nesting in trees. Like most chipmunks the Least Chipmunk is found in woodland but it occurs across a wide range of habitats including more barren tundra and desert areas. Chipmunks are active during the day, particularly in the early morning and evening, when they spend much of their time gathering acorns, nuts and seeds, carrying food to their burrows in large cheek pouches. The Least Chipmunk will also supplement its diet with insects and occasionally small vertebrates. As with most members of the squirrel family, chipmunks store food, but they also hibernate for much of the winter, waking from time to time to feed on their stash. In warmer southern areas the Least Chipmunk will remain more active, hibernating only through the very coldest part of the year. Two or three weeks after emerging in spring, the Least Chipmunk will mate, and a litter of around five young is usually born in May.

The Eastern Chipmunk is common, and the only chipmunk to be found in most eastern states. It is also the largest species of chipmunk and may be quite bold, often visiting gardens in search of food. Its diet consists of acorns, nuts and seeds but also insects and some vertebrates such as young birds, salamanders and small snakes. Like the Least Chipmunk the Eastern Chipmunk constructs an extensive burrow system with a nest chamber and several tunnels for storing food and waste. It hibernates intermittently, waking periodically to feed on its hoard of food, but it tends to hibernate for a longer time, usually from fall through to spring. Mating takes place soon afterwards, and a litter of up to eight young, though usually fewer, is produced in May. In common with all squirrels the tiny offspring are born blind, naked and helpless and spend several weeks in the burrow before emerging.

PLAINS POCKET GOPHER ▼ NORTHERN POCKET GOPHER

Scientific name:	*Geomys bursarius*
Identification:	Medium-sized rodent, light brown to black depending on color of soil in its habitat, underside is paler. Tail is nearly naked and long claws are present on front paws
Length (including tail):	8–14 inches
Weight:	5–12½ oz
Habitat/Range:	Prairies, meadows and lawns in central US
Similar species:	Only gopher in most of its range and has two grooves on upper incisors as opposed to the usual single groove

Scientific name:	*Thomomys talpoides*
Identification:	Brown, but varies greatly in shade and may be nearly gray. White spots beneath chin and dark patches behind ears. Almost hairless tail, large digging claws and incisors
Length (including tail):	6½–9 inches
Weight:	3–4½ oz
Habitat/Range:	Meadows, mountainous areas and sparse woodland across most of southern Canada and the western US
Similar species:	Similar to many gopher species present in the west and which are almost impossible to distinguish by sight. Discernible from the Western Pocket Gopher, which has much larger ears

Gophers are solitary burrowing animals and like moles are rarely seen above ground, but large mounds of excavated earth usually betray their presence. Gophers are well adapted for a subterranean existence, possessing large, strong claws on their forefeet and prominent incisors for digging, and having small eyes and ears. Pocket gophers take their name from the large cheek pouches or "pockets" in which they store food, carrying that which they do not eat straight away into chambers in their burrows. They do not hibernate, but retreat deeper underground in winter, relying on their stores of food for sustenance. Gophers are herbivorous, feeding on roots and tubers which they pull into their tunnels with their teeth. The Plains Pocket Gopher is quite widespread throughout the Great Plains area, preferring loose sandy soils which ease digging, but they also occur in gardens and farmland. Young are born in spring in litters of up to about eight.

The Northern Pocket Gopher is found throughout western states inhabiting a number of different habitats, and like many gophers its coloring is highly variable depending upon location. Gopher fur is rather like that of moles, being short and able to lie in either direction, enabling ease of movement within its narrow tunnels, but the fur of the Northern Pocket Gopher is duller than that of most other Gophers. Highly solitary and territorial, Gophers avoid each other until the breeding season, which for the Northern Pocket Gopher takes place between spring and summer. The gestation period is relatively short; less than three weeks, and Northern Pocket Gophers may produce up to three litters per year of 3-7 young which are born in deep nest chambers. The burrows of this species tend to be quite extensive, resulting in large mounds in open areas.

Ord's Kangaroo Rat ▲ Hispid Pocket Mouse

Scientific name:	*Dipodomys ordii*
Identification:	Red-brown to almost black with a white underside, white spots above eyes and below ears. Long, tufted tail and large, five-toed hind feet
Length (including tail):	8½–11 inches
Weight:	1½–3oz
Habitat/Range:	Desert areas from southern Canada through the mid-west, south to Arizona, New Mexico and Texas
Similar species:	Within its range the Panamint Kangaroo Rat is larger with a longer tail and feet, whilst the Chisel-toothed Kangaroo Rat has a longer, darker striped tail and a grayer coat

Scientific name:	*Chaetodipus hispidus*
Identification:	Coarse brown fur on back and rump, paler underside. Short, bicolored tail, dark on top, white beneath. Large hind feet
Length (including tail):	7–9 inches
Weight:	1–1½ oz
Habitat/Range:	Sparsely vegetated prairies and desert areas in central US
Similar species:	Lacks distinctive tail tuft and spiny hairs on rump common to other related pocket mice

Kangaroo rats are not actually rats, but belong to a separate family of rodents which also contains pocket mice. They have long, powerful hind legs which they use to hop great distances, balancing with their long tails. Ord's Kangaroo Rat can leap up to eight feet in order to escape danger but will also kick sand at potential predators. It is preyed upon by owls, snakes, coyotes, foxes and other carnivorous mammals such as weasels. This species is mainly nocturnal, avoiding desert heat by remaining in its burrow during the day and searching for food when it is cooler. Kangaroo rats are herbivorous, feeding mainly on seeds and green plants from which they absorb moisture. They also store seeds in their burrows, transporting them in external cheek pouches. Reproduction may occur throughout the year if conditions are favorable, usually coinciding with rainfall and therefore an abundance of vegetation.

Pocket mice are found in desert or dry prairie regions and being closely related to kangaroo rats they also have external cheek pouches in which they carry food. The largest pocket mouse, the Hispid Pocket Mouse is quite widespread throughout the central US, but is nocturnal and therefore seldom seen. During the day it retreats to its burrow, where it maintains a supply of food. Hispid pocket mice feed on sunflower, cactus and sagebrush seeds amongst others, but also prey on invertebrates such as grasshoppers. As with kangaroo rats, pocket mice very rarely drink water, if at all, instead absorbing moisture from their food.

Humidity and temperature within the burrow are maintained by plugging entrance holes with soil. The Hispid Pocket Mouse may reproduce throughout the year in the south of its range and once or twice a year further north, giving birth to litters of up to nine young.

WESTERN HARVEST MOUSE▲

Scientific name:	*Reithrodontomys megalotis*
Identification:	Small brown mouse, with lighter colored sides and white belly. Tail is slightly furry and about as long as head and body
Length (including tail):	4½–6½ inches
Weight:	½–¾ oz
Habitat/Range:	Varied habitat of prairies, overgrown meadows, salt marshes, deserts, mixed forests and cultivated fields in the extreme south of British Columbia through much of the western US
Similar species:	Larger than the Eastern Harvest Mouse and Plains Harvest Mouse. Tail of Fulvous Harvest Mouse much longer

Harvest mice are amongst the smallest members of the mouse and rat family *Muridae*, and although found across a range of habitats they are most likely to inhabit overgrown grassy areas. The Western Harvest Mouse typically makes a spherical grass nest in a sheltered spot such as beneath a log, but it is a good climber and also makes its home within tall grass or some way up a bush or shrub. Occasionally the Western Harvest Mouse will occupy a burrow, and as with many rodents, tends to store food underground. Omnivorous, the diet of the Western Harvest Mouse is mainly comprised of seeds and shoots, but it also eats caterpillars and other insects. The Western Harvest Mouse breeds from spring to fall and may produce several litters per year of up to nine, though usually fewer, young.

MEADOW JUMPING MOUSE

Scientific name:	*Zapus hudsonius*
Identification:	Yellow-brown with a darker back and white underside. Very long, almost hairless tail and large hind feet
Length (including tail):	7½–10 inches
Weight:	½–1oz
Habitat/Range:	Marshes, moist fields and woodland throughout most of southern Canada and eastern US as far south as Oklahoma and Georgia
Similar species:	The Woodland Jumping Mouse has a white-tipped tail

The Meadow Jumping Mouse may hibernate for as much as eight months of the year, often within a burrow, but sometimes under a log or in a nest within dense vegetation. It does not hoard food, but puts on a layer of fat prior to hibernation. An omnivorous species, it will eat grasses, seeds, fungi and insects. Upon emerging in spring or early summer males will begin to seek out females, and following mating a litter of four or five young will be born less than three weeks later. Like kangaroo rats, jumping mice have powerful back legs and will leap large distances in order to avoid predators such as weasels and birds of prey. The Meadow Jumping Mouse will usually jump a few times in a zigzag, bounding two or three feet at a time, before stopping still.

NORTH AMERICAN DEER MOUSE

Scientific name:	*Peromyscus maniculatus*
Identification:	Red-brown to gray with white underside and bicolored tail. Two distinct forms are usually noted according to habitat; woodland and prairie, with the woodland form generally being slightly larger
Length (including tail):	4½–8½ inches
Weight:	½–1¼ oz
Habitat/Range:	Very common and widespread across varied habitats throughout Canada and the US, except for southeastern states
Similar species:	There are many similar species and subspecies which can be hard to distinguish. Has a shorter tail than the Northwestern Deer Mouse but longer tail than that of the White-footed Deer Mouse

Deer mice are extremely common rodents, living in woodlands, prairies and cultivated fields and feeding on a diverse range of foods. They are mainly herbivorous, eating seeds, fruits and fungus, but they also eat insects. In turn the North American Deer Mouse is a staple of many predatory species, particularly owls, snakes, foxes and other carnivorous mammals. Deer mice are nocturnal and usually live within hollow logs and tree stumps or in small burrows, where they will store food, emerging at night to forage for seeds before carrying them within internal cheek pouches back to their nests. The North American Deer Mouse reproduces throughout the year if food is plentiful, except during the coldest periods, giving birth to litters of around 5-6 young. It is important to note that this species has been linked to both Lyme disease and the Hanta Virus, and close contact with the animal and its droppings should be avoided.

NORTHERN GRASSHOPPER MOUSE

Scientific name:	*Onychomys leucogaster*
Identification:	Small but thick-set mouse, gray or cinnamon in color with a white underside, feet and tail-tip
Length (including tail):	5½–7½ inches
Weight:	1–2oz
Habitat/Range:	Deserts and prairies from southwestern Canada through much of the western, central and southern US
Similar species:	Larger than the Southern Grasshopper Mouse

This small, nocturnal mouse is amongst the most predatory of all rodents, hunting and eating grasshoppers, other insects, scorpions and spiders. It is not unknown for the Northern Grasshopper Mouse to also prey on small reptiles and mammals. The rest of its diet however consists of seeds and grasses, some of which it will store within its burrow. Burrows may be quite complex, made up of various chambers, including separate areas for nesting, defecation and food storage, and although this species is capable of digging it will often occupy the abandoned burrow of another animal. Highly territorial and protective of its young, the Northern Grasshopper Mouse also marks the boundaries of its range with shallow "signpost" burrows. Up to six litters of around four offspring may be produced each year. Grasshopper mice are known for being vocal, adopting a "singing" position of standing on their hind legs with the head thrown back, emitting long high-pitched calls.

HOUSE MOUSE

Scientific name:	*Mus musculus*
Identification:	Small, gray-brown mouse, long, almost naked tail
Length (including tail):	5–8 inches
Weight:	$\frac{1}{4}$–$\frac{3}{4}$ oz
Habitat/Range:	Buildings and cultivated fields in western and southern Canada, and throughout the US
Similar species:	Lacks white underside of other long-tailed mice

Along with the Black Rat and Norway Rat, the House Mouse is originally from Asia, first colonising Europe before arriving in North America in the 16th Century. Today it is found across the US and much of Canada in both residential and agricultural areas. The House Mouse lives in small colonies, usually outdoors during the summer months, moving into buildings as it becomes colder. Around farmland this species is often found in cultivated fields or barns and grain stores where it can be particularly destructive. Within houses, too the House Mouse can cause a great deal of damage, chewing through wires and ransacking larders. The reproductive ability of the House Mouse is perhaps even greater than that of the Norway Rat, a single female being able to produce almost ten litters a year of four to sixteen offspring which become capable of reproduction after around only six weeks.

▲ EASTERN/FLORIDA WOODRAT

Scientific name:	*Neotoma floridana*
Identification:	Resembles a large deer mouse, gray-brown with lighter or white underside. Relatively short, bicolored tail
Length (including tail):	$12\frac{1}{2}$–17 inches
Weight:	8–16oz
Habitat/Range:	Cliffs, rocky areas, hedges and woodland in southeastern states to central Texas, north to South Dakota
Similar species:	Southern Plains Woodrat is grayer, Allegheny Woodrat occurs north of the Tennessee River

The Florida Woodrat was for some time classified alongside the Allegheny Woodrat as a single species known as the Eastern Woodrat. More recently however, they have become recognised as distinct species, though it is almost impossible to tell them apart by sight. Woodrats have a tendency to construct quite large homes of sticks, leaves and other debris, and are also known as pack rats or trade rats for their habit of dropping what they are carrying in order to pick up other, often shiny, objects which they then incorporate into their nests. The Florida Woodrat often lives in caves but will still construct a "house", leaving the top open if there is enough shelter. In some areas the woodrat may also nest in trees. The Florida Woodrat is herbivorous, mostly eating green plants, fruit and fungi, and in the fall it will store nuts and seeds within its nest. It does not hibernate and breeds throughout the year, producing litters of 2-6 young.

BLACK RAT/"HOUSE RAT" ▶

Scientific name:	*Rattus rattus*
Identification:	Dark gray-brown, gray underside. Long, dark, almost hairless tail
Length (including tail):	12–18 inches
Weight:	4–12½ oz
Habitat/Range:	Urban areas and waterfronts, mainly in south, along both Atlantic and Pacific coasts
Similar species:	Norway or "Brown" Rat has a proportionately shorter tail (less than half its length)

Like the Norway Rat and House Mouse, the Black Rat belongs to the subfamily of Old World rats and mice *Muridae*. It is not a native species but is thought to originate in Asia, first arriving in North America on ships with the first European colonists. It is still concentrated around seaports and cities, faring less well in natural habitats, though it will sometimes nest in trees further inland. The Black Rat is omnivorous but particularly favors grain, causing great damage to stocks and being capable of transmitting a number of diseases. It breeds throughout the year, producing several litters of up to eight young. Other than man, its main enemies are cats, dogs, owls and snakes.

HISPID COTTON RAT

Scientific name:	*Sigmodon hispidus*
Identification:	Coarse, brown fur, grizzled with buff or gray, pale or white underside. Short, scaly, sparsely-haired tail
Length (including tail):	8–14½ inches
Weight:	3–4½ oz
Habitat/Range:	Grasslands and dense vegetation around ditches, ponds and marshes. Found mostly in southeastern US but as far west as New Mexico and Arizona
Similar species:	Yellow-nosed Cotton Rat has an orange nose. Other cotton rats in range are usually larger

Cotton rats are stocky with short tails and although larger, closely resemble voles. Rather than burrowing they also make runways through tall grass in much the same manner as many voles do. The Hispid Cotton Rat is not nocturnal, but tends to be more active at night, moving along its runways in search of food. They mainly eat vegetation, and in agricultural areas can cause a great deal of damage to crops, but they are omnivorous, eating insects, birds' eggs and even chicks. In marshy areas they may eat crayfish and crabs. Spherical nests are constructed from woven grass, and although not colonial, many cotton rats may be present in a fairly small area. The Hispid Cotton Rat is a prolific breeder and although the gestation period is relatively long for an animal of its size, up to fifteen newborn may be produced in one of several litters per year, and juveniles may become sexually mature at six weeks.

NORWAY RAT/BROWN RAT

Scientific name:	*Rattus norvegicus*
Identification:	Gray-brown, gray underside. Scaly tail, lighter on the underside
Length (including tail):	12½–18 inches
Weight:	½–1lb
Habitat/Range:	Urban, suburban and agricultural areas in Southern Canada and throughout the US
Similar species:	Black Rat has a relatively longer tail

Like the Black Rat the Norway Rat is an introduced species, and although it arrived over 150 years later, it has established itself over a far wider range and thrives in a variety of habitats. Hugely adaptable and with great reproductive potential, capable of producing twelve litters a year of up to twenty young, the Norway Rat is incredibly common, particularly in urban areas where food is plentiful. It feeds on insects, carrion, plants and grain, and like the Black Rat causes damage to stockpiled crops in warehouses. This species also carries communicable diseases which can pose a threat to humans. In agricultural areas the Norway Rat tends to live in burrows, whereas in urban areas it will tend to make its home in sewer systems and in and around buildings. It is not strictly colonial, but sheer numbers find them living in close proximity. Mass migrations have been observed when populations become too large for a given area.

MEADOW VOLE

Scientific name:	*Microtus pennsylvanicus*
Identification:	Gray to dark brown, sometimes grizzled with black. Underside is silver-gray
Length (including tail):	5–7½ inches
Weight:	½–2½oz
Habitat/Range:	Densely vegetated meadows, open woodland and marshes throughout Canada and northern US states, south to northeast Georgia and through plains areas to New Mexico
Similar species:	Larger than the Woodland Vole and many other voles within its range and habitat. Longer tail than the Prairie Vole

The Meadow Vole is widely distributed across Canada and the US and breeds at an astonishing rate. A female may bear as many as 100 young in a single year. Mostly active after sunset, voles are preyed upon by many species of mammals, snakes, owls and other birds of prey, as such occupying an important, if somewhat unenviable position in the food chain. The Meadow Vole itself is herbivorous, feeding on flowers, roots and grasses, and when present in great numbers it can cause significant damage to crops. It constructs a ball-shaped nest of grass either below ground in a burrow or along its network of surface runways and does not hibernate but may remain active even under snow, insulated within its home.

SOUTHERN RED-BACKED VOLE ▲

Scientific name:	*Clethrionomys gapperi*
Identification:	Small brightly colored vole, reddish back, yellow-gray sides and pale underside. Tail is short
Length (including tail):	4½–6½ inches
Weight:	½–1½ oz
Habitat/Range:	Damp woodland, meadows and bogs across much of Canada, south into the US through the Rocky Mountains in the west, and south to North Carolina in the east
Similar species:	Western Red-backed Vole has longer tail whilst the Meadow Vole is larger and lacks red coloring

The Southern Red-backed Vole is an abundant species in many woodland and boggy habitats in Canada and the US and is a ground-dwelling species which does not burrow but tends to move along natural runways amongst vegetation, leaf-litter and logs, in meadows and on the forest floor. It will however take advantage of vacant burrows made by other animals, often living in a family group until juveniles mature at around two or three months old. Litters of up to eight young are produced from early spring through to late fall. A herbivorous species, the Southern Red-backed Vole feeds on green plants, berries, and fungi, storing less perishable items such as seeds, nuts and tubers for consumption when other foods may be more scarce. It does not hibernate, continuing to search for food throughout the winter, and it may be seen at any time of day.

SOUTHERN BOG LEMMING

Scientific name:	*Synaptomys cooperi*
Identification:	Vole-like appearance, brown back, silver-gray underside, very short tail
Length (including tail):	4½–6 inches
Weight:	1–2oz
Habitat/Range:	Meadows, grassy woodland areas and fringes of wetlands
Similar species:	Northern Bog Lemming has light patches of fur below ears

Despite its name, the Southern Bog Lemming is rarely found in bogs, being much more common in grasslands and forest clearings. It is vole-like in both its appearance and behavior and occurs alongside voles and similar small mammals, sharing their runways and burrows. Its nest is a spherical grass structure and may be contained within an underground burrow or located amongst dense vegetation. The Southern Bog Lemming feeds mainly on grass, sedges and clover, but also eats fungi, seeds and berries, and may sometimes eat insects. As with many small rodents this species is heavily preyed upon by numerous larger animals such as snakes, birds of prey and carnivorous mammals and though it is capable of rapid and extensive reproduction, populations fluctuate greatly from year to year. This is however, more likely to be dependent upon how much food is available to the lemming rather than due to predation.

MOUNTAIN BEAVER/
SEWELLEL/APLODONTIA

Scientific name:	*Aplodontia rufa*
Identification:	Medium-sized, thick-set rodent, dark brown back, lighter underside. Very short tail and long claws. White spot below ears
Length (including tail):	9½–17 inches
Weight:	1-3lb
Habitat/Range:	Damp forests, particularly near streams. Only found close to the Pacific coast, from British Columbia to northern California and in parts of Nevada
Similar species:	Similar in appearance to the Muskrat, but has a tiny tail

The Mountain Beaver is not closely related to the American Beaver, nor common in mountainous areas; instead, it probably gains its name from its habits of gnawing on bark and cutting and collecting small branches and other vegetation which it stockpiles outside its burrow. On occasion the Mountain Beaver also covers the entrance to its home with twigs and leaves and sometimes diverts streams into its tunnels. It does not hibernate in winter but will usually remain in its burrow, where it will feed on stored vegetation. Mountain Beavers eat grasses, ferns, bark and plants such as nettles which many species will avoid, sometimes climbing trees in order to obtain food. Mating takes place in late winter and 4-5 offspring are born around a month later in early spring. The Mountain Beaver is preyed upon by the Bobcat and larger members of the weasel family.

PORCUPINE

Scientific name:	*Erethizon dorsatum*
Identification:	Large, heavy-bodied rodent with short legs. Front of body covered in long black, brown or yellow hairs, rump and tail covered in long quills
Length (including tail):	25–38 inches
Weight:	Up to 40lb
Habitat/Range:	Forests, tundra and scrubland with some trees, across Canada and the western US, around the Great Lakes and New York in eastern states
Similar species:	None

Perhaps surprisingly given its bulk, the Porcupine is an arboreal species and spends most of its time in trees, climbing with its powerful claws and usually sleeping high amongst the branches during the day. It becomes more active at night, feeding on leaves, buds and bark, stripping away outer layers to eat the preferred cambium layer beneath. Slow and quite clumsy when on the ground, the Porcupine will usually only descend from a tree in order to move to a new food source or to seek shelter within a cave, hollow tree or log. Although more vulnerable on the ground, porcupines have few predators, being well protected by their sharp quills, though some animals, such as the Fisher, have learnt to turn them over, exposing the unprotected underside. When threatened, the Porcupine will turn its back to a potential predator and chatter its teeth. It may also give off a foul-smelling odor. As a last resort, the porcupine will lower its head, present its quills and lash out with its tail. Quills readily detach, becoming embedded in the attacker and can cause serious injury or even death.

AMERICAN PIKA/CONEY

Scientific name:	*Ochotona princeps*
Identification:	Small rodent-like mammal with short legs and small rounded ears. Fur is gray-brown
Length (including tail):	7–8½ inches (No visible tail)
Weight:	4–4½ oz
Habitat/Range:	Rocky alpine slopes throughout the Rocky Mountain range, from British Columbia and Arizona to New Mexico
Similar species:	Collared Pika has a pale band of gray fur around neck

Although the American Pika looks very much like a rodent, it is in fact more closely related to rabbits and hares. It is found at quite high altitudes and lives in colonies amongst boulders and rockslides. The American Pika is active during the day and enjoys basking in the sun, but is likely to be heard before it is seen, emitting a loud bleating call. Pika are strictly herbivorous, feeding on various green vegetation and have an interesting habit of stock-piling grasses and other plants amongst rocks, and allowing them to dry in the sun until they become hay-like. The pika does not hibernate, but will shelter amongst rocks, feeding on this dried plant material. The American Pika breeds in spring, and sometimes again in late summer, giving birth to 2-6 young per litter.

EASTERN COTTONTAIL

Scientific name:	*Sylvilagus floridanus*
Identification:	Gray-brown rabbit with red nape, long ears and a short tail which has a white underside
Length (including tail):	15–18 inches
Weight:	2–4lb
Habitat/Range:	Meadows, brush, woodland, lawns and cultivated fields east of the Rocky Mountains across the eastern US
Similar species:	Desert Cottontail is smaller whilst the Swamp Rabbit tends to be larger and lacks red nape

The Eastern Cottontail is a widespread species and the most common rabbit in most of the eastern US. Like all rabbits it is herbivorous, eating a range of green vegetation when available, tending to eat more woody stems in winter. It also shares the common habit of re-ingesting its droppings, which may allow rabbits to absorb more nutrients, but also enables them to retreat to cover and feed when less exposed to predators. The Eastern Cottontail does not hibernate, but will use the burrows of other animals such as the Woodchuck in winter. It may also make runways beneath snow. Mating takes place between late winter and fall and the Eastern Cottontail is amongst the most prolific breeders, bearing many litters a year of up to nine young. Cottontails give birth in shallow depressions lined with vegetation and fur, and the young are born naked and blind.

BLACK-TAILED JACKRABBIT

Scientific name:	*Lepus californicus*
Identification:	Gray-brown or sandy-colored, with very long, black-tipped ears. Large hind feet. Top of tail has black stripe continuing onto rump
Length (including tail):	18–24 inches
Weight:	6–14lb
Habitat/Range:	Long and short-grass prairies, sagebrush, deserts and cultivated fields in the western US
Similar species:	White-tailed Jackrabbit lacks black tail stripe, Antelope Jackrabbit has white flanks and longer ears without black tips

Despite their name, jackrabbits are actually hares, being more powerfully built than rabbits and generally better adapted to living in sparsely vegetated, open environments. The Black-tailed Jackrabbit is no exception, it has extremely long ears and huge hind feet and legs, being able to detect predators from some distance, it is usually able to outrun them, leaping up to twenty feet and able to reach speeds of over 30 mph (50km/h) in short bursts. Young are born fully-furred with eyes open in quite deep forms, which somewhat unusually for a hare, the female lines with her fur. She also takes the precaution of separating the young soon after birth, presumably to reduce the risk of them all being discovered by predators such as Coyotes, snakes and birds of prey. The Black-tailed Jackrabbit reproduces some three or four times a year, with litters varying in size from 1–8 young.

SNOWSHOE HARE ◀

Scientific name:	*Lepus americanus*
Identification:	Dark brown in summer, white in winter. Large hind feet, soles furred in winter. Tail dark above. Long, black-tipped ears
Length (including tail):	16 – 20 inches
Weight:	2-3 lb
Habitat/Range:	Pine forest across Alaska and Canada, south through the Rocky Mountains in the west, in northern states around the Great Lakes and south through mountainous regions in the east
Similar species:	Smaller than other hares and jackrabbits. Tail of Arctic Hare is all white

Also sometimes referred to as the "Varying Hare", Snowshoe Hares undergo a seasonal color change, turning from brown to white as winter approaches, returning to brown in spring. They are small and shy in comparison to most hares, hiding during the day amongst vegetation, logs or within the burrow of another animal, becoming active mainly at night. This is perhaps due to the large amount of predators which hunt them, including Lynx, Bobcats, foxes, weasels and birds of prey. As with all hares, the young of the Snowshoe Hare are born well developed, furred, with their eyes open, and in the case of this species, able to run almost immediately. Litters of three are most common, produced two or three times a year. Principally, but not strictly vegetarian, feeding on grass, other green plants, bark, berries and buds according to availability, Snowshoe Hares will also feed on carrion.

SWAMP RABBIT

Scientific name:	*Sylvilagus aquaticus*
Identification:	Large rabbit, gray-brown fur with black flecks. White underside and reddish feet
Length (including tail):	18–22 inches
Weight:	4–6lb
Habitat/Range:	Swamps and wetlands in southeastern US
Similar species:	Larger, and lacking red nape of the Eastern Cottontail

The largest of the cottontail rabbits, the Swamp Rabbit is found almost exclusively in swamp regions and is a good swimmer. It feeds on both terrestrial and aquatic vegetation, and like most rabbits eats a number of green plants and the woodier stems of young trees and shrubs. Swamp rabbits are prey to many species, including mammals such as the Long-tailed Weasel and Mink, and they will enter water when chased, sometimes leaving only the nostrils exposed. They are however also eaten by aquatic predators such as alligators. The Swamp Rabbit is not a burrowing species, its home or "form" being a depression in the ground, usually amongst dense vegetation, but it will use the burrows of other mammals. When breeding, females will line the form with fur from their bellies and they typically give birth to around three young. The gestation period is relatively long, about five or six weeks, and like hares, newborns are born with fur and able to open their eyes shortly after birth.

LITTLE BROWN MYOTIS ▲ SILVER-HAIRED BAT

Scientific name:	*Myotis lucifugus*
Identification:	Glossy brown fur on back, lighter underside. Small, round ears
Length (including tail):	3–3½ inches/ Wingspan: 8–10 inches
Weight:	1/16–½ oz
Habitat/Range:	Often close to water. Found throughout most of Canada and the US with the exception of southern California and many southeastern and south-central states
Similar species:	Northern Myotis has longer ears, most other myotis bats in range have a keeled calcar, that is, the bone from the ankle which supports the tail membrane is bowed outwards

Scientific name:	*Lasionycteris noctivagans*
Identification:	Almost black, but flecked with silver hairs. Interfemoral, or tail, membrane is slightly furry. Small rounded ears
Length (including tail):	3½–4 inches
Wingspan:	11 inches
Weight:	¼–½ oz
Habitat/Range:	Woodland throughout southern Canada and most of US, but not present in the Rocky Mountains or many southern states, particularly in the east
Similar species:	Interfemoral membrane is less furred than those of solitary, tree-roosting bats

The Little Brown Myotis is a very common bat, with females and juveniles forming colonies of many thousands of individuals, typically roosting in buildings during the summer, moving eastwards in fall to hibernate in caves. Males are usually solitary until this time, sleeping beneath loose tree bark, but they will roost with females in winter. As is common in many bats, this species mates in fall whilst food is still quite plentiful, but the female delays fertilization until spring, retaining sperm in the reproductive tract during hibernation. During the winter these bats rely on stores of fat, and though they will wake quite frequently, sometimes leaving the roosting site, they will not feed. A single young is born in summer, usually in an attic or similar space, and will not fly for about a month, remaining in the roost while the female catches moths and other small flying insects at night.

Not classified in the genus of solitary tree bats, *Lasiurus*, the Silver-haired Bat is nevertheless usually a solitary forest-dwelling species, though females have been observed roosting together with their young in maternal colonies, and it will hibernate in buildings in winter. It usually roosts in hollow trees or beneath loose bark in summer, migrating southwards in fall to hibernate. When active, this species typically feeds in early evening and has a noticeably slow flight. Like most bats it feeds on moths and other flying insects. The Silver-haired Bat mates in fall and delays fertilization until spring when more often than not, it will give birth to two young.

EASTERN RED BAT

Scientific name:	*Lasiurus borealis*
Identification:	Bright red or orange with white or gray frosting on back and underside. Fur continues across topside of interfemoral, or tail, membrane. Small rounded ears.
Length (including tail):	4–5 inches
Wingspan:	13 inches
Weight:	About ½oz
Habitat/Range:	Woodland habitats from southern Canada throughout central and eastern US. Not found in Rocky Mountains
Similar species:	Western Red Bat and Hoary Bat are larger

The Eastern Red Bat is a solitary, rather than colonial species, but will often form flocks when migrating to southern areas of its range in order to hibernate for the winter. Throughout the warmer months it spends the daylight hours suspended upside-down amongst the foliage of trees, flying at night to hunt for moths, beetles and other insects, usually catching them in flight, but sometimes landing amongst vegetation to capture its prey. It is thought that the Eastern Red Bat also frequently mates on the wing. The female Eastern Red Bat is unique among bats in having four nipples, and rather than the usual single infant, it may produce a litter of four young. Eastern Red Bats will mate in fall but do not give birth until mid-summer.

MEXICAN/BRAZILIAN FREE-TAILED BAT

Scientific name:	*Tadarida brasiliensis*
Identification:	Small bat, dark brown or gray in color. Tail extends well beyond the interfemoral membrane
Length (including tail):	3½–4½ inches
Wingspan:	11 inches
Weight:	About ½ oz
Habitat/Range:	Various habitats depending on location, including desert and farmland. Found throughout the southern US
Similar species:	The Little Free-tailed Bat is around the same size, but can be distinguished by its ears, which meet at the base

The Brazilian Free-tailed Bat (sometimes called the Mexican Free-tailed Bat) is mainly a tropical species which occurs throughout Central and South America. Most North American populations migrate to Mexico during the winter but many in eastern and West Coast areas will hibernate, often in buildings. In Arizona, New Mexico and Texas these bats tend to live in vast colonies in caves, one of their most well known roosts being the Carlsbad Caverns in New Mexico. At one time roosting populations in these caves ran into several million bats, though today it is thought that there are hundreds of thousands. Shortly after sunset the bats leave the caves spiraling high into the air, forming a swarm that may be visible for many miles. They return at sunrise, having spent the night feeding on insects which they catch whilst in flight and with the aid of their tail membranes. The Brazilian Free-tailed Bat mates in spring, usually producing one infant, though sometimes two or three, in early summer.

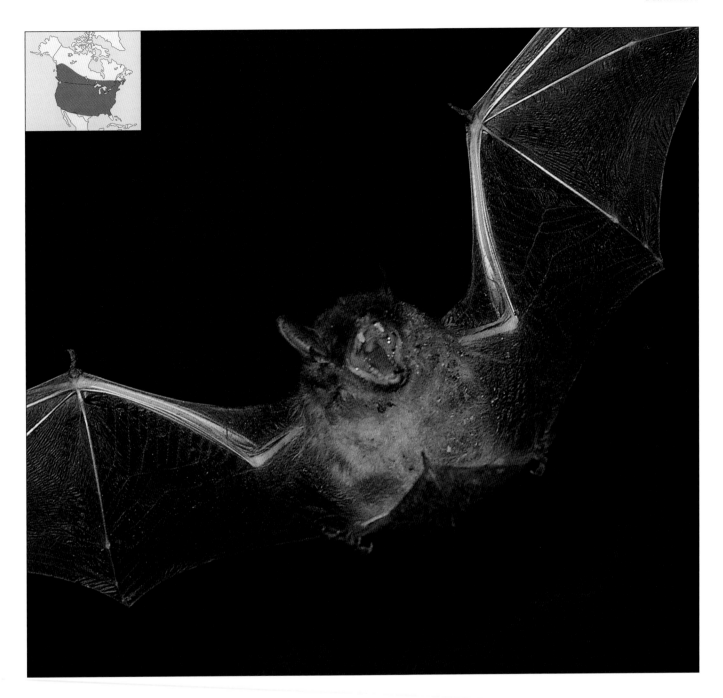

BIG BROWN BAT

Scientific name:	*Eptesicus fuscus*
Identification:	Fairly large bat, brown back, lighter underside. Interfemoral membrane is not furred
Length (including tail):	4½–5 inches
Wingspan:	13 inches
Weight:	About ½ oz
Habitat/Range:	Habitat may be quite varied, from forests to farmland and urban areas. Found across southern Canada and throughout the US except for southern Florida and south-central Texas
Similar species:	Larger than most similar bats within its range

The Big Brown Bat is a very common species across most of North America and often roosts in buildings in urban areas and around farmland. During winter hibernation this species will tend to roost alone or in small groups, but in spring and summer, maternity colonies may number several hundred individuals. In agricultural areas the Big Brown Bat will often make its home in a barn, other man-made structure or sometimes in hollow trees, and it can be a useful ally to the farmer, eating many species of insects which are considered to be pests. It feeds mainly on beetles and other flying insects but is less likely to take moths than many other species. The Big Brown Bat breeds from fall to spring.

MOUNTAIN LION (PUMA/COUGAR)

Scientific name:	*Felis concolor*
Identification:	Large brown or tawny-yellow cat, long black-tipped tail, dark patches on sides of muzzle and back of ears
Length (including tail):	6–8½ feet
Weight:	80–270lb
Habitat /Range:	Mountainous regions and forests in the west, from British Columbia and Alberta, south through Arizona, New Mexico and parts of Texas, into Mexico and beyond. Small population in the Florida Everglades
Similar species:	Largest native North American cat, adults unspotted

Although the Mountain Lion is large and may hunt by day in isolated areas, it is a secretive and solitary hunter and tends to avoid coming into contact with people, hence it is seldom seen. Males of the species are highly territorial with large ranges that may encompass several smaller overlapping female territories. They mark home areas by scraping up piles of dirt and leaf litter, often urinating on them. The Mountain Lion generally travels in search of food, sometimes covering over twenty miles in a day or night, and an adult is powerful enough to bring down large deer. They also eat a variety of smaller mammals including raccoons, beavers, rabbits, hares and mice, but will also eat birds and even large insects. In the case of deer, or other large prey, the Mountain Lion may return to a kill several times, loosely covering a carcass with leaf litter and other debris between feeding sessions. Attacks on humans are rare but a Mountain Lion will attack if particularly hungry or if it is cornered with no obvious means of escape. Usually mating in spring, a male and female will pair up for about two weeks, the young being born about three months later in summer. Litters vary from between one to six cubs which will remain with their mother for up to two years and which have spotted coats for between the first three and six months of their lives. They will start to hunt with the female at about three months old.

BOBCAT

Scientific name:	*Lynx rufus*
Identification:	Fairly large feline, tawny-red to gray back with dark spots, lighter underside. Fur on cheeks extends into a wide ruff. Legs and tail are barred with black. Short, or "bobbed" tail ends in a black tip on top, white below
Length (including tail):	2½–4 feet
Weight:	15–30lb
Habitat/Range:	Scrub, deserts, forests, swamps and cultivated areas from southern Canada across most of the US but not present in some mid-western states
Similar species:	The Lynx has a shorter tail which is black-tipped above and below, longer ear tufts and less distinct spots

Mostly nocturnal, the Bobcat generally spends the day hidden amongst rocks or vegetation and sometimes trees, resting until nightfall when it will emerge to hunt. Unlike the Mountain Lion which may track prey over long distances before stalking to within striking range of its intended victim, the Bobcat tends to find a suitable spot from which to make an ambush and will then wait for a potential meal to arrive. Capable of killing deer, the Bobcat will usually settle for smaller prey however, and will eat a variety of smaller mammals, particularly hares and rabbits, also catching birds and reptiles. Like the Mountain Lion it will return periodically to large kills in order to feed. Solitary other than when breeding, mating takes place in early spring and the female will usually give birth at the beginning of summer in a sheltered spot such as a cave. The young, most commonly born in litters of two or three, will remain with their mother for about a year, learning to hunt independently.

Mountain Lion

(CANADIAN) LYNX

Scientific name:	*Lynx canadensis/Felis lynx/Lynx lynx*
Identification:	Quite large, gray cat with indistinct darker markings, long ear tufts and large ruff. Short tail has black tip
Length (including tail):	2½–3½ feet
Weight:	12–40lb
Habitat/Range:	Coniferous forests throughout most of Alaska and Canada and northern regions of the US, south through parts of the Rocky Mountains
Similar species:	The Bobcat is more brown than gray, with more noticeable markings, shorter ear tufts and a white tip on the underside of its tail

As with other North American cats the Lynx is solitary, elusive and generally nocturnal, resting by day in a sheltered spot amongst boulders, tree roots or within the branches of a tree. The Lynx hunts at night, either stalking or waiting patiently in low branches and other vegetation before ambushing its prey. The Snowshoe Hare forms a considerable proportion of the Lynx's diet, perhaps over two thirds, and like its quarry, the Lynx has large, furry feet which enable it to move swiftly and almost silently across snow. Lynx also feed on other small mammals, particularly rodents, but will tackle much larger animals such as deer, particularly in deep snow or if an animal is weak. A large kill will be revisited and buried beneath snow or leaf litter, and may sustain a Lynx for a considerable time. Lynx come together only to breed, usually in early spring, giving birth to 1-6 young about nine or ten weeks later. Juveniles will remain with their mother for up to a year.

GRAY WOLF

Scientific name:	*Canis lupus*
Identification:	Large canine, commonly gray grizzled with black, but ranges from completely black to white. Long legs, and a long, bushy, black-tipped tail
Length (including tail):	4½–6½ feet
Weight:	60–130lb
Habitat/Range:	Tundra and forests throughout Alaska and Canada, limited to northern regions of the US in Washington and around the Great Lakes
Similar species:	Red Wolf, Coyote and foxes are all smaller

The largest of the North American wild dogs, the Gray Wolf is a sociable pack animal, usually living in a family group of up to fifteen members. Wolf packs adhere to rigid hierarchies under the leadership of a dominant male and cooperate in hunting, enabling them to bring down large prey such as deer and Moose. They will also feed on smaller mammals, birds, fish and insects. Wolves range over vast territories, sometimes covering hundreds of square miles, but they will not chase prey over long distances unless the quarry shows signs of weakness, preferring to ambush or to herd an animal toward other pack members. Wolves are quite vocal and known for their howling, but they also communicate by scent and posture, reaffirming social bonds. The Gray Wolf tends to pair for life, and all members of a pack will care for young. Pups are usually born in a den in spring or early summer, beginning to hunt with the pack at about four or five months old.

RED WOLF

Scientific name:	*Canis rufus*
Identification:	Midway between the Coyote and Gray Wolf in size. Mostly gray or tawny with black and red hairs
Length (including tail):	$4\frac{1}{2}$–$5\frac{1}{2}$ feet
Weight:	40–80lb
Habitat/Range:	Prairies, forests, coastlines and swamps. Reintroduced to parts of North and South Carolina, Mississippi and Florida
Similar species:	Coyote is smaller, Gray Wolf larger

The Red Wolf is a rare species that was on the point of extinction around thirty years ago, but which has been successfully reintroduced in some areas. Its range once covered much of the southeastern US, but by 1900 the Red Wolf was found in small numbers only in parts of Texas and Louisiana. Human persecution and the reduction of their natural habitat were primarily to blame, but interbreeding with feral dogs and Coyotes was also a contributing factor. A breeding program was established in the 1970s and 80s, and by the 1990s there were over 150 individuals beginning to re-establish themselves in the wild. The Red Wolf mates in spring, producing a litter of 2-10 young in early summer. A social animal, Red Wolves are usually found in pairs or small packs, and will hunt small deer, rabbits and other small mammals.

Coyote

Scientific name:	*Canis latrans*
Identification:	Grizzled gray-brown, lighter belly. Bushy black-tipped tail and large ears
Length (including tail):	3½ – 4½ feet
Weight:	20–40lb
Habitat/Range:	Prairies, brush or open woodland and suburban areas from Alaska, southern Canada, and throughout the US
Similar species:	Smaller than both the Red and Gray Wolf

The Coyote was once found almost exclusively on western prairies, but the disappearance of the larger Gray Wolf from much of its original habitat has enabled the Coyote to extend its range eastwards. It is also highly adaptable, living alongside human populations quite happily, a trait which has seen the Coyote moving into suburban and even urban areas. Usually found alone or in pairs, Coyotes will occasionally form groups in order to hunt large prey such as deer, but they are typically opportunistic hunters and scavengers, feeding on a range of small mammals, birds, reptiles, amphibians, insects and carrion. Sometimes pairing for life, Coyotes mate in late winter or early spring, with up to twenty, though usually fewer, pups being born in spring or early summer. Pups are born in sheltered dens such as caves, or the vacant burrows of other large mammals, though a female may dig her own. Coyotes communicate over long distances with a range of calls, the most familiar being a long howl preceded and followed by a succession of barks.

RED FOX

Scientific name:	*Vulpes vulpes*
Identification:	Usually rusty-red with white chin and underside, black legs and feet and a bushy white-tipped tail
Length (including tail):	3–3½ feet
Weight:	8–15lb
Habitat/Range:	Woodland, meadows, cultivated areas and suburbs throughout most of Canada and the US, but absent from parts of the west
Similar species:	Common Gray Fox has gray back and black topside of tail without white tip

The Red Fox is both common and widespread and although it will often live in close proximity to man, it is mainly nocturnal and quite shy. When seen, the Red Fox is usually easy to identify due to its distinctive coloring, though variations include black, black and silver, and "cross" in which dark markings extend from the underside across the back and shoulders. A single litter may contain any of these variations. Mostly solitary, adult Red Foxes come together to mate from late winter to early spring and many will pair

for life. At the start of the breeding season this fox is at its most vocal as males and females call to each other. The young are born in a den in spring or early summer, usually the enlarged burrow of another animal such as a badger, though sometimes amongst rocks or in a similar concealed location. At about one month the juveniles will emerge from the den for short periods, to begin with, being fed regurgitated food by the parents, but being brought live food and then joining their parents on hunting trips as they grow, remaining with them for six months or more. The Red Fox is omnivorous and its diet contains quite a large amount of vegetation, particularly in summer, when it will eat various fruits, and grasses, increasingly eating small mammals and birds in winter.

The **Common Gray Fox** (*Urocyon cinereoargenteus*), is found mainly in the eastern US, but also in western and southwestern states where the Red Fox may be largely absent. Very similar to the Red Fox in habit, the Common Gray Fox usually prefers denser cover however, and is the most adept climber of the dog family, scaling trees in order to seek cover or to reach birds' eggs and fruit such as cherries. Around the same size and build as the Red Fox, this species is sometimes confused with its relative, but it differs in color, being largely grizzled gray with reddish sides, legs, feet, back of head and underside of tail. The top of the tail is black, as is the tip.

KIT FOX/SWIFT FOX

Scientific name:	*Vulpes velox*
Identification:	Small, slender fox with very large ears. Sandy-gray with white underside and bushy black-tipped tail
Length (including tail):	2–3 feet
Weight:	4–6lb
Habitat/Range:	Desert and shortgrass prairies in southwestern states, north through the Dakotas to parts of southern Canada
Similar species:	Smaller than both the Red and Gray Fox

The Kit Fox and Swift Fox were at one time regarded as separate species but are now often classified together as *Vulpes velox*. As with most foxes the Kit Fox is generally solitary, though will pair for life, with adults coming together in late winter to mate and remaining as a family group until juveniles become independent in fall. The young are born in an earthen den in spring, usually a disused Marmot, Prairie Dog or American Badger burrow, though females may dig their own. Kit Foxes are mainly nocturnal, hunting at night for small animals such as rodents and rabbits, birds and large insects like crickets and grasshoppers. They will also eat vegetation such as berries, grasses and in desert regions, the fruit of cacti. Numbers have declined due to human encroachment and poisoned baits intended for the control of Coyotes, but populations have recently begun to increase in areas such as South Dakota where they have been almost absent for many years.

ARCTIC FOX ▶

Scientific name:	*Alopex lagopus*
Identification:	Small short-legged fox with rounded ears. Color varies from gray-brown in summer to white in winter. Coastal foxes sometimes blue-gray, lighter in winter
Length (including tail):	2½–3 feet
Weight:	6–9lb
Habitat/Range:	Coastlines, forest edges, open tundra and ice floes in north and west Alaska and northern Canada
Similar species:	Only Red Fox occurs within the same range

Like the Snowshoe Hare, the Arctic Fox undergoes a seasonal moult during which its coat usually changes color from gray-brown to white in order to camouflage it against the winter snow. The pads of the feet also become more densely furred to protect the fox from the cold and to enable ease of movement across snow and ice. In summer when food is more abundant the Arctic Fox will feed on a variety of small mammals such as lemmings and voles, birds and their eggs, and some vegetation, mainly berries. When food is scarce they will rely more heavily on carrion, following Polar Bears out onto the ice and scavenging from their kills. The Arctic Fox may also migrate long distances to the south of its range in search of food. Young are born in spring or summer in a den and are cared for by both parents until late summer.

Grizzly/Brown Bear

Scientific name:	*Ursus arctos*
Identification:	Large bear, light - dark brown, often grizzled with white-tipped hairs. Distinct shoulder hump, long front claws (up to four inches)
Length (including tail):	6–7 feet
Weight:	300–1000 lb+
Habitat / Range:	Open mountainous grassland, forests and tundra in Alaska and northwestern Canada. Isolated populations in remote areas of the Rocky Mountains in the US
Similar species:	Black Bear is smaller with no shoulder hump

The Grizzly Bear is large and extremely powerful and is probably the most unpredictable and potentially dangerous bear in North America, sometimes weighing well over 1000lb, and able to run as fast as a horse over short distances. The subspecies *Ursos arctos Middendorffi*, known as the Alaskan Brown Bear or Kodiak Bear, may weigh almost 2000lb. Bears tend to avoid human contact, but can be at their most dangerous in areas where they have grown used to man's presence, or at other times when surprised, feeding, with young, or if injured. The Grizzly Bear is in fact the biggest terrestrial predator, but is omnivorous, and as well as eating small mammals, fish and insects, it also feeds on vegetation such as roots, leaves, shoots, fruit and fungi. They are however, capable of catching prey as large as deer and Moose. Grizzly Bears dramatically increase their bodyweight prior to hibernation, and though they do not sleep as deeply as many mammals, will hole up in a cave, or hollow for the winter months. Mating takes place in summer with the young usually being produced in late winter or early spring. Weighing only about 1lb at birth and around the size of rats, bears develop extremely quickly.

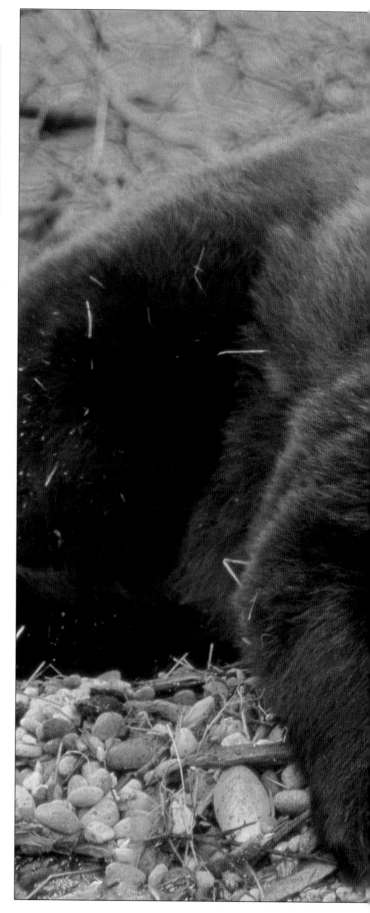

BLACK BEAR

Scientific name:	*Ursus americanus*
Identification:	Black – light brown with a pale snout, and convex facial profile
Length (including tail):	4½–6 feet
Weight:	200–550lb
Habitat/Range:	Forests, swamps and mountainous woodland in much of Canada and Alaska, south through Rocky Mountains to New Mexico and along the Pacific Coast in the west. In the eastern US, found in Great Lakes area, and through Appalachian Mountains to Florida
Similar species:	Grizzly Bear is larger with more concave facial profile, large shoulder hump and longer claws

Black Bears are classed as carnivores, but most of their intake consists of various vegetable matter, including roots, buds, leaves, fruit, nuts and the inner bark of trees. They also eat various insects, ripping open rotten logs and beehives, from which they will also eat honey. The remainder of the Black Bear's diet is composed of fish and small mammals but they can be dangerous to man, particularly where there are sources of food close to human habitations, such as waste dumps, where bears may have overcome their fear of people. Like Grizzly Bears, the Black Bear hibernates during the winter in a cave, hollow log or other large, secluded spot, emerging in spring, with mating occurring between early and mid-summer. Two cubs are usually born six or seven months later in a den and may be cared for by their mother for up to a year.

POLAR BEAR

Scientific name:	*Ursus maritimus*
Identification:	Very large bear, white or yellowish fur, long neck and legs, relatively small head and ears
Length (including tail):	7–11 feet
Weight:	700–1200lb
Habitat/Range:	Pack ice, ice floes and coastlines in northern Canada and Alaska
Similar species:	Unmistakable

The Polar Bear is the most carnivorous of the North American bears, chiefly due to the lack of vegetation within its range, hunting and feeding on fish, seals and Walrus. It is a powerful swimmer, but lacks the agility to catch swimming seals, instead stalking and catching them on the ice or waiting for them to come up for air at their breathing holes. Polar Bears also eat carrion, birds and smaller mammals, and in summer, or when otherwise available, will supplement their diet with vegetation. Often hunting by day, probably due to their camouflage, the Polar Bear is sometimes also active throughout the year, holing up in a den in the snow for a few months in winter during the most inhospitable weather. Females tend to retire for longer periods, particularly if giving birth, which occurs from around November to January. Litters typically contain two cubs, which remain with the female for about eighteen months.

COMMON/NORTHERN RACCOON

Scientific name:	*Procyon lotor*
Identification:	Gray or reddish-brown flecked with black, black around eyes, bordered with white. Tail is bushy and ringed with black
Length (including tail):	2–3 feet
Weight:	12–45lb
Habitat/Range:	Woodland, wetlands, rural, suburban and urban areas from southern Canada throughout most of the US, but absent from areas of the Rocky Mountains and desert regions in the southwest
Similar species:	The Ringtail and the White-nosed Coati are both smaller and more slender with proportionally longer tails. The Ringtail also lacks a black eye mask.

The Common Raccoon is a highly adaptable mammal, successful across a wide range of habitats. It can both swim and climb well, eats a huge range of foods and has great dexterity with its forepaws. Able to open doors and lift the lids from garbage cans, the Common Raccoon often flourishes alongside man, scavenging for food amongst our waste. In the natural surroundings of wooded areas it will most commonly be found close to streams or lakes where it will catch insects, other invertebrates, fish, amphibians and reptiles, seeming sometimes to wash its food, but in fact, breaking it up in the water. The Raccoon also eats a range of vegetable matter, particularly fruit and nuts, and hunts for small mammals, birds and their eggs. Raccoons put on a great deal of weight as winter approaches, and although they may sleep for long periods at a time, do not truly hibernate. They will however shelter in a den, usually a hollow tree, sometimes in large groups. Dens are also used in spring and summer when nursing young.

WHITE-NOSED COATI

Scientific name:	*Nasua narica*
Identification:	Dark brown with long, white snout and white around eyes. Feet dark or black. Tail is long and slender, ringed, but indistinctly so
Length (including tail):	3–4½ feet
Weight:	17–27lb
Habitat/Range:	Mountainous woodland and rocky areas in southern parts of Texas, New Mexico and Arizona
Similar species:	The White-nosed Coati can be distinguished from both the Common Raccoon and Ringtail due to its size and coloring

The White-nosed Coati is essentially a tropical species, but its range extends from the Central Americas into North America, with quite large populations in Arizona. Males tend to be solitary, but females and their offspring will often form fairly large groups, sometimes numbering twenty or more individuals. Excellent climbers, coatis do not use dens except during the breeding season, but spend much of their time in trees, either resting in the shade or foraging for fruit, which is a favorite food. Coatis also spend the night sleeping in trees, being active during the day. As well as fruit, the White-nosed Coati eats insects, birds and small mammals, and will defend itself aggressively if threatened by larger animals such as dogs. Young are born in spring in sheltered dens amongst rocks or hollow trees.

RINGTAIL

Scientific name:	*Bassariscus astutus*
Identification:	Small, slender and catlike with gray fur and a long, bushy, black-ringed tail with a black tip. Its large eyes are surrounded by white rings
Length (including tail):	2–3 feet
Weight:	2–2½lb
Habitat/Range:	Rocky, sometimes wooded areas in the southwestern US
Similar species:	Raccoon is heavier-bodied with black eye mask. White-nosed Coati is larger, brown rather than gray and its tail bands are much less pronounced

Though not a member of the cat family, the Ringtail is cat-like in appearance and is sometimes called the "Miner's Cat" as it was used in mines to kill rats and mice. It is in fact related to the Common Raccoon and shares a similarly omnivorous diet. In addition to small mammals, the Ringtail will eat reptiles, amphibians, birds, fruit and some large invertebrates. It is incredibly agile, able to jump and climb well, and to squeeze through narrow gaps that might restrict other predators. It usually hunts at night, resting by day in a tree or secluded den, often amongst rocks or tree roots. Ringtails mate in spring, producing a litter of 2 – 4 young. Once weaned, both parents will participate in caring for their offspring. By the end of summer, the young Ringtails will be hunting alone. As well as "Miner's Cat", they are also known as "Cacomistles", derived from a Mexican Indian name meaning "half mountain lion", and also as "Civet Cats" since, like the African Civet, they can produce a strong musk.

NORTHERN RIVER OTTER

Scientific name:	*Lutra canadensis*
Identification:	Long and slender with short legs, long tapering tail and webbed feet. Coat is dark brown, lighter or silvery on throat
Length (including tail):	3–4 feet
Weight:	12–30lb
Habitat/Range:	Rivers, lakes, marshes and sometimes estuaries across most of Canada and much of the US, but now largely absent from many Midwestern states
Similar species:	The Sea Otter is larger and stockier with a shorter tail, and is found in sea water along the Pacific Coast

The Northern River Otter is mainly nocturnal, usually spending the day in a bank-side burrow, but where undisturbed it may be abroad in daylight hours, hunting for fish and invertebrates, or playing in and around the water. Otters are noted for their playful behavior, often chasing each other and sliding down banks of mud or snow. Quite comfortable on land, the Northern River Otter excels when in the water and is agile and powerful enough to catch quite large fish. Well adapted to aquatic life, swimming with webbed feet and its powerful tail, the Northern River Otter is capable of remaining submerged for several minutes at a time and is able to seal its ears and nostrils. In addition to fish and insects, otters will eat small mammals and the nestlings of aquatic birds. The Northern River Otter mates in spring, but as with some other mammals, female otters delay the implantation of the fertilized ova and will not give birth until the following March or April. The male is usually driven away until the young are about six months old, but will then care for them with the female until they become independent, usually a few months prior to the birth of a new litter.

SEA OTTER

Scientific name:	*Enhydra lutris*
Identification:	Dark brown, with a gray head and underside, becoming whiter in older males. The tail is short and feet are webbed, the hind feet being much more flipper-like
Length (including tail):	3–5½ feet
Weight:	25–75lb
Habitat/Range:	Coastal waters, particularly shallow kelp beds along the Pacific Coast
Similar species:	The Northern River Otter is found in fresh water, is smaller and has a longer tail

The Sea Otter dwells in rocky coastal shallows where its food is most abundant and it is rarely found more than a mile from the coast. However, it also hardly ever comes ashore; feeding, sleeping and even giving birth at sea, usually taking to land only when threatened by severe storms. Well adapted for a marine existence, the Sea Otter is not surprisingly a good swimmer, but it is most likely to be seen floating lazily on its back, preening itself or feeding. Sea Otters lack the blubber of other marine mammals, instead relying on their dense fur for insulation and buoyancy, and they therefore spend a great deal of time grooming and cleaning their coats. Whilst the Sea Otter's webbed hind feet may make it clumsy when out of the water, its forepaws are hand-like and Sea Otters display a high level of dexterity, being amongst the few animals that use tools. When diving for shellfish they will also collect a stone with which to crack open their prey, a task performed lying on their backs, with the stone placed against their chest. Favorite foods include abalone, crabs and sea urchins, but they will also feed on other invertebrates and fish. Sea Otters may breed at any time of year if conditions are favorable, but young are usually born in late winter or spring, following a gestation period of up to nine months.

MINK

Scientific name:	*Mustela vison*
Identification:	Long and slender with dark brown or black fur, a small white patch on chin and a long, bushy tail
Length (including tail):	18–28 inches
Weight:	2–3½lb
Habitat/Range:	Close to freshwater; lakes, rivers, streams and marshland throughout most of Canada and the US, except for arid southwestern regions
Similar species:	American Marten is around the same size but has a light, or orange-colored throat, longer tail and larger ears

AMERICAN MARTEN ▶

Scientific name:	*Martes americana*
Identification:	Long and slender, brown back with lighter face and underside, with orange or yellow patch on throat. Tail is long and bushy
Length (including tail):	20 – 27 inches
Weight:	1½–3½lb
Habitat/Range:	Mainly coniferous forests across much of Canada and Alaska. In the US, found south to New York in the east, and to northern California, and the Rocky Mountains in the west
Similar species:	Mink is darker, lacks throat patch and has a shorter tail. The Fisher is much larger

The Mink is semi-aquatic and is always found close to water, hunting for its prey either along the banks, or in the water itself. A good swimmer, with partially webbed feet, Mink are capable of catching fish, but eat a wide variety of small animals, preying on reptiles, amphibians, waterfowl, and a range of mammals, up to the size of rabbits and muskrats. Mink are fierce predators, but they are also solitary and highly territorial, and except when coming together to breed, will fight when they encounter another of their own species. Mating takes place from late winter to April, with young males typically mating with a number of females, being inclined to become more monogamous with age. Females give birth to up to ten young in a den, usually a muskrat burrow, from spring to early summer, and they are weaned at about six weeks. Like skunks and many other members of the weasel family, or *Mustelidae*, the Mink is capable of producing a noxious discharge from its anal glands, and does so when threatened or marking territory.

The American Marten is mainly nocturnal and an extremely good climber, often resting in a hollow tree during the day, sometimes in the former nest of a squirrel or woodpecker, though it will also den in a log or amongst rocks. When active, martens spend much of their time hunting on the forest floor, particularly for voles and other rodents, but they have a varied diet, taking rabbits, squirrels, birds, reptiles and insects, also eating vegetation such as seeds and berries. Like the mink, the American Marten is generally solitary and it scent marks its territory, being aggressive to other martens outside of the breeding season. Martens mate in summer, but implantation into the uterine wall is delayed for around seven months, with a litter of three to four, blind, helpless young being born in spring.

FISHER

Scientific name:	*Martes pennanti*
Identification:	Long, but stocky, with thick, dark brown fur, sometimes flecked with gold or silver hairs, particularly on head. Long bushy tail
Length (including tail):	2½–3½ feet
Weight:	3–16lb
Habitat/Range:	Dense, mainly coniferous forest across the southern half of Canada, south to northern California and the Rocky Mountains in the west, and to New York in the east
Similar species:	Larger, darker and more heavily built than the American Marten, also lacks throat patch. Larger than the Mink

The Fisher resembles a large, powerful Mink, and perhaps it was given its name due to being confused with its more aquatic relative, for though it can swim it rarely eats fish. It is however a voracious predator, frequently hunting small to medium-sized mammals such as squirrels and Snowshoe Hares. It is also one of the few animals that will kill and eat Porcupines, attempting to avoid the Porcupine's sharp quills by circling its slower quarry, launching attacks on its face and attempting to roll it over. As well as eating mammals, the Fisher also climbs trees in search of birds' eggs, fruit and nuts. Fishers tend to wander over quite large territories, and as such, they do not usually have a permanent den or burrow, but may have a number of temporary hiding places amongst vegetation, hollow logs or tree roots. Females will use a den when expecting to give birth, most commonly making a nest within a hollow tree, where a litter of up to six young will be born.

WOLVERINE

Scientific name:	*Gulo gulo*
Identification:	Quite bear-like in appearance, heavily built, with short legs and a fairly short, bushy tail. Fur is dark, but two light, or yellow bands extend from the shoulders to the tail and there are light patches above the eyes
Length (including tail):	3–3½ feet
Weight:	20–40lb
Habitat/Range:	Forests and tundra in Alaska and northern Canada. Also found in remote, mountainous parts of the western US
Similar species:	Similar build to the American Badger, though usually larger and lacking distinctive white facial markings

The Wolverine is the largest member of the weasel family, and is sometimes known as the "Glutton" on account of its seemingly vast appetite. It moves almost constantly through its territory searching for food, covering an area of hundreds of square miles. Wolverines are omnivorous, eating a wide range of smaller animals, vegetation and particularly carrion, but they are powerful enough to bring down young, weak or snowbound Moose, and are fierce enough to drive much larger predators, including Mountain Lions and bears away from their kills. Unlike many carnivores that will bury excess food or carry it to a den, the Wolverine instead scent-marks any surplus with a repellent musk, ensuring that it is unattractive to other scavengers. Wolverines are solitary, but may mate at any time from spring to fall, probably because the male and female seldom encounter one another. They do not hibernate, but the female tends to delay implantation until winter, with a litter of up to five cubs being born in a cave or burrow the following spring. The young may stay with their mother for up to two years before dispersing.

AMERICAN BADGER

Scientific name:	*Taxidea taxus*
Identification:	Broad and stocky, with shaggy, gray fur, short legs and distinctive black and white facial markings. A white stripe usually runs from the nose to the back of the neck, but may extend to the tail, particularly in southwestern populations
Length (including tail):	2–2½ feet
Weight:	8–25lb
Habitat/Range:	Mainly open grasslands, sometimes in marshy areas or near woodland. Found throughout much of the US, west from the Great Lakes in southern Canada, south to Mexico, but largely absent from eastern states
Similar species:	The Wolverine shares a similar build, but is larger, with longer legs and lacks white cheeks and facial stripe

Amongst the larger members of the weasel family, the American Badger is squat and powerfully built, with strong claws for digging. It is primarily nocturnal, usually spending the day in an underground burrow. Badgers may have several such dens throughout their territory, and will wander between them at night in search of food, often staying in a particular burrow for only a day or so at a time. The American Badger eats a range of small animals including reptiles, insects and birds nesting on the ground, but it is especially well adapted to catching small subterranean mammals such as ground squirrels and prairie dogs, which it will dig from the soil. Leftover food is stored in one of its burrows. Though it has few predators and can be aggressive, a threatened American Badger may attempt to dig a burrow on the spot, in much the same way as an Armadillo. Solitary outside of the breeding season, the male will seek a mate in late summer, with the young being born in spring. The mother gives birth to up to five young in a fairly complex maternity burrow, and they are weaned in about two months.

Above: The long-tailed weasel

WEASELS

The three species of North American weasels vary somewhat in appearance and distribution, but are similar in behavior and habitat. All are voracious predators, capable of killing creatures much larger than themselves if smaller, less challenging prey is not available. They are often found in forests and around farmland, and although they are useful in controlling rodents, poultry farmers regard them as pests. Weasels tend to make homes in the burrows of small mammals such as chipmunks and ground squirrels, sometimes having eaten the former occupants. They line the nest chamber with the fur and feathers of their prey.

The **Long-tailed Weasel** (*Mustela frenata*) is slim with a brown back, legs and feet; the underside is lighter and the tail has a black tip. It is 11-20 inches long and weighs 4-11 ounces. This species is found across southern Canada and the US, but is absent from the arid areas of the southwest.

The **Short-tailed Weasel** (*Mustela erminea*) is slender with a dark brown back, white underside and feet, and a black-tipped tail. It is 7½-13 inches in length and weighs 2-6½ ounces. Its range covers much of Canada, western US and the Great Lakes.

The **Least Weasel** (*Mustela nivalis*) is very small and has a short tail. It is brown, with white feet and underside. It is 6½-8 inches long, and weighs a mere 1¼-2 ounces. This species is found across most of Canada, ranging south to the Great Lakes and the Appalachian Mountains.

The two larger species will kill and eat mammals as big as rabbits, but the Least Weasel, North America's smallest carnivore, feeds almost exclusively on voles and mice. Long-tailed and Short-tailed weasels mate in summer, but delayed implantation ensures that offspring do not appear until the following spring. The Least Weasel, however, may produce several litters in one year. Weasels may be active by day or night, and individuals of all three species may turn white in winter in the northern parts of their ranges; the Long-tailed and Short-tailed retain their black tail-tips, the Least becomes completely white. The Short-tailed is sometimes called the Ermine, particularly in its winter coloring, and is referred to as the Stoat at other times. "Ermine" is sometimes applied to any weasel that has turned white.

BLACK-FOOTED FERRET

Scientific name:	*Mustela nigripes*
Identification:	Long and slender, light brown or sandy-colored , with black feet, raccoon-like eye mask and black tail tip
Length (including tail):	20–23 inches
Weight:	19–22oz
Habitat/Range:	Dry prairie regions around Prairie Dog towns in South Dakota and surrounding areas
Similar species:	May be distinguished from similar species by black mask across the eyes

Once found across much of the Great Plains region, the Black-footed Ferret is currently one of the rarest species in North America, found in small numbers in western prairie areas around Montana and South Dakota. Highly dependent on Prairie Dogs as a source of food, Black-footed Ferret populations were devastated as Prairie Dogs were culled in many areas. They are however beginning to be slowly re-established with the aid of captive breeding and release programs. The Black-footed Ferret often lives amongst Prairie Dog towns, sometimes enlarging the burrows of its prey, where it usually remains during the day, emerging at night to hunt. In addition to Prairie Dogs, it will take other small rodents, reptiles and ground-nesting birds, killing, as weasels do, with a bite to the back of the neck. Although the Black-footed Ferret has a relatively short gestation period in comparison to many other members of the weasel family (around forty days), it produces only one litter per year. Three to five young are usual, and they will become sexually mature at about one year.

SKUNKS

Those members of the weasel family (*Mustelidae*) known as skunks are chiefly noted for their boldly patterned fur and their defensive strategy. Their striking black and white coloration issues a warning to would-be predators; if the warning is unheeded, skunks can release a spray of foul-smelling, irritant fluid over a distance of ten feet and more. This is an effective deterrent in most cases, although birds of prey, particularly the Great Horned Owl, may surprise and kill a skunk without a confrontation. Skunks are omnivorous, feeding on small mammals, amphibians and invertebrates, fruit and vegetable matter. Although skunks do not hibernate, they may become less active in cold weather, taking to a burrow or other shelter. They also use dens when bearing and raising young.

The **Striped Skunk** (*Mephitis mephitis*) is usually black with two white stripes on its back. These meet at the neck and the base of the tail, which is bushy and tipped or fringed with white. This species is 20-30 inches long and weighs 7-15lb. The Striped Skunk is widely distributed across the US and southern Canada. When threatened or disturbed, it will display its tail and chatter and stomp the ground, spraying its musk as a last resort.

The **Eastern Spotted Skunk** (*Spilogale putorius*) and the **Western Spotted Skunk** (*Spilogale gracilis*) are small animals, black with white stripes on the neck and flanks, which break into spots on the back and rump. Both measure 14–21 inches and weigh 1–1½ lb. The Eastern Spotted is found through central midwestern and southeastern states; the Western Spotted is located to the west of this range. They overlap in Wyoming.

Skunks usually mate in late winter and early spring, and in the Striped Skunk there is a short delay in implantation. Litters of up to seven are born in late spring and early summer. The Western Spotted Skunk is sometimes classified separately from its eastern relative because of its different breeding pattern; it tends to mate in late summer and fall, bearing young in spring following delayed implantation.

In addition to the more common skunks, there are two forms of Hog-nosed Skunk and the Hooded Skunk; these are similar in behavior to other skunks, and inhabit rocky, arid terrain or scrubland in Arizona, New Mexico and Texas.

Below: The Striped Skunk
Opposite: The short-tailed weasel in its winter coloring.

HOOFED
MAMMALS

COLLARED PECCARY

Scientific name:	*Tayassu tajacu*
Identification:	Fairly small pig-like animal with a large head, long snout and downward-pointing tusks. The coat is coarse and grizzled gray or black with a pale collar around the neck and shoulders. Tail is short and inconspicuous
Length (including tail):	3–3½ feet
Weight:	30–60lb
Habitat/Range:	Desert, and dry brush or rocky areas in parts of Arizona, New Mexico and Texas
Similar species:	Similar to feral pigs and the wild boar, but smaller and lacking clearly visible tail. Tusks curve downwards rather than up

Although feral pigs and the European Wild Boar may be encountered in North America, the Collared Peccary is the only pig-like animal native to the US. This species is subtropical and found south through the Americas to Argentina, but its range extends into some southern states of the US. Once much more numerous, the Collared Peccary would at one time have been found in huge herds, but today groups tend to number up to around thirty animals. Territorial and led by a dominant male, Collared Peccaries move around in the early morning and evening in search of food, sometimes breaking into smaller groups to feed. They secrete a strong musk as they do so, probably as a means of locating each other or for marking territory. Mainly herbivorous, peccaries feed on a number of different succulent plants, cacti, fruit and roots, but they will also eat insects, small mammals and reptiles from time to time. The Collared Peccary may breed throughout the year, but females usually only produce one litter each, the dominant male mating with several herd members. Litters number up to about six young, born after a gestation period of around five months.

MOUNTAIN GOAT

Scientific name:	*Oreamnos americanus*
Identification:	Stocky, short-legged bovid with thick, yellow-white fur, which is shaggier in winter. Male has short beard, both sexes have fairly short, black horns, only slightly curved
Length (including tail):	4 – 5½ feet
Weight:	120–180 lb (Male larger than female)
Habitat/Range:	Rocky, mountainous terrain in western and northwestern parts of Canada and the US
Similar species:	This species can be most easily distinguished from mountain sheep by its almost straight, rather than coiled horns

Although Mountain Goats may be found nearer to the timberline in winter, in summer they retreat high into the mountains away from potential predators, and spend their time in alpine meadows or deftly moving about steep, craggy cliff faces in search of vegetation. Usually most active in the morning and evening, the Mountain Goat may be seen in small groups, sometimes dust-bathing in the summer months. Males and females remain apart until fall when mating takes place, and though males will often challenge each other or engage in sparring, serious fights tend not to occur, as the horns and skull of this species are relatively frail. Due to the nature of the terrain that the Mountain Goat inhabits, few predators pose a threat, accidental falls and landslides being a greater danger. Golden Eagles however, may kill kids.

BIGHORN SHEEP

Scientific name:	*Ovis canadensis*
Identification:	Thickset, brown sheep with white nose, rump patch and underparts. Male has large spiraling horns, those of the female are smaller and less curved
Length (including tail):	4½–6 feet
Weight:	80–300lb (Male larger than female)
Habitat/Range:	Sparsely vegetated, rocky slopes from alpine meadows to desert areas. Found in scattered populations in the west, from British Columbia south to New Mexico
Similar species:	The Mountain Goat occurs within parts of its range but is smaller, and white or yellowish with straighter horns

Spending much of its time on high mountain slopes, the Bighorn Sheep has specially adapted hooves with soft soles and is able to traverse almost sheer surfaces. It feeds by day on grasses and other vegetation, and sleeps in a scrape or depression at night. For most of the year males and females herd together in small groups, but as it gets colder Bighorn Sheep migrate down into valleys, with females forming much larger herds. Throughout fall, males seek out potential mates within these herds, engaging in duels with each other, running and butting their heads together with considerable force. In spring the Bighorn Sheep return to higher ground, and it is here that the females give birth. The lambs are born well developed and are able to move around confidently within a matter of days.

(American) Bison/ Buffalo

Scientific name:	*Bison bison*
Identification:	Huge bovid, with males standing up to six feet tall at their humped shoulders. The forequarters are covered in a shaggy mane that extends down the front legs. Both sexes have relatively short, black horns
Length (including tail):	7–12½ feet
Weight:	800–2000lb (Male larger than female)
Habitat/Range:	Mainly open short-grass prairie areas, occasionally woodland. Some free-ranging populations in Alaska and Canada, but largely confined to national parks
Similar species:	Unmistakable

The American Bison or Buffalo is North America's largest land-dwelling animal, and at one time it was also amongst the most numerous. It was invaluable to the Native Americans, for whom it not only represented a source of food, but also provided them with materials for clothing, tools and fuel. However, by around 1900, settlers with guns had hunted the American Bison almost to extinction. It now survives only in relatively small numbers in national parks and on private ranches. American Bison are diurnal, but will rest during the hottest part of the day, preferring to graze in the morning and evening, eating grasses and similar vegetation. As with many bovids, the sexes tend to herd separately outside of the breeding season, often in quite small groups of up to twenty individuals. During the rut however, mixed herds of many thousand may congregate. Males will seek out females in heat and attempt to separate them from the herd, a behavior known as "tending". At this time, males become aggressive to one another and may fight. This usually involves butting, but bulls may also gore each other with their horns, which can potentially lead to fatal injuries. Mating is followed by a gestation period of around nine months, and the well-developed newborn calves are able to stand within an hour of birth. They initially remain with the mother, but may then group together in a nursery herd.

MUSKOX

Scientific name:	*Ovibos moschatus*
Identification:	Large longhaired bovid, cattle-sized but otherwise quite sheep-like in appearance. Hair is shaggy and dark brown with a light saddle on the back. Both sexes have brown, downward curving horns, but those of the male are larger
Length (including tail):	6½–8 feet
Weight:	400–900lb (Male larger than female)
Habitat/Range:	Open tundra in northern Canada, some semi-domesticated herds located in Alaska
Similar species:	Unmistakable

The Muskox lives primarily in the northernmost reaches of Canada and on the surrounding Arctic islands, protected from the cold by a thick, shaggy coat that reaches almost to its feet. Males and females group together in small herds, remaining on the tundra throughout the year, but spend the summer in sheltered, grassy meadows, braving more inhospitable, windswept slopes in winter, where vegetation is likely to be exposed. Muskox feed on grasses, sedges and willow when available, eating hardier, woody plants in winter. The Muskox does not actually produce musk, as its name might suggest, but produces powerful-smelling urine, particularly during late summer and fall when breeding occurs. At this time the dominant male will attempt to force other males from the herd, and may mate with all the females. Breeding typically takes place once every two years, and the gestation period may last up to nine months. Wolves are the main threat to young or weak Muskox, but when confronted, this species forms into a defensive circle, with the formidable horns facing outwards, and the young protected in the middle.

MOOSE

Scientific name:	*Alces alces*
Identification:	A massive dark brown deer with long, pale legs, a shoulder hump and a huge head with a fleshy muzzle. Males develop antlers up to 5 feet across and have a large dewlap beneath the chin
Length (including tail):	7–10 feet
Weight:	700–1400lb (Males around twice the weight of females)
Habitat/Range:	Forests, particularly in marshy areas. Found across most of Canada and through the Rocky Mountains
Similar species:	Discernible from other deer by its size, broad, pendulous nose and huge palmate antlers

The Moose is the largest member of the deer family and is easily recognized by its considerable size, elongated head, dewlap and large, overhanging snout. In summer males also develop huge flattened antlers, shedding them during the winter months. Moose are often found in marshy areas, and though generally solitary outside of the breeding season, a group may congregate near water to feed on aquatic vegetation in spring or summer. In winter the Moose tends to eat more woody vegetation such as twigs and bark. Mating takes place in fall and may be preceded by highly vocal behavior, particularly between males vying for the attention of a female. Fighting sometimes occurs between bulls, and can prove fatal, but it is usually avoided, with one male backing down from a challenge. The successful male will remain with the cow for one or two days, during which time they will mate. Pregnancy lasts for around eight months, at the end of which one or two, lightly colored calves are born in early summer. Moose are often shy, but are potentially dangerous, being most aggressive during the breeding season or when they are with calves.

ELK/WAPITI

Scientific name:	*Cervus elaphus*
Identification:	Large brown deer with pale rump and yellowish tail, grayer in winter. Males have large branching antlers from summer to spring
Length (including tail):	7–10 feet
Weight:	500–1000lb (Male larger than female)
Habitat/Range:	Mountainous woodlands and pastures in the western US and Canada
Similar species:	Larger than other deer except the Moose, which is heavier-bodied and has palmate antlers, a dewlap and larger muzzle

CARIBOU ▲

Scientific name:	*Rangifer tarandus*
Identification:	Large deer with branching antlers which also extend over the brow. Coat is shaggy and varies from white, to brown with white underparts.
Length (including tail):	$4\frac{1}{2}$–8 feet
Weight:	150–650lb (Male larger than female)
Habitat/Range:	Open tundra and mountainous forests across most of Canada
Similar species:	This species may be distinguished from the elk by its white, rather than reddish throat, and by the forward-pointing tines on its antlers

The Elk is also known by the Shawnee Indian name "Wapiti", which means white, or pale, deer. The Elk is a large tan or brown species that becomes more gray in winter, but there are also paler subspecies found along the Pacific coast and in parts of the Rocky Mountains. Male Elk develop large, branching antlers during the summer in time for the breeding season, which takes place from late summer until fall. Elk are very social, often forming herds numbering hundreds of individuals, particularly in open country. The main body of the herd consists of cows and their calves, whilst the bulls tend to herd together at the fringes of the group. During the rutting season males become highly vocal, emitting high-pitched whistling sounds, and they also joust, clashing antlers to establish dominance. Bulls attempt to herd many cows together and may mate with fifty or more in a season. Gestation lasts for some nine months, with the newborn then relying on its mother's milk for at least a month, gradually moving onto a diet of vegetation. The Elk is chiefly a grazing species but will feed on a variety of plants, including woody material and lichen.

The Caribou, known as the Reindeer in Europe, is unusual amongst deer species in that both the male and female develop antlers, with those of the male being larger and more broadly flattened. Males tend to lose their antlers following mating in fall, whereas the females keep theirs until summer. Caribou are a gregarious species, usually forming single-sex groups in winter, forming much larger, mixed herds prior to migration in spring. Those animals that dwell on the open tundra move northwards to their feeding grounds, where the females will give birth throughout the summer. The Caribou graze on various grasses, also consuming lichen, fruit and fungi, eating mainly lichen and other hardy vegetation in winter. In fall, the Caribou mate, with much fighting between males, who will mate with numerous females before migrating south for the winter. The Caribou is well adapted to its harsh habitat, being able to swim well and run at high speed even across snow, with its feet becoming densely haired in winter to aid traction on snow and ice.

MULE DEER

Scientific name:	*Odocoileus hemionus*
Identification:	Red-brown in summer, gray in winter, undersides paler, throat and rump white. Males have fairly large, branching antlers from summer to late winter. Large ears, black-tipped tail, top of tail black in some populations
Length (including tail):	4½–7 feet
Weight:	70–450lb (Male larger than female)
Habitat/Range:	Varied; brush, forests, desert and mountains in western Canada and US
Similar species:	The White-tailed Deer lacks black tail-tip and has smaller ears

The Mule Deer may be found in a variety of habitats, but in mountainous regions, they usually spend the winter amongst the more sheltered foothills where cover and food are most plentiful, moving to higher altitudes in spring and summer. They eat a range of vegetation, including fruits, but subsist mainly on twigs in winter. Males are often solitary, whilst females tend to form small family groups with fawns and the previous year's offspring. Females will attempt to avoid other does and may fight upon meeting. Males engage in threat displays during the breeding season, sometimes resulting in conflicts whereby they will lock antlers in displays of strength. Following mating in fall however, deer of both sexes may herd together until spring. The young are born in summer and are spotted to aid camouflage. They remain hidden in cover for around their first month of weaning, but as with adult deer, the young may fall prey to wolves, big cats or bears. As a defense against predators the Mule Deer has a good sense of hearing, aided by its large, highly mobile, mule-like ears.

WHITE-TAILED DEER

Scientific name:	*Odocoileus virginianus*
Identification:	Medium-size red-brown or tan deer, grayer in winter. Underparts, throat and edges of tail white. Males' antlers spread to around 3 feet
Length (including tail):	4½–7 feet
Weight:	90–300lb (Male larger than female)
Habitat/Range:	Woodland, brush, farmland, marshes and suburban parks and gardens across most of US and southern Canada
Similar species:	Similar to the Mule Deer, but has smaller ears and a white-fringed tail which lacks black tip

Although it remains a popular game animal, the White-tailed Deer is a widespread and common species, flourishing in areas where its numbers were once in serious decline. As with the Mule Deer, females are usually found in a family group with their young, but the males are much more sociable, forming small bands together until the breeding season. At this time they will begin to separate and challenge each other for potential mates, but they may also join large, mixed herds for the winter. Young are born in spring or summer following a six-month gestation period and are weaned within about two months, though they may stay with the mother for up to two years. White-tailed Deer feed on all kinds of green plants when they are plentiful in summer, consuming more nuts in fall and woody vegetation during the winter months. They are also good swimmers and are often found in marshy areas where they will feed on aquatic plants.

PRONGHORN

Scientific name:	*Antilocapra americana*
Identification:	Deer-like, with long legs. Black horns, reddish coat with white on flanks, rump and underside
Length (including tail):	4–4½ feet
Weight:	80–130lb (Male larger than female)
Habitat/Range:	Grassland and brush in the western US, north to southern Alberta and Saskatchewan
Similar species:	Distinctive markings and horns distinguish this species from deer

Although sometimes referred to as the American Antelope, the Pronghorn in fact, belongs to the ancient family *Antilocapridae*, of which it is the only surviving species. Both sexes have distinctive black horns, with those of the male being much larger, and having a forward-pointing prong from which the animal gains its name. Once common in large herds across the western prairies, groups seldom exceed ten individuals in summer, though in winter herds may swell to one hundred. Summer groupings are usually divided into females with fawns and young males, whilst older males tend to form territories from as early as spring and may fight to defend them. Mating takes place in fall with births occurring in summer. A single fawn is usually produced in a female's first year of reproduction, with twins common in subsequent years. The mother will separate twins and graze at a distance from them in order to minimize the chances of them being attacked by predators. The Pronghorn is amongst the fastest of terrestrial animals, relying on its speed and good eyesight to avoid predators such as Coyotes, striking with its hooves if confronted.

MARINE MAMMALS

EARED SEALS

There are four species of eared seals found in North American waters, including the massive **Northern Sea Lion** (*Eumetopias jubatus*) and the threatened **Guadalupe Fur Seal** (*Arctocephalus townsendi*). All are found along parts of the Pacific Coast, with the Northern Sea Lion and Northern Fur Seal occurring as far north as Alaska. The Guadalupe Fur Seal however, is confined to the coastal islands of southern California and Mexico, breeding only on Guadalupe Island. As their name suggests, the eared seals have visible external ears. They are also more agile on land than other seals, able to walk on their large, mobile, flippers, and they tend to be fairly slender, with long necks.

The **California Sea Lion** (*Zalophus californianus*) is perhaps most familiar as the trained "circus seal", and is in fact very inquisitive and playful in the wild, sometimes playing with large fish or found objects and leaping clear of the surface whilst swimming at speeds of up to 25 mph (40 km/h). At times this curiosity threatens the California Sea Lion however, and many are killed or injured by discarded fishing line and nets. Usually hunting at night, this species preys mainly on small schooling fish, squid, rockfish, flatfish, hake, lamprey, and salmon, spending the day basking on the shore. The California Sea Lion is a gregarious species, often found in large single-sex groups outside of the breeding season. Females remain in southern California, nursing their pups for up to a year at a time, whilst bulls typically congregate in the north of their range until summer. Breeding males head south to establish territories in May or June and will fight to defend them, barking almost constantly. The females will come ashore to give birth around this time, and then mate about one month later. The males will return north in late summer or early fall. Chief predators of the California Sea Lion include large sharks and the Killer Whale.

The **Northern Fur Seal** (*Callorhinus ursinus*) is quite solitary and spends almost all of its time in the open ocean, usually only coming ashore to breed. It is also rarely seen on the mainland, instead utilising islands in the Pacific, particularly the Pribilof Islands, where over a million seals may gather in summer. Bulls tend to arrive first and begin to establish territories from late May to early June. Pregnant females arrive in June and July to give birth, and bulls will attempt to herd them into harems, aggressively guarding perhaps thirty or forty females from other males. The females nurse their newborn young for about 10 days before mating, and will then go to sea to feed on fish, squid and octopus for four or five days. As with most seals, the bulls do not feed during the breeding season. Females then begin to feed for longer periods, nursing the young for one or two days at a time. The pups are weaned after about four months. Year-old males and females come ashore to mate in late summer, and they will have all dispersed by fall, some migrating as far as California or even Asia.

Opposite: **Northern Fur Seals**
Above: **A group of Californian Sea Lions**

HAIR SEALS (*Phocidae*)

The hair seals, or true seals, are the most common carnivorous, marine mammals in North American waters, with some ten species present, ranging from the small Ringed Seal (*Pusa hispida*) to the huge Northern Elephant Seal (*Mirounga angustirostris*). Unlike sealions and fur seals, hair seals lack external ears and are less agile on land, unable to support their weight with their relatively small flippers. This family is so called due to their haired flippers, which are also fully clawed and well adapted for swimming. With the exception of the West Indian Monk Seal (*Monachus tropicalis*), the Northern Elephant Seal, and the Harbor Seal, hair seals almost exclusively inhabit cold, northern waters off Alaska and Canada, dwelling on and around the pack ice.

The **Harbor Seal** (*Phoca vitulina*) is the only seal commonly found along the US mainland coasts and is present in both the east and west, as well as being found in Arctic waters. Unlike most seals, which remain on land for about a month after birth, the pups of the Harbor Seal are able to swim with the mother almost immediately. However, they are amongst the most sociable of all seals and spend much of their time basking on the shore, sometimes in groups of thousands. The Harbor Seal typically rests between tides, entering the water to feed as high tide approaches. As with most seals, this species feeds mainly on fish, mollusks and crustaceans, and is able to remain submerged for around half an hour. In spring the Harbor Seal may ascend upstream in pursuit of spawning fish, and there are landlocked populations that now live exclusively in freshwater lakes.

In contrast, the **Harp Seal** (*Pagophilus groenlandius*) undertakes massive migrations in Arctic waters, often following shoals of cod. In fall as the bays become increasingly frozen, the Harp Seals travel from the far north and from Hudson Bay in order to winter along the Newfoundland coast, where they will spend much of the time hunting for food. In late winter these seals breed, forming huge colonies on the pack ice around Newfoundland and southern parts of Greenland. Mating takes place at sea, with the pups being born on land in early spring. Initially white, the distinctive, dark, harp-shaped markings form over many years and moults, and in the intermediate stages the Harp Seal is usually silver-gray with spots or blotches.

The **Ribbon Seal** (*Histriophoca fastiata*) is comparable in size and shape to the Harp Seal, and also exhibits distinctive markings. Rather than a dark saddle however, this species is dark overall, with white rings around its rump, neck and front flippers. It is generally solitary and seldom comes close to the shore, but bears its young on ice floes in spring or early summer.

Opposite: The Common or Harbor Seal
Above: The Harp Seal

The large **Bearded Seal** (*Erignathus barbatus*) is also usually solitary, but may be found in groups of forty to fifty individuals during May when they gather to breed. Bearded Seals are highly vocal, particularly during the mating season, and the males may also fight. This species uses its claws for digging out mollusks and crustaceans, and for clearing breathing holes in the ice.

The **Gray Seal** (*Halichoerus grypus*) is another large species and is often found further inland than other seals, congregating on large islands to breed and to bear young. Also quite vocal, males make threat displays to each other during the mating season and may fight, biting at the neck of opponents. The young of the Gray Seal are weaned after a few weeks, and are then left to fend for themselves, usually remaining on land for a further month while developing their adult coat. Young seals are particularly prone to predation, but adult seals also face many dangers, and are at risk from Polar Bears, Sharks, Killer Whales and even Walruses.

NORTHERN ELEPHANT SEAL

Scientific name:	*Mirounga angustirostris*
Identification:	A huge brown or gray seal with a large rounded head. Males develop trunk-like nose by adulthood, and are often heavily scarred from fighting
Length (including tail):	10–15+ feet
Weight:	1000–4000+lb (Male larger than female)
Habitat/Range:	Open ocean for much of the year, from the Gulf of Alaska to Mexico, breeds on Californian coast and surrounding islands
Similar species:	Size and distinctive snout make this species unmistakable

The Northern Elephant Seal is the world's second-largest seal, smaller only than the Southern Elephant Seal (*Mirounga leonina*), which inhabits Antarctic waters. It occurs in the Pacific Ocean from Mexico to Alaska and may be found on both islands and remote parts of the mainland, preferring sandy beaches in temperate or warm waters when breeding and molting. The mating season lasts from winter to spring, and begins with males arriving at the breeding beaches in Mexico and California around December. Here the males fight for territory in advance of the arrival of the females. Displays involve much bellowing and the inflation of the trunk-like nose, frequently leading to quite savage fighting. The females arrive soon after and give birth to pups that may weigh up to eighty pounds. The young are weaned after about one month, after which mating will take place. Following this, the Elephant Seals leave the young and return to the sea to feed, returning to molt in summer. The Northern Elephant Seal can remain submerged for over an hour and feeds at depths of up to 5000 feet. It eats a variety of deep-sea fish and squid. Due to their considerable size, adults have few natural enemies, though large sharks and Killer Whales will prey on young or weak individuals.

WALRUS

Scientific name:	*Odobenus rosmarus*
Identification:	Large, seal-like animal with pink or brown skin. Walruses have a fine layer of hairs but lack fur. Large tusks extend from heavily bristled muzzle
Length (including tail):	7½–12 feet
Weight:	800–3000+lb (Male larger than female, also Pacific individuals larger than those found in the Atlantic)
Habitat/Range:	Relatively shallow waters around pack ice. In the Atlantic, around Hudson Bay and Greenland, in the Pacific, found off Alaska in winter, but some migrate across the Bering Sea
Similar species:	Unmistakable

The Walrus is the only species in the family *Odobenidae*, and although it does not have visible ears, it is thought to be more closely related to the eared seals than to the hair seals, being able to rotate its hind flippers to walk on land. It spends a great deal of its time on shorelines and ice floes, feeding in the morning and basking throughout the day. Walruses are highly gregarious and are usually found in mixed groups of many hundred animals. The Walrus is primarily a bottom feeder, using its sensitive vibrissae, or whiskers, to find crustaceans and mollusks on the ocean floor, dislodging them with the aid of its tusks. It also feeds on some fish and carrion, and has even been known to kill and eat seals, impaling them with its tusks. Tusks are also used in defense, and are a sign of social standing between males, who may use them in territorial disputes during the breeding season. In contrast to seals, females do not mate in the same year as they bear young. Mating takes place in winter, and calves are born from spring to summer. They will remain with the mother for up to two years while their tusks develop. Walruses are very protective of their young, and as with some other herd animals, will also defend adults from attack, though healthy individuals have few enemies. Indigenous peoples are entitled to hunt the Walrus for subsistence, and Killer Whales and Polar Bears may attack juveniles or injured animals.

(WEST INDIAN) MANATEE

Scientific name:	*Trichechus manatus*
Identification:	Huge cigar-shaped body, walrus-like head with bristled, cleft upper lip. Skin is gray to brown and almost hairless. Forelegs are adapted into large paddles, hind legs into a single fluke. Lacks external ears
Length (including tail):	8–12 feet
Weight:	1000–3500lb
Habitat/Range:	Coastal shallows, estuaries, rivers and lagoons on the east coast, particularly around Florida
Similar species:	No similar species in range

Perhaps surprisingly, the Manatee and other members of the order *Sirenia* are not closely related to other aquatic mammals such as seals, but rather to hoofed mammals, and elephants in particular. The Manatee is a herbivorous species, browsing on aquatic vegetation such as lilies and water hyacinth, and though it never hauls itself completely out of the water as seals do, it may graze on bank-side grasses and other plants, sometimes grasping them with its flippers. Only found in warm water, Manatees tend to move further upstream in winter, and may be attracted to power station outflows, though food is often more scarce in such areas. They are fairly sociable, gathering in small groups, particularly when seeking warmer waters or when breeding. There is no fixed breeding season, and females reproduce only every few years or so, probably when conditions are most favorable. Females may attract several males, and mate more than once. Gestation is long, lasting for a year or more, and results in the birth of a single calf. A few hours after birth, Manatees begin to nurse their young. The nipples are located under the pectoral (front) flippers, and suckling takes place underwater. The calf will begin to eat vegetation after the first few weeks of weaning, and though it may be weaned by the end of the first year, it usually stays with the mother for up to two years. Slow-moving and inquisitive, Manatees were once heavily hunted in the US, but are now protected. Dangers are still presented by boats however, and sharks, crocodilians and Killer Whales may attack the young.

BALEEN WHALES (*Mysticetes*)

Whales are broadly divided into two groups, the baleen whales (*Mysticetes*) and the toothed whales (*Odontocetes*). Baleen whales lack teeth, and instead their upper jaws are lined with rows of baleen plates that filter zooplankton and other small animals from the water. In spite of feeding off this often microscopic prey, baleen whales tend to be huge, and consume tons of food each day. Other distinguishing features of this group include a double blowhole and tiny or absent dorsal fins. Most of the baleen whales found in North American waters are further classified in a group known as rorqual whales, based upon their method of feeding. They expand their pleated throats in order to take in huge mouthfuls of food and water, before forcing the water out through the baleen plates.

The smallest and most abundant of the rorqual whales is the **Northern Minke Whale** (*Balaenoptera acutorostrata*), which is found on both coastlines, often close to the shore. It grows to around thirty feet, and may be identified by white markings that extend from the belly to the center of its back, and white bands on its fins. It also has the largest dorsal fin relative to its body size.

Other rorquals are far less common, and most have failed to make a significant recovery, having suffered greatly from commercial whaling in earlier centuries. The **Fin Whale** (*Balaenoptera physalus*) is no exception, but it may come close to the shore during its migrations from warmer southern waters to the north Atlantic in summer. It is quite often seen surfacing, though it rarely raises its tail fluke above the water as some species do. The Fin Whale grows to around eighty feet in length and is exceeded in size only by the **Blue Whale** (*Balaenoptera musculus*), which may reach over 100 feet and weigh over 300,000 pounds (150 tons). Despite its immense bulk however, the Blue Whale is highly streamlined. It is usually blue-gray in color with a lighter underside and large white-tipped fins. The dorsal fin is small and set close to the tail fluke. Although found in the Atlantic, this species is most common in the Pacific, and the Californian coast has the highest density of Blue Whales anywhere in the world, with a population of around 2000.

Amongst the most distinctive of the rorqual whales are the **Right Whale** (*Eubalaena glacialis*) and the **Humpback Whale** (*Megaptera novaeangliae*). Both average around fifty feet in length and are predominantly black, the Humpback Whale having white undersides

and very long, narrow, mottled fins. It has a small dorsal fin quite close to the tail, which gives the whale a humped appearance when it dives. The Right Whale has no dorsal fin, having a characteristic, smooth back, and a distinctive shape provided by the narrow, highly arched upper jaw. It is not commonly seen however, and is amongst the rarest of all whales. The Humpback is also endangered, but is familiar as the most acrobatic and vocal of the large whales, often breaching, that is leaping clear of the water, and slapping the surface with its fins and tail fluke. It is also more gregarious than other rorqual whales, and cooperates in catching fish and krill using a unique method of "bubble net" feeding. One or more whales release a string of bubbles to encircle prey, before swimming through them, gulping in large amounts of water as usual.

The **Gray Whale** (*Eschrichtus robustus*) is a baleen whale, but unlike the rorqual whales, it feeds on bottom-dwelling invertebrates by filtering mud that it sucks in at the sides of its mouth and then expels through its baleen plates. It grows to about forty or fifty feet, with the males usually being smaller than the females. Gray Whales tend to remain quite close to the shore, and live along the west coast, migrating from Alaska to Baja California, Mexico in fall, returning north in spring.

Baleen whales tend to reproduce once every few years, usually producing one calf after a gestation period of about a year. Calves typically nurse for between six months and a year, though may remain with the mother for longer.

Above: Minke Whale
Opposite: Humpback Whales

TOOTHED WHALES (*Odontocetes*)

Aside from having teeth, toothed whales or *Odontocetes*, are generally smaller and faster-swimming than the baleen whales, and are able to feed on larger prey, hunting for fish and other animals, rather than sifting huge amounts of water to obtain food. They also have a single blowhole opening, and are usually more gregarious, sometimes hunting in packs. Toothed whales navigate by sonar, and most species have characteristically domed heads that contain an organ known as a melon, through which sound is directed. This group includes the dolphin family, *Delphinidae.*

The **Beluga**, or **White Whale** (*Delphinapterus leucas*) is small at 10-15 feet, and weighs 2200-3300lb, males being larger than females. It is entirely white with a distinctive domed head, and lacks a dorsal fin. Calves are four or five feet long at birth, blue-gray or brownish, and become paler with age. Most are born in spring and suckle for one to two years whilst their teeth are developing. About a year after birth they begin to eat fish, mollusks and crustaceans. Belugas feed mainly in shallow water, on or near the seabed. They use echo-location at frequencies beyond the range of human hearing, and also employ a selection of audible calls, giving rise to the alternative name "sea canary". They have mobile, seemingly expressive features, and can move their heads from side to side and up and down, as their neckbones are not fused as they are in other whales. Belugas are found in Arctic waters, usually close to the shore or to ice floes, and can also be seen in fresh water, in rivers such as the St Lawrence in Canada and the Yukon in Alaska.

The **Killer Whale** (*Orcinus orca*), sometimes called the "Orca", is the biggest member of the dolphin family (*Delphinidae*), 20-30 feet long and weighing 3000-12000 lb, males being larger than females. Distinctive black and white coloration and a large dorsal fin make this the most easily recognized of all whales. They often live in groups (pods) of up to fifty members, and different pods tend to have specific characteristics and identities, including distinct vocalizations, feeding habits and migratory patterns. Groups exhibiting these behavioral differences have been categorized as "resident", "transient" and "offshore", the last-named living in the open oceans in the largest groups. Transient populations are thought to roam wide territories, hunting in packs, feeding mainly on seals, other whales and dolphins. Resident populations are smaller family groups whose members may remain together for life, moving seasonally between well-defined areas and eating mainly fish. Killer Whales inhabit all oceans at various temperatures and depths; in North American waters they are most often seen in temperate areas, but they can also be found in the Arctic. Mating usually occurs in fall and winter, when many pods may congregate, sometimes resulting in the formation of new groups.

Above: The Killer Whale

SPERM WHALE

Scientific name:	*Physeter macrocephalus*
Identification:	Large, square-headed whale, light brown to dark gray in color. Lacks dorsal fin, but has a series of ridges from dorsal hump to tail fluke. Fins are relatively small
Length (including tail):	40–60 feet
Weight:	40, 000–80, 00lb (Male larger than female)
Habitat/Range:	Deep, temperate waters in the open ocean, particularly where currents converge. Found in both the Pacific and Atlantic Oceans
Similar species:	Large, blunt head makes this whale distinct from other whales

The Sperm Whale is the largest of the toothed whales, and has a huge head that comprises about a third of its length. The mouthparts are usually white, and the lower jaw contains around fifty teeth. Sperm Whales are highly sociable, often forming pods of forty or more individuals, usually segregated into groups of females and young males. Adult males though, tend to be solitary. The Sperm Whale mates in spring or summer, usually in tropical or subtropical waters, and males may attempt to herd females, sometimes challenging each other for dominance. A single calf is born after some fourteen months, and may stay with the maternal pod for many years. Sperm Whales feed at great depths, sometimes many thousands of feet below the surface, eating mainly large squid and octopi.

SHORT-BEAKED COMMON DOLPHIN

Scientific name:	*Delphinus delphis*
Identification:	Small, slender dolphin, with dark back, white belly, and an "hourglass" pattern on the flanks in yellow and gray. Colors and markings vary however
Length (including tail):	6½–8½ feet
Weight:	155–250lb
Habitat/Range:	Temperate and warm waters along both coastlines, usually at some distance from the shoreline
Similar species:	Long-beaked Common Dolphin (*Delphinus capensis*) more slender, less brightly colored, with a less pronounced forehead and longer beak

The Short-beaked Common Dolphin is often found in large groups, sometimes numbering hundreds or even thousands of individuals. They are highly active, fast swimmers, and are noted for riding the bow waves of boats, commonly breaching in unison. Highly inquisitive, common dolphins also frequently associate with other whale and dolphin species, and also with schools of Tuna. They feed on small schooling fish and mollusks such as squid, often cooperating when feeding by herding fish together. Like many other dolphin species, the common dolphin will sometimes also follow trawlers, feeding on fish escaped from nets or discarded by fishermen, and such activity can prove perilous, with dolphins being accidentally caught in nets and drowned. Short-beaked Common Dolphins reach sexual maturity at about four years old, but breeding seasons vary from cool to warmer waters. Off the coast of southern California, mating and births occur mainly in fall, with pregnancy lasting about one year.

BOTTLE-NOSED DOLPHIN ▼▶

Scientific name:	*Tursiops truncates*
Identification:	Fairly large dolphin, gray to brown back, with lighter flanks and pale belly. Short but distinct beak, central dorsal fin
Length (including tail):	9–12 feet
Weight:	400–1000lb (Male larger than female, also Pacific individuals larger than those found in the Atlantic)
Habitat/Range:	Found primarily in coastal and inshore regions of temperate waters, including harbors and estuaries, in both the Pacific and Atlantic Oceans
Similar species:	Easily distinguished from other dolphins by its gray color, lack of markings, and short beak

The Bottle-nosed Dolphin is amongst the most abundant dolphin species in US waters, common along both coastlines, and it is also the most familiar and well-studied dolphin. Pacific populations of Bottle-nosed Dolphins are sometimes regarded as a separate species however, and are known as Gill's Bottle-nosed Dolphin (*Tursiops Gillii*). Furthermore, distinctions have been made between dolphins in the Atlantic, identifying small coastal, and larger pelagic subspecies. All exhibit similar behaviors, though bottle-nosed Dolphins in the open ocean probably feed at greater depth. Patterns of migration also seem to vary somewhat, according to geographical range and localized conditions. Generally though, the Bottle-nosed Dolphin is found close to the shore, and is a sociable, playful and inquisitive animal. Often found in small groups, these dolphins may be observed leaping clear of the water whilst riding in the bow waves of boats. At times, several pods may congregate together. The Bottle-nosed Dolphin feeds mainly on small fish, mollusks and crustaceans.

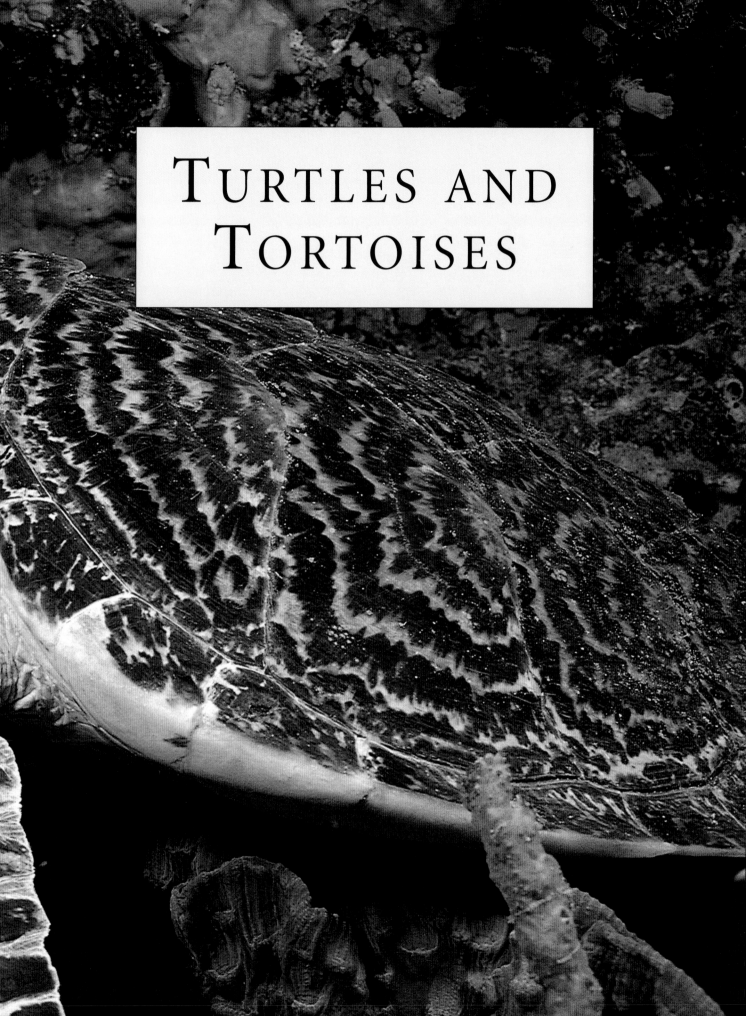

TURTLES AND TORTOISES

MUSK AND MUD TURTLES (*KINOSTERNIDAE*)

The mud and musk turtles belong to the same family, and are quite difficult to tell apart when viewed from above, tending to be similar in size and coloring. However, the two groups can be distinguished by viewing the underside, the lower shell, or plastron, being much smaller in musk turtles. Both are sometimes referred to generically as "stinkpots", though the term is more specifically applied to the **Common Musk Turtle** (*Sternotherus odoratus*). All members of this family are capable of producing a powerful musk from glands on the sides of the body, most likely to deter predators, as they do so when handled. They may also attempt to bite. Both musk and mud turtles are concentrated in eastern states, with the **Common Musk Turtle** and the **Yellow Mud Turtle** (*Kinosternon flavescens*) being amongst the most common and widespread examples of the two genera. They are found in a variety of freshwater habitats, but prefer slow moving or still water, usually with a muddy bottom. Both are highly aquatic and seldom leave the water, spending much of their time searching for food on the bottom. They may be seen partially exposed in shallows however, and occasionally, the Common Musk Turtle will ascend gently sloping waterside trees in order to bask. The Yellow Mud Turtle is also sometimes found on land, especially during rains, or when seeking a new body of water. This species is more inclined to use temporary habitats than the Common Musk Turtle, including ditches and drains. Both are around 3 - 6 inches in length and have distinctive facial markings. The Common Musk Turtle has two thin, yellow stripes on each side of the head, whilst the Yellow Mud Turtle sports a yellow chin and throat.

ALLIGATOR SNAPPING TURTLE ▲

Scientific name:	*Macroclemys temmincki*
Identification:	Very large freshwater turtle, prominent hooked beak, and long tail. Shell is gray-brown and rough, with well defined keels or ridges
Length (including tail):	1½–2 feet
Weight:	40–200 lb
Habitat/Range:	Deep lakes or rivers with muddy bottoms. Found from northern Florida, east to Texas and as far north as Iowa
Similar species:	Common Snapping Turtle is smaller with a knobbly tail

The Alligator Snapping Turtle is the largest freshwater turtle in North America and inhabits large, deep bodies of water such as lakes and rivers. It spends much of its time submerged, surfacing to breathe, but seemingly never basking. As with sea turtles, it is thought that only the female leaves the water, doing so in order to lay eggs. This species mates from late winter to spring and lays one clutch of eggs in a hollow at the water's edge. The hatchlings emerge some three to four months later. Alligator Snapping Turtles are mainly nocturnal, patrolling the lake or riverbed at night in search of food. During the day they are more likely to lie in the mud waiting to ambush prey. They have a useful adaptation in order to do this; a worm-like growth on the tongue, which they use as a lure to attract fish. Alligator Snapping Turtles also feed on invertebrates, birds, mammals and other reptiles, including smaller turtles. Snappers may become aggressive if disturbed and the jaws are large, hooked and capable of delivering a powerful bite.

COMMON SNAPPING TURTLE

Scientific name:	*Chelydra serpentina*
Identification:	A fairly large freshwater turtle with powerful jaws, black to brown carapace has three distinct keels. Tail is long and saw-toothed
Length (including tail):	8–18 inches
Weight:	10–45lb+
Habitat/Range:	Varied freshwater habitats across southern parts of Canada, eastwards from Alberta, south to the Gulf across the central and eastern US
Similar species:	Alligator Snapping Turtle is larger and lacks prominent tail ridges

The Common Snapping Turtle is smaller than the Alligator Snapping Turtle and though it eats a variety of aquatic vegetation it remains a formidable predator, eating fish, invertebrates, birds, reptiles and small mammals. It is also more likely to be encountered out of water than its larger relative, sometimes traveling some distance to nesting sites or to new bodies of water. At such times they may be particularly aggressive. The Common Snapping Turtle is found in still or slow-moving lakes and rivers, usually with dense vegetation. They spend much of their time buried in mud and also lure fish with a growth on the tongue. This species mates from spring to fall, but it is capable of delaying fertilization for many years. It lays up to fifty eggs, which are incubated for between two to four months.

PAINTED TURTLE

Scientific name:	*Chrysemys picta*
Identification:	Green to black, unkeeled carapace, brightly marked with yellow and red. Limbs and neck usually striped and head often bears yellow spots
Length (including tail):	4–7 inches
Habitat/Range:	Still or slow-flowing water with abundant vegetation and basking places. Common across southern Canada and the US, but largely absent from southwestern states
Similar species:	Similar to the Redbelly Turtle, *Pseudemys rubriventris*, but smaller

The Painted Turtle is amongst the most common and widespread of North American turtles and belongs to the group known as the basking turtles. Although all reptiles warm themselves in the sun, these species exhibit a particular prevalence for such behavior, spending much of their time resting out of the water on rocks, logs or other convenient perches. A gregarious species, large numbers may be encountered basking together, sometimes piled on top of each other where space is limited. Like most turtles however, they are timid and are likely to enter the water if disturbed. The Painted Turtle favors shallow, densely vegetated, still or slow-moving water, and is found in a range of such habitats. Though there is only one species, four subspecies exist, usually discernible by their range and appearance. However, where ranges overlap, characteristics are often shared. The Eastern subspecies (*Chrysemys picta picta*) is notable for having almost perfectly straight rows of dark scutes across its back, usually outlined with yellow, whilst the Western Painted Turtle (*Chrysemys picta bellii*) is often more colorful, with an intricately patterned carapace. Painted Turtles tend to be omnivorous, eating a range of vegetation and invertebrates, but become more herbivorous with age.

(POND) SLIDER

Scientific name:	*Trachemys scripta*
Identification:	Brown or green, slightly keeled carapace, frequently striped, as are the legs and neck. Often has a prominent spot behind eye
Length (including tail):	5–10 inches (Female larger than male)
Habitat/Range:	Varied, quiet waters with vegetation, from Illinois to Virginia, south to northern Florida and Texas
Similar species:	Lower jaw is rounded, distinguishing this species from otherwise similar species

The Slider, or Pond Slider, is quite commonly seen basking and is closely related to the Painted Turtle. It was once frequently sold in pet stores. There are three subspecies; the Yellowbelly Slider (*T. s. scripta*), Red-eared Slider (*T. s. elegans*) and Cumberland Slider (*T. s. troostii*), all of which are very similar, but vary slightly in their markings. In older males particularly, differentiation may be quite difficult, as patterns tend to become less distinct with age, although Sliders usually have an orange, red or yellow spot behind each eye. Gregarious and often found basking in groups, Sliders are found in lakes, rivers, ponds and ditches, and prefer soft, sandy or muddy bottomed stretches, usually where there is an abundance of vegetation. When young, their diet consists of various insects, mollusks and crustaceans, but Sliders generally become more herbivorous as they reach adulthood. The Slider mates in spring or summer, laying around ten to twenty eggs at a time in a nest in the ground. The young hatch about two months later, but may remain in the nest until the following spring.

(COMMON) MAP TURTLE

Scientific name:	*Graptemys geographica*
Identification:	Olive-green or brown, keeled carapace with intricate markings. Yellow spot behind eye. Head of female is particularly large
Length (including tail):	4–10 inches (Female larger than male)
Habitat/Range:	Lakes and large, slow rivers with dense vegetation. Found from the Great Lakes, south to Alabama and Arkansas
Similar species:	Painted Turtle has unkeeled carapace, lower jaw of Slider is rounded

Map Turtles are so called due to the intricate and somewhat map-like patterns found on the carapace, though in adults, especially in females, markings become more vague. There are ten species of Map Turtle, of which the Common Map Turtle is the most widespread, with many species being highly localized. All have keeled shells to some extent and some possess spines along this dorsal ridge. The Common Map Turtle, however, usually only has slight bumps. Although not classed as basking turtles, Map Turtles are highly sociable and spend a considerable amount of time hauled out on rocks, logs or stumps, basking together in groups. The Common Map Turtle is found mainly in large bodies of water such as lakes and rivers, where it feeds on various plant material, invertebrates and carrion. They are equipped with powerful jaws, and the females, which may be twice the size of males, have a particularly enlarged head, enabling them to feed on large freshwater snails and shellfish.

WOOD TURTLE

Scientific name:	*Clemmys insculpta*
Identification:	Rough, "sculptured", pyramid-shaped scutes. Legs and neck usually orange or red
Length (including tail):	5–9 inches
Habitat/Range:	Woodland streams, marshes and meadows, primarily in the northeast
Similar species:	Carapace is similar to that of the Diamondback Terrapin which is found in brackish water in coastal areas

The Wood Turtle is a member of the genus *Clemmys*, also known as the pond turtles, and although it hibernates underwater, often remaining close to water in spring, it is highly terrestrial, spending much of its time in woodland and meadows. It may travel quite far overland in search of food, and is also a good climber. The Wood Turtle is omnivorous, feeding on a variety of insects, fruit and other vegetation. The Latin name of this species refers to the distinctive sculptured appearance of its carapace, which is highly keeled, with large, rough scutes or scales. It is also sometimes known as "redlegs" on account of its orange-red limbs. The female Wood Turtle lays her eggs in early summer and they hatch in fall, though as with many turtles, the young may spend the winter within the nest, especially in the northernmost parts of its range.

CHICKEN TURTLE AND BLANDING'S TURTLE

The Chicken Turtle (*Deirochelys reticularia*) and Blanding's Turtle (*Emydoidea blandingii*) belong to separate genera, *Deirochelys* and *Emydoidea* respectively, and though they display various differences in shell structure, markings and range, it is thought that they are probably quite closely related. Both species are around five to ten inches in length, with long tails and extremely long necks. They inhabit still, shallow waters, typically in swamps or marshland, favoring highly vegetated areas, although they are also quite commonly found on land, either basking or searching amongst undergrowth for food such as insects, slugs and snails. Both species are quite easily recognized on account of their long necks, but have other distinctive features. The Chicken Turtle has a yellow striped neck and legs, and a fairly narrow shell, patterned with yellowish, web-like markings. Blanding's Turtle is typically darker, but has a yellow throat and irregular yellow markings on the carapace. Neither species has a keeled shell except when very young. The Chicken Turtle is found mainly in southeastern states, from Texas to Florida, and as far north as Missouri in the west, and Virginia in the east. It may reproduce throughout the year in the warmer parts of its range. In contrast, Blanding's Turtle is found further north, inhabiting the Great Lakes area, and though it is able to tolerate the cold quite comfortably, sometimes even swimming below ice, it generally reproduces in summer.

Above: **Blanding's Turtle**

DIAMONDBACK TERRAPIN

Scientific name:	*Malaclemys terrapin*
Identification:	Keeled, gray-brown or black carapace with sculptured appearance. Gray head, neck and limbs, spotted with black
Length (including tail):	4–9 inches (Female larger than male)
Habitat/Range:	Brackish lagoons, estuaries and salt-marshes along the Atlantic coastline
Similar species:	Habitat is distinctive; snapping turtles may enter brackish water, but are much larger

Unusual amongst the semi-aquatic turtles, the Diamondback Terrapin chiefly inhabits coastal waters, living in and around brackish floodplains and estuaries. The carapace of this species is dorsally keeled, and the characteristic scutes usually display obvious growth rings. Once widely hunted for food, Diamondback Terrapin populations became severely depleted but they remain fairly common in certain areas. There are seven subspecies found along the Atlantic Coast, all of which vary somewhat in appearance, being perhaps best distinguished from each other by range. Breeding tends to take place in summer, though usually earlier in the south than in the north. Eggs are typically laid in sandy soil close to water and are less spherical than those of many species. The Diamondback Terrapin is carnivorous and feeds on insects, mollusks, crustaceans and small fish.

SPINY SOFTSHELL ▲

Scientific name:	*Trionyx spiniferus/Apalone spinifera*
Identification:	Olive green to brown
Length (including tail):	5–20 inches (Female larger than male)
Habitat/Range:	Mainly found in fast-flowing rivers, but also in marshy areas and still water. Range extends through central and eastern US
Similar species:	Smooth Softshell lacks any projections on shell and has no ridges on nostrils, Florida Softshell has bumps rather than spines or tubercles

The most noticeable feature of the Spiny Softshell is the fact that its carapace lacks the hard, bony plates or scutes common to other turtles. Instead, its shell is rather flat and disc-shaped, with a leathery covering. In females, small spines are usually present along the front edge of the carapace, whilst males may develop quite a rough texture, with small projections occurring all over the shell. Some six subspecies of Spiny Softshell have been identified, but all share similar characteristics and are perhaps best told apart by geographical range. Primarily river-dwelling, the Spiny Softshell is highly aquatic and swims powerfully, though it can also move quickly on land. It spends much of the time however, partially buried in the mud or sand of the riverbed, extending its long neck and snorkel-like nose to the surface in order to breathe. This species feeds mainly on invertebrates such as crustaceans and mollusks, but is agile enough to catch small fish.

EASTERN BOX TURTLE AND WESTERN/ORNATE BOX TURTLE

Despite being terrestrial and superficially similar, the box turtles are more closely related to many of the semi-aquatic species than they are to tortoises. The shells are variable in color, and are highly domed with distinct growth rings on the scutes, but the carapaces of box turtles are hinged at both ends, and can be closed more tightly than in other species. The **Eastern Box Turtle** (*Terrapene carolina*) is found mainly in damp fields and woodland across much of the eastern US, whilst the **Western**, or

Ornate Box Turtle (*Terrapene ornata*) inhabits drier, more central and western areas, and is chiefly plains-dwelling. Both species are diurnal and omnivorous, feeding on a variety of insects, fruit, green plants and carrion, but the Western Box Turtle is usually more carnivorous. The ranges of the two species overlap slightly, and as they were both once widely kept as pets, there have been escapes and releases outside of their natural ranges. They are both similar in size, up to about five inches in length, but can usually be distinguished in such areas by the shape and markings of the shell. The Western Box Turtle lacks a keel and possesses a more distinct pattern of radiating lines. However it is known that the species do interbreed, and hybrids may share characteristics with both. Breeding takes place in summer, with up to eight eggs being laid in sandy soil from May to July, at a depth of a few inches.

Below: The Eastern Box Turtle

GOPHER TORTOISE AND DESERT TORTOISE

The **Gopher Tortoise** (*Gopherus polyphemus*) and **Desert Tortoise** (*Gopherus agassizii*) are medium-sized terrestrial turtles (up to about fourteen inches), which both occupy dry, sandy terrain, and make their homes in burrows. The Gopher Tortoise is an eastern species, which ranges from eastern parts of Louisiana to Florida and South Carolina, and it is usually found living close to grasslands and forests. The Desert Tortoise tends to live in more arid desert and scrubland, occurring in the west in California, Nevada and Arizona. Both have long, broad, well-scaled forelegs which are adapted for digging, and which are also used as protection for the head when they retreat into their shells. The burrows of these species may be up to thirty feet in length, wide enough for turning, and usually ending in a chamber where they will spend the hottest part of the day. The Gopher Tortoise in particular is known for sharing its burrow with various other species, including snakes, mammals and burrowing owls. Herbivorous, feeding normally takes place in the morning when it is cool, and these tortoises feed on a variety of fruit, flowers, cacti and green vegetation, from which they absorb most of their water. They mate in spring, laying between two to fourteen eggs, with the Desert Tortoise typically laying more than one clutch. The hatchlings emerge from summer to fall. Although they are long-living creatures, adult females do not reproduce until they are approaching twenty years of age, and therefore these species, which are endangered in most of their ranges, have been slow to recover in significant numbers from the impact of the pet trade and a loss of habitat.

LEATHERBACK

Scientific name:	*Dermochelys coriacea*
Identification:	Huge, dark-colored turtle. Lacks scales, but has several keels along length of both carapace and plastron
Length (including tail):	4–7 feet
Weight:	650–1000lb+
Habitat/Range:	Pelagic, but found around both the Pacific and Atlantic coastlines, mainly in tropical waters, though further north in summer
Similar species:	Unique carapace easily distinguishes this species from other turtles

The Leatherback is the largest turtle in the world and belongs to a separate family from all other sea turtles, namely *Dermochelyidae.*

Although hatchlings are scaled, these are shed as the turtle grows, and the adult Leatherback possesses a unique, leathery, blue-black carapace, with seven distinctive keels. The plastron, or lower shell has five such ridges. Although it may be found in bays quite close to the shore, the Leatherback is unlike other sea turtles in that it is a wandering, open ocean species. It is a powerful swimmer, traversing huge distances at sea, feeding mainly on quite small jellyfish. This species is also capable of regulating its body temperature more efficiently than other turtles and it occurs along the length of the Atlantic coast, and is sometimes found as far north as Alaska on the Pacific coast. It nests further south, however, around the Gulf of Mexico and Florida, coming ashore to lay its eggs at night, at any time from spring to fall, but particularly in summer. The female may lay almost two hundred eggs at a time, and returns over a period of weeks, producing several clutches. As with all sea turtles, the Leatherback is regarded as an endangered species.

LOGGERHEAD

Scientific name:	*Caretta caretta*
Identification:	Quite large, with a brown, heart-shaped carapace. As with all sea turtles, the males have tails extending beyond the carapace
Length (including tail):	3–4 feet
Weight:	180–400lb
Habitat/Range:	The Loggerhead is found at sea and in coastal bays along the Atlantic and around southern California in the Pacific
Similar species:	The Hawksbill often has overlapping scales or laminae, whilst the Green Turtle has one, rather than two pairs of scales between the eyes

Although endangered and not particularly widespread, the Loggerhead is the most common sea turtle found along the North American coast. It is most likely to be seen on summer nights when females come ashore to lay their eggs, usually in the warm waters around the Gulf, but also further north. As with other sea turtles, the males also usually come inshore at this time, and mating takes place just before or after the eggs are deposited. The female may lay over one hundred eggs before returning to the sea, but many of the hatchlings will fail to reach adulthood. A fully grown Loggerhead is by no means small, but there may once have been much larger specimens, possibly weighing as much as 1000 lb and being up to seven feet in length. Such examples could represent a subspecies, or be the result of exaggerated estimation, but there have been no reports of them in recent years. The Loggerhead is an omnivorous turtle and feeds on various marine invertebrates and plants.

GREEN TURTLE

Scientific name:	*Chelonia mydas*
Identification:	Fairly broad, sometimes mottled carapace, with four laminae on each side
Length (including tail):	3–5 feet
Weight:	250–500lb
Habitat/Range:	Vegetated coastal shallows in warm Atlantic waters and around southern California
Similar species:	The Loggerhead has two pairs of scales between the eyes, whilst the Hawksbill often has overlapping scales on its carapace

In spite of its common name, the Green Turtle is in fact usually brown, though it may sometimes be a dark olive color. Its name actually derives from a green fatty substance, which this turtle was once extensively killed for, and which was commonly used as an ingredient in turtle soup. The Green Turtle was also hunted for its meat, leather and for use in the manufacture of cosmetics. Although now protected, illegal trade in Green Turtles persists and populations remain seriously depleted. Green Turtles are amongst the most herbivorous of the sea turtles, though they also feed on small invertebrates. They spend the first year of their lives in the open ocean before returning to coastal shallows where they usually remain for many years, before migrating to the breeding grounds where they were born.

ATLANTIC HAWKSBILL ▲

Scientific name:	*Eretmochelys imbricate*
Identification:	Keeled, mottled, green-brown carapace with overlapping scutes. Mouth is hooked and beak-like
Length (including tail):	2½–3 feet
Weight:	100–170lb
Habitat/Range:	Coastal shallows, estuaries and bays, particularly around rocks and reefs
Similar species:	Beak-like mouth and overlapping scales are distinctive

Another sea turtle which has suffered extensively at the hands of man, the Atlantic Hawksbill is considered endangered throughout the Atlantic coastal states. It was hunted for food, but also in great numbers for its attractive shell, the source of "tortoiseshell" jewelry and other similar items. Trade in its shell is now severely restricted, but as turtles are slow to reach sexual maturity and breeding cycles are relatively long, population recovery is a lengthy process. The Atlantic Hawksbill prefers warmer waters and is usually found in tropical or subtropical shallows, where it feeds mainly on marine invertebrates. It may be found as far north as Rhode Island and Massachusetts however. The subspecies, the Pacific Hawksbill (*Eretmochelys imbricata bissa*), is sometimes found around southern California.

ATLANTIC RIDLEY/KEMP'S RIDLEY

Scientific name:	*Lepidochelys kempii*
Identification:	Small sea turtle with round shell. Gray-green in color
Length (including tail):	2–2½ feet
Weight:	80–100 lb
Habitat/Range:	Mainly tropical or subtropical coastal shallows, particularly around the Gulf of Mexico
Similar species:	Smaller than all other species of sea turtle

The Atlantic Ridley, sometimes known as Kemp's Ridley, has many distinctive characteristics. Perhaps most noticeably, it is the smallest species of sea turtle and has the most circular shell, but it also displays distinctive behavior. It is the most highly carnivorous of the sea turtles, and has the shortest breeding cycle, reproducing every year or two. It is almost unique too, in that the females tend to lay their eggs during the day. It nests in spring or summer, laying one hundred or more eggs at a time, usually producing two or three clutches. This species once congregated in its thousands at nesting sites along the Gulf coast, but it is thought that today there are perhaps as few as 1000 breeding females remaining, with nesting sites now limited to a much shorter stretch of coastline. The Atlantic Ridley is most frequently found in the warm shallows of the Gulf, but may range much further north at times. The slightly larger Pacific subspecies, *Lepidochelys olivvacea*, is found along the coast of California, but also occurs in the Caribbean Sea.

LIZARDS AND SNAKES

SKINKS (*Scincidae*)

Skinks are generally highly active, diurnal, terrestrial lizards, and many species, particularly amongst the striped skinks, are burrowing animals. The **Broad-headed Skink** (*Eumeces laticeps*), however, is highly arboreal, living in damp woodlands throughout much of the eastern US, where it hunts for insects amongst the branches of trees. It is also large enough to eat birds' eggs and will even take nestlings. It may make its home in a hollow tree or stump, although it is also found on the ground in loose soil or leaf litter. It is a large skink, up to a foot long, the only larger example being the **Great Plains Skink** (*Eumeces obsoletus*), which can reach up to around fourteen inches. This species is found throughout the Great Plains region, and in the more arid parts of its range, will tend to

be found close to a constant source of water. It feeds chiefly on insects, but may also eat other reptiles, and small mammals such as mice. The **Five-lined Skink** (*Eumeces fasciatus*) is a considerably smaller species, growing to about eight inches in length. Like the Broad-headed Skink it is mainly found in eastern woodlands, and though it is able to climb trees, it is considerably more terrestrial. Although the three species discussed here differ in size as adults, they are otherwise very similar in appearance, and may be difficult to distinguish. The juveniles are usually dark, with distinct stripes and bright blue tails, becoming more uniformly brown or olive-colored with age. Their patterns tend to fade and the tails become grayer. The Broad-headed Skink, as its name would suggest, has a proportionally larger head than the other two species, whilst the Great Plains Skink has a unique arrangement of scales. The rows on the back run in parallel, horizontal bands, but those on the flanks slant diagonally. All three species mate from spring to early summer, and the females lay up to about twenty eggs in a sheltered spot. They nest with the eggs until August when the hatchlings normally emerge.

Below: The southeastern Five-Lined Skink
Opposite: The Broad-headed Skink

WESTERN BANDED GECKO ▲

Scientific name:	*Coleonyx variegates*
Identification:	Small, slender gray-brown or greenish lizard with dark bands, and spots. Eyes are prominent
Length (including tail):	4½–6 inches
Habitat/Range:	Scrub and rocky desert areas in the southwestern US, east as far as New Mexico
Similar species:	Banded geckos are difficult to distinguish from each other without close inspection of spurs found at the base of the tail, but differ from other geckos in having moveable eyelids

Geckos belong to a large family of lizards, with some 650 species worldwide, around ten of which are native to North America. Most are known for their climbing ability, able to traverse walls and ceilings, but the Western Banded Gecko is a ground-dwelling species and climbs comparatively rarely. It is found in scrub and desert areas, and is primarily nocturnal, spending the day holed-up amongst rocks. It hunts at night, preying on spiders and other invertebrates. The female Western Banded Gecko produces eggs in pairs from summer to fall, sometimes in two or three clutches. Hatchlings emerge about a month and a half later. Geckos are often quite vocal, in fact the name "gecko" originates from the sound made by a member of this family. Western Banded Geckos may squeak if caught or threatened, but as with many lizards they have a useful adaptation to avoid capture; the tail detaches easily if seized.

DESERT NIGHT LIZARD

Scientific name:	*Xantusia vigilis*
Identification:	Small, olive-brown and speckled with soft skin. This species lacks visible eyelids and has vertical pupils
Length (including tail):	3–5 inches
Habitat/Range:	Rocky areas in southwestern desert regions
Similar species:	Not unlike the Western Banded Gecko, but lacks bold markings and moveable eyelids

The Desert Night Lizard is found in arid scrub and desert areas, and although it may avoid the main heat of the day by hiding amongst rocks or vegetation, sometimes hunting after twilight, it is in fact mainly diurnal. Generally shy and well camouflaged however, it may be difficult to spot. A terrestrial species, the Desert Night Lizard feeds on ants, termites and various other small insects which it finds on the ground, hunting around fallen trees or other decaying plant matter. It is mainly associated with yucca logs, and may in fact spend its entire life in the same area of cover if it is not significantly disturbed. No doubt this secretive lifestyle helps prolong life expectancy but its potential for reproduction is low. Unlike most lizards this species does not lay eggs, but gives birth to between one and three live young in fall, mating having taken place in summer.

SLENDER GLASS LIZARD

Scientific name:	*Ophisaurus attenuatus*
Identification:	Very long-tailed, legless species. Brown, green or gray, with dark stripes, grooved sides, moveable eyelids and external ear openings
Length (including tail):	2–3½ feet
Habitat/Range:	Woods and grasslands in central plains areas, east to Florida and Virginia
Similar species:	Other glass lizards lack stripes below the lateral groove

The Slender Glass Lizard is a legless species and is serpentine in appearance. However, unlike snakes, it has ear openings and moveable eyelids. It is also somewhat stiffer than a snake, its scales being supported by bony plates. The tail in particular is exceptionally brittle, and whilst many lizards have readily detachable tails, that of the Slender Glass Lizard may break into many pieces if it is struck or restrained. It will wriggle strenuously if caught, and few adults retain their original tails, instead the tail is regenerated, somewhat shorter, and usually with slightly different coloring. This species is mainly active by day, feeding on insects, the eggs of ground-nesting birds and small vertebrates, hunting amongst grass or leaf litter. The Slender Glass Lizard is capable of burrowing, but typically only does so when hibernating in winter. Mating and egg-laying take place in summer, and the female will guard her eggs.

CALIFORNIA LEGLESS LIZARD

Scientific name:	*Anniela pulchra*
Identification:	Silver-gray or brown legless lizard with dark stripes
Length (including tail):	6–9 inches
Habitat/Range:	Sand dunes, beaches, mixed woodlands with sandy soil. Occurs in California, south to northern parts of Baja California
Similar species:	No similar species in range, glass lizards are found in the eastern US and have ear openings

The California Legless Lizard is restricted to a fairly small area, much of which remains quite warm for most of the year. It is able to tolerate cool conditions however, and is a nocturnal, burrowing species, which lives just below the surface of the soil or amongst leaf litter, particularly in sandy habitats. It is well adapted for such an existence, having a blunt snout and tail, tiny, smooth scales and no external ear openings. It feeds on subterranean insects and their larvae, but will often surface in the evening or at night to forage for spiders and other invertebrates, and may be found amongst vegetation, beneath logs or discarded boards. It does not usually hibernate except in the northernmost parts of its range, but it may become inactive for short periods in winter. Mating takes place in summer, and up to four live young are born in fall.

GREEN ANOLE

Scientific name:	*Anolis carolinensis*
Identification:	Slim, often bright green, though color is variable. Has a pink throat fan
Length (including tail):	5–8 inches
Habitat/Range:	Varied arboreal areas including suburbs. Occurs from Virginia, throughout south eastern states to eastern Texas
Similar species:	An introduced brown variety (*Anolis sagrei*) is found in much of Florida. Its throat fan is usually yellow or red, and it is a more terrestrial species

The Green Anole is the only member of its family native to North America, and although it is usually bright green, it is sometimes referred to as a chameleon due to an ability to change its color, through various greens to gray or brown. It also possesses a striking, pink, throat fan, which it displays to potential mates or rivals. This fan is more greatly pronounced in males. It is a very common species in much of its range and is often found in suburban areas, climbing amongst trees and shrubs, or on fences. Although mainly arboreal, Green Anoles also spend time on the ground and feed on a variety of small invertebrates. Anoles lay their eggs on the ground too, usually in a relatively secluded location amongst leaf litter or rocks. Mating takes place from spring to fall, and the Green Anole produces a single egg every two weeks during this period.

WHIPTAILS AND RACERUNNERS (*Teiidae*)

These lizards belong to a large family native only to the Americas and includes species which are unisexual, reproducing asexually. The **Six-lined Racerunner** (*Cnemidophorus sexlineatus*) and **Western Whiptail** (*Cnemidophorus tigris*), also known as the Tiger Whiptail, reproduce sexually however. These species are closely related and share many characteristics, though their ranges are quite distinct. Both are slender with extremely long tails, and although they may shelter in extreme heat, they are seemingly constantly active when abroad, moving rapidly in a somewhat agitated manner. In North America, almost all members of this family are confined to arid western scrublands, prairies, deserts or forest edges, and although the Six-lined Racerunner is found in similar habitats; open woodlands and dry grasslands, it is an inhabitant of eastern states. Both species are capable of burrowing and hole-up at night or when it is cold. In northern parts of their ranges, or at altitude, they may hibernate. They also sometimes dig for prey. Both feed on insects, whilst the slightly larger Western Whiptail also tackles scorpions. It grows to around a foot long, about two inches longer than the Six-lined Racerunner. Although they are physically similar, the coloration of these two species is quite different. The Western Whiptail is usually gray or sandy-colored with tiger-like markings, hence its alternative and Latin names, whereas the Six-lined Racerunner is usually greenish brown to black, with six (sometimes seven), light, longitudinal stripes. In males the throat and snout may be predominantly green or blue. Juveniles of both species have blue tails. Breeding takes place from late spring to summer, usually resulting in two clutches of between one and six eggs which hatch by fall.

Below: **The Six-lined Racerunner**

DESERT IGUANA ▲

Scientific name:	*Dipsosaurus dorsalis*
Identification:	Large, stocky lizard with dark head, lighter body and tail, often spotted with gray or white. Low crest along center of back
Length (including tail):	10–16 inches
Habitat/Range:	Sandy scrub, creosote flats and rocky foothills throughout the Mojave and Colorado deserts
Similar species:	Chuckwalla lacks dorsal crest

Whilst most iguanids are almost exclusively carnivorous, the Desert Iguana is mainly herbivorous. It feeds heavily on creosote bushes and other vegetation, but will supplement its diet with small invertebrates and carrion. It is active during the day, basking and feeding at temperatures which force most other desert creatures to seek shelter. Should the ground become too hot underfoot however, it will ascend a bush or take refuge amongst rocks, or perhaps in the enlarged burrow of a rodent. It also uses burrows at night, when hibernating, and when threatened by predators such as large snakes or birds of prey. Whilst occupying a burrow, the Desert Iguana often blocks the entrance, perhaps serving to regulate temperature and to deter predators. Adults are usually active from spring to mid or late summer, mating soon after emerging from dormancy. Up to eight eggs are produced soon after, hatching during the summer. The young are around three to four inches long upon hatching and tend to remain active until fall.

SIDE-BLOTCHED LIZARD

Scientific name:	*Uta stansburiana*
Identification:	Brown back with varied markings, dark spot behind each foreleg, single skin fold on throat
Length (including tail):	4–6 inches
Habitat/Range:	Dry, sparsely vegetated areas in the western US
Similar species:	Generally similar to the Lesser Earless Lizard, but has visible ear openings

The Side-blotched Lizard belongs to the family *Phrynosomatidae*, which also includes the earless, spiny and horned lizards. It is a fairly small species, and is relatively slow-moving, but it has a large appetite for its size, and once it has warmed itself by basking, it will spend the rest of the day seeking food. It eats all kinds of insects, as well as spiders and scorpions. Though it is capable of climbing, most of its hunting is done on the ground, amongst vegetation or rocks. As with many terrestrial lizards, the Side-blotched Lizard utilizes the burrows of small mammals, usually remaining close to such shelter, for being small it is preyed upon by a variety of larger animals. Its range extends into mountainous regions, and at higher altitudes, or simply in more temperate northern parts, this species may become dormant during the winter months, breeding in the summer. In the south it is often active throughout the year and may reproduce at any time. Females of this species may produce more than one clutch of eggs from a single mating, storing sperm for several months.

Long-nosed Leopard Lizard

Scientific name:	*Gambelia wislizenii*
Identification:	Large, gray-brown lizard with dark, scattered spots and white lateral bars
Length (including tail):	8½–15 inches
Habitat/Range:	Arid plains and desert regions throughout western states
Similar species:	Size and markings distinguish this species from others in range

A close relative of the Collared Lizard, this species is also found in arid southwestern states where it preys on invertebrates, small mammals, and lizards, sometimes tackling quite large specimens. It is however omnivorous, and will eat a range of plants. It is usually found in areas of sparse vegetation, seeking shade or waiting in ambush for a potential meal, and it moves quickly from one area of cover to another, rising onto its hind legs as it gains speed. At night, or during the hottest part of the day, the Long-nosed Leopard Lizard may retreat to a burrow, and it also hibernates over winter. Mating occurs in spring with around four or five eggs being laid from early to mid-summer. Sometimes a second clutch is produced towards the end of the season. Females carrying eggs display bright red or orange markings on their sides.

Chuckwalla

Scientific name:	*Sauromalus obesus / Sauromalus ater*
Identification:	Large and stocky with loose folds of skin, particularly about the throat. Black foreparts becoming gray or yellow to the tip of the tail
Length (including tail):	11–16½ inches
Habitat/Range:	Rocky outcrops in creosote bush scrub or desert. Found in southwestern US
Similar species:	Desert Iguana has low dorsal crest

Amongst the largest of North American lizards, the Chuckwalla is rather sluggish for much of the day, spending the morning basking on rocks until its body temperature reaches around 100° F. It then becomes active, when it will begin to forage for food in the afternoon sun. It is a strictly herbivorous species and feeds upon creosote bushes and the leaves, buds, flowers and fruits of various other desert plants. Despite their size, Chuckwallas are quite timid and display an unusual characteristic when alarmed, wedging themselves in crevices and inflating their bodies by swallowing air. They are active from early spring to late summer or fall, but may also be seen on warm winter days. When food is abundant, large males may become territorial. Breeding takes place in summer, but may occur only once every two years, perhaps depending on the amount of food available.

COLLARED LIZARD

Scientific name:	*Crotaphytus collaris*
Identification:	Fairly large, brightly colored, usually greenish, with varied markings on body and two black collar bands. Head appears enlarged
Length (including tail):	8–14 inches
Habitat/Range:	Rocky hillsides with sparse vegetation from Utah to Illinois, southwest to Texas and Arizona
Similar species:	Crevice Spiny Lizard (*Sceloporus poinsetti*) has a single black collar and spiny scales

Collared Lizards are highly variable in color, but are usually bright yellow, green or blue, with spots or stripes. They have two distinctive black bands around the neck. Females tend to be slightly duller and may be brownish, but develop striking red or orange markings when carrying eggs. The heads of both sexes are disproportionately large. Collared Lizards are omnivorous, but feed mainly on other smaller reptiles and insects, and though they may flee if approached, they are generally aggressive and capable of delivering a painful bite. When moving at speed from a threat or in pursuit of prey, the Collared Lizard will often adopt a bipedal stance, running solely on its hind legs. It reproduces in summer, laying up to twelve eggs in a sheltered spot.

SPINY LIZARDS

The spiny lizards represent a large group of species, all of which have rough, pointed scales along their backs and tails, though these are more pronounced in some species than in others. They are generally found from Texas, west to the Pacific Coast, with the **Eastern Fence Lizard** (*Sceloporus undulatus*), being a notable exception. It is in fact, the most widespread lizard in North America, ranging from Pennsylvania and Delaware, west to Utah, and south to northern Florida and Arizona. There are a number of subspecies, including varieties referred to as prairie and plateau lizards. Most share a similar appearance, being up to seven inches in length with a gray or brown ground color and a number of stripes. Colors and variations in markings are common however. In prairie areas this species tends to be mainly terrestrial, but elsewhere it is highly arboreal, climbing with ease, and it is often seen on trees, fences or log piles. The **Northern**, or **Common**

Sagebrush Lizard (*Sceloporus graciosus*), is a close relative of the Eastern Fence Lizard but occurs only in western states. As its name would suggest it is found chiefly in sagebrush areas, but also lives in open forests, though it rarely climbs. This species will seek cover in vegetation or in a burrow, rather than ascending trees. Both are similar in appearance, but the Common Sagebrush Lizard is usually slightly smaller, and lacks dark markings and overlapping scales on the rear of its thighs. Males of both species have blue areas on the belly and throat, those of the Sagebrush Lizard being more mottled. They are both diurnal and insectivorous, feeding by day on beetles and other small invertebrates. Mating occurs in spring, following winter hibernation and the hatchlings appear in summer or early fall. The Sagebrush Lizard produces only one clutch of eggs, as do young Fence Lizards, but older females may lay up to four clutches.

Below: Eastern Fence Lizard

TEXAS HORNED LIZARD ▲

Scientific name:	*Phrynosoma cornutum*
Identification:	Small and flat, mottled red, brown or orange, with a short tail. Bears characteristic spines and horns
Length (including tail):	2½–6 inches
Habitat/Range:	Arid, sparsely vegetated terrain in Texas and surrounding states
Similar species:	This species can be distinguished from other horned lizards by the two enlarged spines at the back of the head

The Texas Horned Lizard is amongst the strangest and most striking of all North American lizards. Sometimes referred to as the "horned toad", it is rather wide and flat, and is adorned with a number of large spines, particularly along its back, sides and around the head, from the center of which, two long spines project backwards. The spines no doubt act as a deterrent to many potential predators, but this species mainly relies on its camouflage whilst in the open. If threatened however, it may attempt to hide amongst rocks, vegetation or in a burrow, though it will sometimes display more curious defensive behavior; hissing, moving towards its attacker and even squirting blood from the corners of its eyes. Despite these traits, it may be eaten by larger lizards, snakes, birds of prey and coyotes. The Texas Horned Lizard is diurnal and able to withstand high temperatures. It forages during the day for small insects and is particularly fond of ants. Breeding takes place in summer, with large clutches of eggs (sometimes thirty or more) being produced in a burrow.

LESSER EARLESS LIZARD

Scientific name:	*Holbrookia maculatum*
Identification:	Small gray-brown lizard with dark bars, light spots and stripes on back. Male has a pair of dark patches on underside
Length (including tail):	4–5 inches
Habitat/Range:	Sandy, open grasslands through the Great Plains region, west to Arizona
Similar species:	The Side-blotched Lizard is quite similar but has external ear openings

The Lesser Earless Lizard is an inhabitant of prairies, scrub and desert grasslands and is well adapted to living in such conditions. It is small, with tiny, smooth scales, and has long hind legs and toes which allow it to move rapidly over the loose sandy soil which it prefers. As its name suggests, it also lacks external ear openings, allowing it to burrow headfirst into sand. It is a diurnal species, but will usually seek refuge during the hottest part of the day, often amongst vegetation or in a rodent burrow. The Lesser Earless Lizard is insectivorous, preying upon beetles, grasshoppers and spiders. In turn it is eaten by larger lizards, snakes and birds of prey. It mates in spring and summer, and as with many lizard species, gravid, or egg-carrying, females develop red or orange markings on their sides. Eggs are laid from spring through to fall, with hatchlings emerging from early summer to around October.

GILA MONSTER ▶

Scientific name:	*Heloderma suspectum*
Identification:	Very large, stocky lizard with a short tail. Small bead-like scales are black and yellow, orange-red or pinkish. The tongue is black and forked
Length (including tail):	1½–2 feet
Habitat/Range:	Scrub, desert and juniper-oak woodland in parts of Utah, Nevada, Arizona and New Mexico
Similar species:	Unmistakable

The Gila Monster is one of only two venomous lizards in the world, and the only one which is found in North America, the other being the Beaded Lizard (*Heloderma horridum*) of Mexico. The Gila Monster is also the largest lizard in the US, easily recognized by its stout body, short, thick tail and distinctive coloration. Its venom is used both defensively and in subduing prey. It usually remains amongst rocks or in a burrow by day, feeding at night on reptiles, small mammals, ground-nesting birds and their eggs. Unlike snakes, this species does not inject its venom, instead it is secreted from glands in the mouth and flows into wounds as the Gila Monster chews on its victim. The toxin is not usually fatal to humans. The female produces up to five eggs, laid in her burrow in fall or winter.

FLORIDA WORM LIZARD

Scientific name:	*Rhineura floridana*
Identification:	Cylindrical, limbless, worm-like reptile with circular bands of scales. Lacks external ear openings and eyes
Length (including tail):	7–12 inches
Habitat/Range:	Well-drained, sandy soil, in woodland. Occurs only in central Florida
Similar species:	No similar species

Another highly unusual reptile, the Florida Worm Lizard is the only Amphisbaenid occurring in North America. It is closely related to, but in a separate Suborder from both snakes and lizards. At first glance it looks very much like a large earthworm, being pink, and lacking limbs, external ear openings and eyes. Upon closer inspection, though, it is scaly, and despite lacking in facial features has a definite, lizard-like head with a recessed mouth. It lives an almost entirely subterranean existence, burrowing through sandy soil, where it feeds on insects, their larvae and other invertebrates. It may however, be unearthed by birds or cultivation, and will occasionally surface after heavy rain. It lays up to three eggs in summer which hatch by fall.

GARTER SNAKES

Garter snakes are common across North America, and the **Common Garter Snake** (*Thamnophis sirtalis*), is the most widespread snake of all, occurring from coast-to-coast, absent only from the most arid southwestern regions. It is also found further north than any other reptile, with its range extending into much of Canada. A fairly slender species, the Common Garter Snake may grow to over four foot long, and though its color is variable, like most garter snakes it has prominent longitudinal stripes. It occupies a range of habitats, including woodlands, meadows and gardens, often being found close to water. It feeds on invertebrates and amphibians, sometimes also catching small fish or rodents. The **Eastern Ribbon Snake** (*Thamnophis sauritus*), is a more highly aquatic species, frequently swimming at the surface of ponds or streams, and subsisting almost exclusively on amphibians and small fish. It is the most streamlined of the garter snakes and is usually dark, with three bold stripes. It is somewhat shorter than the Common Garter however, reaching about two and a half feet. It is found throughout the eastern US, from the Mississippi to the Atlantic coast and north into southern Ontario. Both the Common Garter Snake and Eastern Ribbon Snake tend to mate in spring, producing live young in the summer. Garter snakes are harmless, but may struggle and release musk if handled. The Common Garter Snake is also likely to bite, but may tame quite quickly.

Below: **The Eastern Ribbon Snake**

COMMON/NORTHERN WATER SNAKE

Scientific name:	*Nerodia sipedon*
Identification:	Fairly large, usually dark snake, with darker bands on neck, becoming alternating blotches along back and sides
Length (including tail):	2–4½ feet
Habitat/Range:	Freshwater habitats across the eastern US
Similar species:	The Southern Water Snake (*Nerodia fasciata*), has dark markings between the eyes and mouth, the Cottonmouth is larger and swims with its head above water

The Common or Northern Water Snake is often mistakenly persecuted due to its superficial similarity to the venomous Cottonmouth. It is however, a non-venomous species, but will bite if threatened. It is active both by day and night, and frequents almost any freshwater habitat, though prefers still or slow-moving water. Often seen basking on rocks, a stump or overhanging branch, the Common Water Snake is a strong swimmer and will slip into the water if disturbed. It feeds on invertebrates, frogs and other amphibians, small fish, reptiles and occasionally small mammals. Mating occurs in spring or summer and this species may give birth to over one hundred young, although the average number is probably closer to twenty. Pregnant females are often heavily distended. The young are born in late summer or fall, and are vividly patterned. Adults usually darken with age and may become uniformly black.

RINGNECK SNAKE

Scientific name:	*Diadophis punctatus*
Identification:	Usually gray or olive with a yellow, orange or red collar and underside. The belly is also often spotted
Length (including tail):	1–2½ feet
Habitat/Range:	Woodland, prairies and scrub, often close to water. Found across the US, but distribution is more patchy in the west
Similar species:	Brown Snake (*Storeria dekayi*) juveniles have yellow collar, but scales are keeled rather than smooth

Some twelve subspecies of the Ringneck Snake have been identified in North America. All vary somewhat in color and pattern, particularly on the underside, where the occurrence, number and size of spots are useful characteristics for differentiating between them. Otherwise, they are much alike, and exhibit similar behavior. Ringnecks favor moist woodlands, hillsides and open grasslands, being found close to pools or streams in more arid regions. It is not an aquatic species, but feeds heavily on amphibians, as well as consuming invertebrates and small reptiles. The Ringneck Snake spends much of its time concealed amongst logs, rocks, bark or leaf litter, and is seldom seen in the open. Those subspecies which have a red belly, including the Prairie Ringneck (*Diadophis punctatus arnyi*), may twist themselves to expose their underside when disturbed. The female produces a clutch of up to ten eggs in summer, often in a communal nest.

WESTERN SHOVEL-NOSED SNAKE

Scientific name:	*Chionactis occipitalis*
Identification:	Small light-colored snake with dark cross bands and flattened snout
Length (including tail):	1–1½ feet
Habitat/Range:	Desert and scrub in southwestern states
Similar species:	Banded Sand Snake (*Chilomeniscus cinctus*) is almost identical, but rarely exceeds 10 inches

A fairly small, burrowing species of southwestern desert areas, the Western Shovel-nosed, as its name might suggest, is well adapted for moving through loose soil and sand. Its smooth belly and head are flattened, and the tapering snout is equipped with valved nostrils. They are occasionally encountered during the day, but are primarily nocturnal, hunting at night for insects and arthropods, feeding on crickets, centipedes, spiders and scorpions. The Western Shovel-nosed Snake is quite temperamental and will often strike repeatedly if disturbed, but its teeth are very small, and its bite is ineffectual to humans. Females of this species usually only produce two to four eggs, which, as is the case with most snakes, are laid in summer.

EASTERN HOGNOSE SNAKE ▲

Scientific name:	*Heterodon platyrhinos*
Identification:	Fairly stout with a wide neck. Snout is upturned. Color is variable, but blotches are usually present on back and sides. Underside is pale and lightest along the tail
Length (including tail):	2–4 feet
Habitat/Range:	Sandy grasslands and forest edges throughout most of the eastern US
Similar species:	Western species (*Heterodon nasicus*) has dark markings on underside of tail

PLAINS BLACKHEAD SNAKE

Scientific name:	*Tantilla nigriceps*
Identification:	Small, light brown or yellowish snake with black cap
Length (including tail):	7–14 inches
Habitat/Range:	Rocky scrub and grasslands from Nebraska, south through parts of Texas, Arizona and New Mexico
Similar species:	Not unlike the Ringneck Snake, but lacks collar

The Eastern Hognose Snake is harmless to humans, and although it may strike, it very rarely bites. Instead it displays dramatic defensive behavior, hissing loudly, spreading its wide neck and inflating its body; traits which have earned this snake the name "Puff Adder". If this fails to deter a predator or other intruder, it will then play dead, rolling onto its back with an open mouth. It favors sandy grasslands and forest edges, often burrowing through loose soil in search of toads, upon which it feeds almost exclusively. It will also eat frogs, piercing its prey with two enlarged fangs in the rear of its upper jaw. Juveniles however, may feed on invertebrates. The female Eastern Hognose Snake lays her eggs in summer, producing perhaps as many as sixty, which will be hidden in a hollow in the ground.

A small burrowing snake found in the south of the Great Plains area and surrounding arid regions, the Plains Blackhead Snake is rarely seen in the open. By day it usually remains hidden in a burrow, amongst rocks, vegetation or leaf litter, and it hunts at night, moving through similarly covered areas. It feeds on subterranean insects and their larvae, centipedes and spiders, and though it is not considered venomous to man, it has grooved rear fangs and is thought to use a mild toxin to subdue its small prey. It hibernates below ground in winter, mates in spring and produces eggs in spring or summer.

KINGSNAKES

There are several subspecies of Kingsnake in North America, with the **Common Kingsnake** (*Lampropeltis getula*), having the widest distribution. Varieties are found across most of the southern half of the US, extending further north in the east and along the Pacific Coast. Amongst the largest of the kingsnakes, this species is heavy-bodied and may grow to over six feet in length. It is usually dark brown or black, with variable, light bands or blotches, although a chain-link pattern is common. It is found across a wide range of habitats, from arid desert to swamps and woodlands, and is chiefly diurnal, although it is also likely to be active on warm summer nights. The **Prairie Kingsnake** (*Lampropeltis calligaster*), is a more nocturnal species. Less inclined to bask, it usually spends the day hidden amongst debris, sometimes retreating to a burrow. It inhabits open grasslands and woodland from Nebraska to Maryland, south to eastern Texas and Florida. Smaller than the Common Kingsnake, this species is quite slender and reaches a length of about four feet. It is also generally lighter in color, but its blotched markings become increasingly indistinct with age, and the ground color, usually light brown or gray, also darkens. Both species are constrictors, feeding on rodents, birds and amphibians, but are also well known for eating bird and reptile eggs, and also adult snakes. They are seemingly unaffected by the venom of species upon which they prey. Breeding occurs in spring and summer, with females laying up to around twenty eggs.

Below: Eastern Kingsnake

MILK SNAKE

Scientific name:	*Lampropeltis triangulum*
Identification:	Medium-sized snake, varies from gray with brown blotches outlined with black, to "coral snake mimics" with red, black and yellow bands. Some have a V or Y-shaped marking on the neck
Length (including tail):	2–3 feet
Habitat/Range:	Extremely varied, found in both arid and damp conditions, from woodlands, grasslands and rocky foothills to suburban areas. Occurs east of the Rocky Mountains to the Atlantic
Similar species:	Some are colored like the venomous Eastern Coral Snake, but the red areas are bordered by black rather than yellow. The nose also tends to be red as opposed to black

A close relative of the Kingsnakes, the Milk Snake is a widespread and common species, but as with many snakes, it is rarely seen during the day. It prefers to seek shelter amongst rocks, logs, or in farm buildings until nightfall, when it will emerge to feed. Its name is derived from a mythical belief that it suckles milk from cows, but in reality its diet is very similar to that of the Kingsnakes. It eats rodents, birds and reptiles, including venomous snakes. It is not venomous itself however, instead it kills by means of constriction. This species mates in spring and lays a clutch of around ten eggs in summer, often under a log-pile. The young hatch around two months later and range from about five to ten inches in length.

▲ SCARLET SNAKE

Scientific name:	*Cemophora coccinea*
Identification:	Slender, with wide red and yellow bands divided by black
Length (including tail):	1–2½ feet
Habitat/Range:	Mainly open woodland with sandy soil. Found in the eastern US, particularly along coastal states
Similar species:	Much like the venomous Eastern Coral Snake, but the rings of the Scarlet Snake are incomplete, and its red areas are bordered by black rather than yellow. The nose is also red as opposed to black

The Scarlet Snake is closely related to the Kingsnakes and Milk Snakes, and is often similar in appearance. However, it also closely resembles the poisonous Eastern Coral Snake, particularly in terms of its coloration, a trait which perhaps serves to keep would-be predators at bay. It is a reclusive and nocturnal species, usually hiding by day, spending much of its time when active burrowing through soil and leaf litter. It may however be observed after heavy rainfall or exposed by the plowing of fields. It constricts small mammals and reptiles, but seems to favor eating eggs, particularly those of other snakes, which if small enough are swallowed whole.

BULLSNAKE

Scientific name:	*Pituophis melanoleucas*
Identification:	Large, light-colored snake with dark blotches along back and sides
Length (including tail):	4–8 feet
Habitat/Range:	Mainly grasslands, from the Great Plains throughout the western US, north to the Great Lakes and British Columbia. Separate populations in Florida and surrounding area
Similar species:	May be mistaken for a rattlesnake due to its threat display

Known in various parts of its range as the Pine Snake or Gopher Snake, the Bullsnake is a large, heavy constrictor which is often aggressive when encountered. Like the Corn Snake and Rat Snakes it vibrates its tail and hisses loudly when alarmed, and it will also readily bite. It is mainly diurnal, but becomes increasingly active at night during the summer. It is usually found hunting amongst vegetation or animal burrows, feeding mainly on rodents. It will also eat birds and eggs. Sometimes making its home in a tortoise burrow, the Bullsnake also frequently hibernates with other species, including Rat Snakes and rattlesnakes.

CORN SNAKE

Scientific name:	*Elaphe guttata*
Identification:	Slender, often orange, though also gray or brown. Large blotches on back alternate with smaller ones on sides. Slightly keeled scales. Some individuals have a checkered underside and an arrow-shape on head
Length (including tail):	2–6 feet
Habitat/Range:	Varied habitats, from woodlands, grassland and cultivated areas, to rocky hills. Occurs in east from New Jersey to Texas and eastern Colorado, with separate population in western Colorado and Utah
Similar species:	Kingsnakes and Milk Snakes may be similarly marked, but their scales are smooth

The Corn Snake belongs to the genus *Elaphe*, also known as Rat Snakes, and in common with other members of this group, it has a predilection for consuming small rodents. This trait makes it a useful ally to the farmer. It is a constrictor, and also feeds on birds, bats, reptiles and amphibians. Mainly nocturnal and terrestrial, the Corn Snake becomes active in the evening, hunting along the ground or in the burrows of small mammals. It is a good climber however, aided by keeled scales, and will readily ascend trees and bushes in pursuit of prey. It is not a dangerous species, but will often adopt a defensive posture if surprised, vibrating the tail, coiling and rearing up to strike.

▼ RAT SNAKE

Scientific name:	*Elaphe obsoleta*
Identification:	Large, heavy-bodied snake, often uniformly black. Yellow, brown and gray, striped or blotched varieties occur in parts of range. Scales slightly keeled
Length (including tail):	3½–8 feet
Habitat/Range:	Forests, swamps, dry grasslands, hillsides and farms throughout eastern states, west into Texas and prairie regions
Similar species:	Racer is smooth and slender

The Rat Snake, or Eastern Rat Snake, is widespread across the eastern US, with four subspecies, varying from yellow to gray, inhabiting localized areas. The predominant form however, which is found throughout the region, is black, often with some white or gray patterning, usually between the scales. It is a large constricting snake, and preys on small mammals, birds, reptiles and eggs, often climbing high into trees in search of food. It is also not unknown for this species to establish a home in a hollow tree trunk or branch. Like the Corn Snake it may be aggressive when encountered and will vibrate its tail, but it is not considered to be dangerous. In winter however, this species may hibernate with venomous snakes such as the Copperhead and rattlesnakes, a habit which has earned it the nickname "Rattlesnake Pilot".

ROUGH GREEN SNAKE ▲ RACER

Scientific name:	*Opheodrys aestivus*
Identification:	Very slender, uniformly green snake with keeled scales. Underside may be yellowish
Length (including tail):	2–3½ feet
Habitat/Range:	Amongst trees and vines in moist habitats, often close to ponds and streams
Similar species:	Smooth Green Snake (*Opheodrys vernalis*), has flat scales

Scientific name:	*Coluber constrictor*
Identification:	Long and slender, back uniformly black, brown or dark green in adults. Underside pale. Moves very quickly
Length (including tail):	3–6 feet
Habitat/Range:	Extremely varied habitat. Found in southern Canada and throughout much of the US. Absent from the most arid southwestern regions
Similar species:	Indigo Snake is more powerfully built, Coachwhip is generally lighter in color

A highly distinctive, brightly colored snake, the Rough Green Snake may however, be difficult to spot. Its chief means of defense is its camouflage, and it blends in well amongst the vines and foliage where it spends its time. It is an excellent climber and is highly arboreal, moving through trees and bushes in search of its insect prey of grasshoppers, caterpillars and spiders. A diurnal species, the Smooth Green Snake usually sleeps amongst branches at night. It is often found in vegetation which overhangs streams or ponds and it swims well, sometimes entering water if disturbed. It is a passive snake and will very rarely bite, but it may open its mouth to display the black interior. Mating generally takes place in spring, and females deposit their eggs in summer. The eggs are usually concealed in a hollow tree or stump, amongst logs, or sometimes on the ground beneath rocks. Females commonly share nesting sites for their eggs.

Despite its Latin name, the Racer is in fact not a constrictor at all, and though it may restrain its prey with its coiled body, it usually swallows its victims live, and whole. It is a long, slender and very fast-moving snake, and is active by day, hunting down large invertebrates, birds, rodents, amphibians and reptiles. It moves swiftly as it hunts, and relies heavily on its eyesight, holding its head well above the ground. Although it is primarily terrestrial, the Racer is extremely agile and may climb trees and bushes in search of a meal. Racers are widespread throughout the US, and although some eleven subspecies have been identified, distinguishing between them is difficult. All are very much alike and may interbreed where their ranges overlap. Mating occurs in spring or early summer, and the resultant eggs have a rough texture.

EASTERN INDIGO SNAKE ▼ COACHWHIP

Scientific name:	*Drymarchon corais couperi*
Identification:	Very large, black or blue-black snake. Sides of head and throat may be cream or orange
Length (including tail):	5–8½ feet
Habitat/Range:	Dry grasslands and open woodland, often near water. Found in southeast in Florida and adjacent areas
Similar species:	Western, or Texas Indigo Snake is almost identical, but has dark lines below the eyes and often brownish foreparts

Scientific name:	*Masticophis flagellum*
Identification:	Long and thin, often light brown with a darker head and neck. Fast-moving
Length (including tail):	3–8½ feet
Habitat/Range:	Dry, open prairie and woodland areas throughout the southern US
Similar species:	Racer is similarly built, but usually darker overall

The Eastern Indigo Snake is amongst the largest of all North American snakes, and may react defensively when disturbed, hissing and shaking its tail. It is easily tamed however, and has long been a popular species at carnivals, fairs and amongst animal dealers, though wild populations are in decline. It is diurnal, hunting by day and sleeping at night, usually in an underground den. It is often found within the burrows of Gopher Tortoises, sometimes sharing their homes with rattlesnakes. In cold weather the Eastern Indigo Snake will remain below ground for extended periods, but it may be active on warm winter days. It is non-venomous and not a constricting species, instead it swallows its prey whole, feeding on small mammals, birds, amphibians and reptiles.

Like the closely related Racer, the Coachwhip is known for its speed and agility, being perhaps the fastest-moving snake in North America. It is terrestrial, mainly hunting on the ground, but it is also a good climber and may seek prey, refuge or a basking site amongst the branches of a tree or shrub. At night it will frequently retreat to a burrow. It feeds on small mammals, birds and reptiles, but will also eat invertebrates such as grasshoppers, swallowing its prey whole. Though it will usually attempt to escape if threatened, and will occasionally play dead, caution should be exercised as this species can be highly aggressive and will often strike at the face. This species mates in spring and lays eggs in summer. The eggs are usually one to two inches long and have a grainy surface.

Above: The Rubber Boa

BOAS

Most of the species of snake found in North America, and indeed the world, belong to the family *Colubridae* and are considered to be "advanced" snakes. The two species of boa native to the US however, are of the family *Boidae*, which includes the pythons and the Boa Constrictor of more tropical climes. The **Rosy Boa** (*Lichanura trivirgata*), is found in arid scrublands and desert in southern California, Arizona and south into Mexico, commonly close to a source of water. It grows to between two, and three and a half feet in length, is quite heavy-bodied and ranges in color from gray to brown or red, with three dark brown stripes from head to tail. It is mainly terrestrial, but may ascend bushes in search of prey. Like the **Rubber Boa** (*Charina bottae*), it hunts at night, feeding on

small birds, mammals and reptiles, and kills by means of constriction. The Rubber Boa is a similarly thick-set species with a blunt head and tail, but it is somewhat shorter, attaining a maximum length of just under three feet. It has a rubbery appearance and is uniformly colored, usually some shade of green or brown. It prefers more moist, temperate conditions than the Rosy Boa, and is an inhabitant of woodlands and grasslands from California, north to British Columbia. It often burrows, but is also an adept climber and swimmer. Following mating, which takes place in summer, both of these species produce up to about eight live young in fall. Both are quite docile and will tend to curl into a ball if handled.

EASTERN CORAL SNAKE

Scientific name:	*Micrurus fulvius*
Identification:	Distinctive black and red bands separated by yellow, black snout
Length (including tail):	2–4 feet
Habitat/Range:	Pinewoods, rocky hills, and woodland with dense vegetation mainly in southeastern coastal states
Similar species:	Scarlet Snake and similarly colored Milk Snakes have red areas divided by black, not yellow, and their snouts are also red

A member of the family *Elapidae*, the Eastern Coral Snake has fixed fangs at the front of its upper jaw which it uses to administer a powerful neurotoxin. Although it is not usually aggressive, and the mouth and teeth are small, its bite can prove fatal to humans and it should therefore never be handled. It is active by day, often in the morning, when it hunts mainly for small reptiles. When resting, it will usually seek cover amongst leaf litter or logs. It lays eggs in summer which hatch in fall, and it is the only oviparous venomous snake in North America. All members of the viper family are live-bearing.

COPPERHEAD

Scientific name:	*Agkistrodon contortrix*
Identification:	Heavy-bodied, brown or pinkish, with copper head and broad dark brown bands
Length (including tail):	2–4 feet
Habitat/Range:	Woodland, rocky hills and marshy areas throughout most of the eastern US
Similar species:	Broad head and facial pits distinguish this species from similar Colubrid snakes such as Milk Snakes or Corn Snakes

Like the Cottonmouth and rattlesnakes, the Copperhead belongs to a group of the viper family known as the pit vipers, so called, due to sensory pits located on the face. These act as heat sensors, and enable the snake to strike accurately at warm-blooded prey. All pit vipers are venomous, and may be aggressive if approached. It is therefore advisable to avoid close contact, and never to handle these species. The Copperhead is common in much of the eastern US, and though mainly diurnal, tends to be fairly sluggish, basking motionlessly or moving slowly around walls, sawdust mounds, woodpiles and similar covered areas in search of food. It feeds on rodents, frogs and invertebrates. This species is seldom aggressive, and its venom not usually life-threatening, but it may strike if provoked.

COTTONMOUTH ▲

Scientific name:	*Agkistrodon piscivorus*
Identification:	Large, heavy, aquatic snake with keeled scales. Head is broad and lining of mouth is white
Length (including tail):	2–6 feet
Habitat/Range:	Swamps, marshes, rivers and lakes, particularly in wooded areas. Found from Texas to Florida, north to Virginia and Illinois
Similar species:	Other aquatic snakes often smaller and more retiring. Swims with head above water

The Cottonmouth, sometimes also known as the Water Moccasin, is a large, heavily built water snake. It hunts mostly at night, but may be seen basking by day. Unlike other aquatic species which will usually take to water if disturbed, the Cottonmouth will frequently stand its ground, and if particularly agitated will vibrate its tail, before opening its mouth widely to expose the white lining. It is often aggressive and is dangerous, its venom may prove fatal to humans. It can usually be distinguished from other aquatic species whilst swimming as it holds its head clear of the water. It feeds primarily on fish and amphibians, but also eats small aquatic reptiles, birds and mammals. Young are born in late summer or fall and may be over a foot long.

EASTERN DIAMONDBACK RATTLESNAKE

Scientific name:	*Crotalus adamanteus*
Identification:	Powerfully built rattlesnake. Large head is marked with two diagonal lines on each side. Back is patterned with large, dark diamonds, bordered with lighter scales
Length (including tail):	3–8 feet
Habitat/Range:	Dry habitats in southeastern states
Similar species:	Other rattlesnakes are generally smaller

One of the most deadly snakes in the world, and along with its smaller western relative *Crotalus atrox*, the Eastern Diamondback Rattlesnake is the most dangerous snake in North America. It is also the largest venomous snake found in the US. It will usually not retreat from a threat, but will issue a warning by vibrating its rattle; the hard, terminal sections of its tail. It inhabits lowland coastal woodlands, farmland and dry sandy terrain, often sharing the burrows of Gopher Tortoises in winter. It may also swim in the sea, and is found on the Florida Keys. This snake is an ambush hunter, lying in wait for potential prey amongst long grass or other vegetation, striking at animals which come within range. It preys upon squirrels, cotton rats and other large rodents, rabbits and birds. The female Eastern Diamondback Rattlesnake produces offspring every other year, giving birth to as many as twenty young in late summer or fall.

OTHER RATTLESNAKES

Although the Diamondback Rattlesnakes are perhaps the best known and most feared, there are several other rattlesnake species present in North America, ranging from the small pigmy rattlesnakes of the genus *Sistrurus*, which includes the Massasauga (*Sistrurus catenatus*), to the larger crotalus species, which includes the Diamondbacks, the Western Rattlesnake (*Crotalus viridis*), and the Timber Rattlesnake (*Crotalus horridus*). A greater variety of rattlesnakes is found in western states, particularly in the southwest, but the group is represented by at least one species in almost every state. The Western Rattlesnake, which may reach a length of five feet, has the largest range, and occupies a variety of habitats from southern Canada, throughout the western US and Great Plains region into Texas, whilst the slightly smaller, more venomous Mojave Rattlesnake (*Crotalus scutulatus*), is restricted to southwestern desert and grasslands. The Timber Rattlesnake

meanwhile, is a large species, up to around six foot long, which is found across most of the eastern US. Although these species may vary in distribution, size and color, they share much in common. All are equipped with heat-sensing facial pits, folding fangs and venom, and though some are more poisonous and aggressive than others, they are all potentially dangerous. Adults usually have well developed rattles, but they may be absent on occasion, and under-developed in juveniles. They are terrestrial snakes, feeding on small mammals such as rodents, birds and other reptiles, often ambushing their prey from the cover of vegetation. Most are active from spring to fall and are fairly diurnal, becoming more nocturnal in summer. In winter they may experience long periods of inactivity. In northern and mountainous areas some species will hibernate in large groups. All produce live young, usually in late summer or fall, in litters of up to about twenty.

Opposite: The Timber Rattlesnake
Above: The Western Rattlesnake

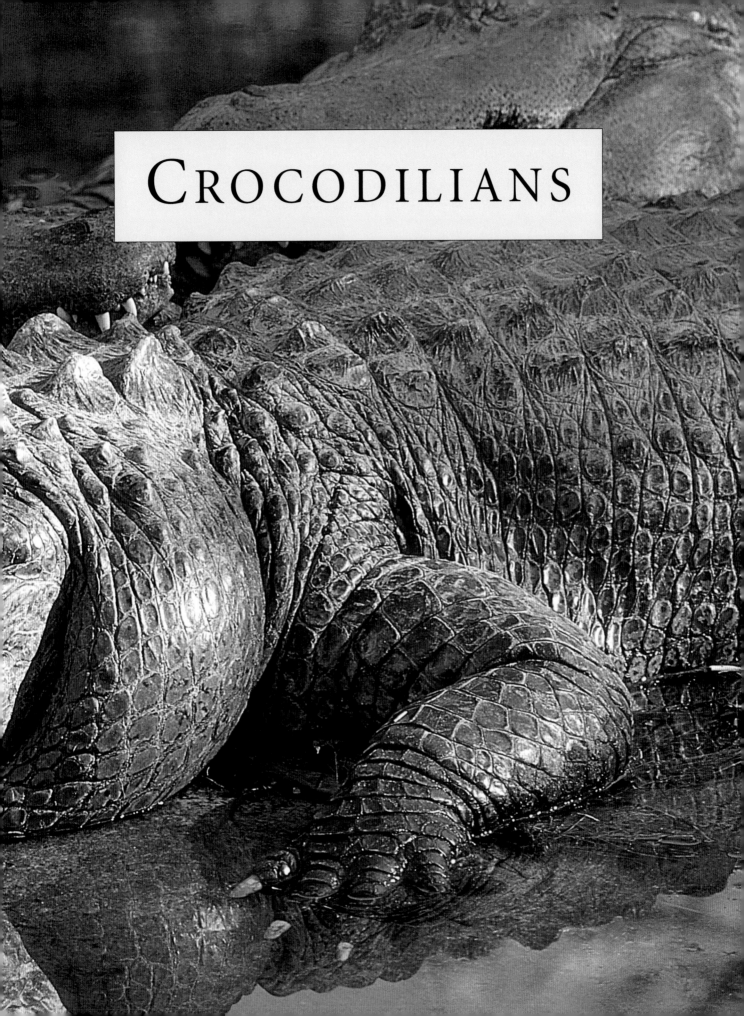

CROCODILIANS

AMERICAN ALLIGATOR

Scientific name:	*Alligator mississippiensis*
Identification:	Vast, armored, lizard-like reptile. Black or gray in color, sometimes with traces of light markings. Snout is broad and rounded
Length:	6–18 feet
Habitat/Range:	Freshwater; swamps, marshes, lakes and rivers throughout the southeastern coastal plain from North Carolina to Texas. Also found in the Florida Keys
Similar species:	The snout of the American Crocodile is more narrow and tapered, and the fourth tooth in the lower jaw protrudes when the mouth is closed. The Spectacled Caiman has a prominent ridge across its snout in front of the eyes

The American Alligator is the largest reptile found in North America, with a powerful, muscular body and a record length of over nineteen feet. Once far more numerous, it was heavily hunted for its skin, and although now protected, earlier persecution and continued encroachment upon its habitat have left populations greatly reduced. Much maligned, indeed Alligators are fearsome predators which should be treated with caution, this species is however, beneficial to the ecology of its habitat. In times of drought Alligators dig out deep "gator holes" which may sustain various other aquatic life. Female Alligators are also highly maternal, guarding their eggs until hatching, when they will carry their offspring to the water in their mouths. The young may then stay with the mother for over a year. About forty eggs are laid in summer in nests of rotting vegetation, where they are incubated for about two months. The American Alligator preys on fish, reptiles, birds, amphibians and small mammals.

AMERICAN CROCODILE

Scientific name:	*Crocodylus acutus*
Identification:	Large green or brown crocodilian with darker bands. Its snout is tapered, and a tooth remains exposed on each side when the mouth is shut
Length:	7–12 feet +
Habitat/Range:	Brackish water in swamps, lagoons and in coastal bays. Found only in southern Florida and the Keys
Similar species:	Snout of the Alligator is much broader, whilst that of the Spectacled Caiman has a bony ridge

The American Crocodile is a rare species which occurs in both saltwater and freshwater habitats. In the US it is confined to southern Florida and the Keys, being mainly found in the Everglades National Park, but it is also found in South America. Much of its decline has been due to urban expansion, hunting and disruption to water systems, for the young are only able to survive in freshwater. Although it is now protected, there are perhaps only five hundred individuals remaining. It is much like its relatives in terms of behavior, feeding on various smaller reptiles, amphibians, birds and mammals, and it has powerful jaws. Breeding takes place in summer, with eggs being deposited in a nest. The young are carried to the water by the mother upon hatching.

SPECTACLED CAIMAN

Scientific name:	*Caiman crocodilus*
Identification:	Yellowish, olive-green or brown, with dark bands on back and tail. Bony ridge just in front of eyes
Length:	3½–7 feet
Habitat/Range:	Marshland, ponds, streams and canals in southern Florida
Similar species:	Smaller than the native crocodilians, but ridge on snout is most distinguishing feature

The Spectacled Caiman is in fact not native to North America, but has been introduced from Central and South America, and become established in parts of southern Florida. This population is most likely descended from released or escaped individuals once kept as pets. Although it is usually smaller than the American Crocodile and Alligator, it remains potentially dangerous and may be aggressive. Like other crocodilians, this species spends much of its time basking and conserving energy. For reptiles of their size, they may feed comparatively rarely, and may appear sluggish, but they are capable of sudden bursts of speed in order to obtain a meal, or in response to a perceived threat. The Spectacled Caiman feeds on fish, amphibians, invertebrates, birds and small mammals. Like the Alligator, the Caiman lays its eggs in a nest of vegetation in summer.

FROGS, TOADS
AND SALAMANDERS

GREEN FROG

Scientific name:	*Rana clamitans*
Identification:	Green, brown or bronze, with prominent eardrums and ridges along sides
Length:	2–4 inches
Habitat/Range:	Mainly shallow ponds and streams in southeastern Canada and the eastern US
Similar species:	Very similar to the Mink Frog, but has bands on hind legs and does not produce odour when handled

A very common species, the Green Frog is found in various habitats, from small bodies of water to the shallows of larger ponds and lakes. It is abundant in marshland, and may wander away from the water into damp woodlands or meadows in search of invertebrate prey. In the south of its range it tends to be more bronze-colored, and indeed is usually known as the Bronze Frog, whereas in the northern US into Canada, it is often very dark. Blue individuals have also been identified. This species breeds in spring or summer, at which time males become territorial and highly vocal. As with most frogs, the female lays her spawn amongst aquatic vegetation.

PICKEREL FROG ▶

Scientific name:	*Rana palustris*
Identification:	Distinctive, with prominent ridges on sides and almost square blotches. Undersides of its legs are bright orange or yellow
Length:	2–3 inches
Habitat/Range:	In northern part of range, often found in cold streams, but inhabiting warmer swamp areas further south. Occurs in the eastern US from South Carolina and Texas, north into Canada
Similar species:	Leopard Frogs have more rounded spots

The Pickerel Frog is closely related to the Leopard Frogs, and is also frequently found in damp meadows, sometimes at a distance from water. However, it seldom, if ever, ventures as far as the Northern Leopard Frog. It is found in a variety of situations, having a wide, if somewhat patchy distribution, but prefers areas with quite dense vegetation. It is also sometimes found within caves. As with other frogs, it feeds on small insects, slugs and other invertebrates. It is less heavily preyed upon than some other frogs, secreting a particularly toxic substance through its skin.

NORTHERN LEOPARD FROG

Scientific name:	*Rana pipiens*
Identification:	A medium-sized frog, brown or green with dark spots
Length:	2–5 inches
Habitat/Range:	Marshes, damp meadows, ponds, lakes and rivers throughout much of Canada, south to Kentucky, Nebraska and Arizona
Similar species:	Other Leopard Frogs are almost identical, but in this species, the vocal sacs of the male are not visible unless it is calling

Sometimes known as the "Meadow Frog", the Northern Leopard Frog is often found a considerable distance from water, particularly following hibernation and breeding when it may make long migrations between aquatic habitats. They typically breed in small pools in spring, roaming through wet fields in summer to find larger ponds and lakes where they will hibernate in winter. The mass of eggs produced by this species is often secured to vegetation, but may also be laid on the bottom of a suitable pool. This frog is well known as the species commonly used in laboratory dissections.

MINK FROG

Scientific name:	*Rana septentrionalis*
Identification:	Usually green or brown with dark blotches. Eardrum is quite prominent
Length:	2–3 inches
Habitat/Range:	Ponds, streams and lakes with dense aquatic vegetation, particularly lilies. Found in north-eastern US around the Great Lakes, north into Canada
Similar species:	The Green Frog is similar, but has bands rather than blotches on hind legs

The Mink Frog is so called due to a habit of expelling a mink-like musk if not handled with great care. It is a northern species, inhabiting cold waters, and may often be found where streams flow into larger bodies of water. It also prefers highly vegetated areas, hiding by day amongst plants at the shore, and venturing out onto lily pads at night, where males will often emit low-pitched croaks. Like other frogs of its size, it feeds on small insects and other invertebrates. This species lays its eggs in summer, attaching them to vegetation below the water.

WOOD FROG

Scientific name:	*Rana sylvatica*
Identification:	Dark to light brown or reddish, with dark markings behind the eyes. Light dorsal stripe is often present
Length:	1¼–2¼ inches
Habitat/Range:	Woodlands and grasslands, to tundra in northernmost parts of range. Found from South Carolina, north to the Great Lakes, and through Canada to Alaska
Similar species:	Northern Chorus Frog has similar facial markings, but is usually smaller, with three bold stripes on back

The Wood Frog is found further north than any other amphibian, occurring on tundra within the Arctic Circle, and though it hibernates in forests in the winter, it will enter icy water in early spring in order to reproduce. At such times, many frogs will gather, often in quite shallow pools, but unlike most species which will take up residence for a period of weeks, breeding usually only lasts for a matter of one or two days. The Wood Frogs then disperse. A diurnal species, this frog may be found roaming quite far from water during the day, particularly in summer.

BULLFROG ▶

Scientific name:	*Rana catesbeiana*
Identification:	Large yellow-green or brown frog, sometimes blotched. Eardrums are large and prominent
Length:	3½–7 inches
Habitat/Range:	Lakes, ponds, slow-moving streams and rivers, mainly throughout the eastern US, but also along the Pacific Coast
Similar species:	The Pig Frog (*Rana grylio*) is another large species, but its nose is more pointed and its toes are more fully webbed

The Bullfrog is North America's largest frog, with the biggest specimen recorded being eight inches long. It is also more carnivorous than other species, and in addition to eating invertebrates, it will eat other frogs, small fish, birds and even small snakes. Unfortunately, where it has been introduced to areas outside of its natural range, it has often caused something of an imbalance in the ecology of habitats, threatening or displacing other aquatic and semi-aquatic fauna. It is often found in quite large bodies of water, but is perhaps less aquatic than some frogs, spending much of its time on, or close to the shore, usually amongst vegetation.

TREEFROGS

Treefrogs are specially adapted for a more or less arboreal lifestyle. Most are small and light enough to be supported by even the thinnest stems and leaves of waterside plants and trees, and they have long limbs and rounded toe pads which aid in climbing. As with other amphibians, they require water for breeding, and like other frogs, have moist skins. As such, they are rarely found far from ponds or streams.

The **Green Treefrog** (*Hyla cinerea*) is an abundant species in densely vegetated swamps and marshes along much of the eastern coast, often congregating at the edges of pools in large numbers. It is about $1\frac{1}{4}$ to $2\frac{1}{4}$ inches long, and usually bright green with a white or yellow stripe along each side. Some individuals have gold speckles on their backs. It is nocturnal, resting amongst leaves during the day and becoming active in the evening. In suburban areas it may often be found at windows feeding on insects attracted by house lights. The **Barking Treefrog** (*Hyla gratiosa*), occupies a similar, though slightly smaller range, and although its habits vary somewhat from those of the Green Treefrog, the two species are known to interbreed. It is grows to about two and a half inches long, and is quite rotund. It is however an excellent climber, spending a great deal of its time high up in waterside treetops from where it gives a bark-like call. In dry conditions

though, it often burrows into soil to seek moisture. Another species known to burrow is the **Pacific Treefrog** (*Hyla regilla*), which inhabits marshes and waterside areas from California, north to British Columbia. This species is about two inches long, varies from green, to brown or black, and has quite warty skin. A dark stripe through the eyes is another distinctive feature. It is often found on the ground amongst rocks, vegetation or in burrows, but also climbs into the lower branches of trees or shrubs. Its high-pitched call is a familiar nighttime sound along the Pacific coast, though this treefrog is also active by day. Perhaps the most arboreal and least aquatic members of the genus **Hyla** are the **Gray Treefrogs** (*Hyla versicolor and Hyla chrysocelis*), two almost identical frogs which can only be told apart in the field by their calls; that of *Hyla versicolor* being slower and lower-pitched. They are rarely seen on the ground or in water except when breeding, spending their time in trees and shrubs which grow in or close to water. In fact, they may be difficult to see at all, having rough, gray or brown skin that acts as excellent camouflage. Both are found throughout the eastern US. All the species mentioned breed from spring through to late summer or fall, although the Gray and Pacific Treefrogs may begin breeding in the winter in warmer parts of their ranges.

Below: **The Green Treefrog**
Opposite: **The Lesser Gray Treefrog**

SPRING PEEPER

Scientific name:	*Pseudacris crucifer/Hyla crucifer*
Identification:	A small gray, brown or reddish treefrog, usually lacking distinct blotches or stripes, but with a dark cross on its back
Length:	$\frac{3}{4}$–$1\frac{1}{2}$ inches
Habitat/Range:	Woodland pools, swamps and marshes throughout the eastern US, into Manitoba, Ontario, Quebec and Nova Scotia
Similar species:	Most similar species have blotches or stripes, the Pine Woods Treefrog (*Hyla femoralis*) has spotted thighs

The Spring Peeper is closely related to the Chorus Frogs, but has well developed, round toe pads and climbs more readily. It shares various characteristics with both the Chorus Frogs of the genus *Pseudacris*, and the treefrogs of the genus *Hyla*, and there remains some discussion as to with which group it should be classified. Although it is common, it is also secretive, hiding amongst vegetation in woodland thickets, close to ponds or flooded areas. As such it is not often seen, but it may be abroad in more open areas following heavy rain. The presence of a group of these frogs is also announced by loud, high-pitched "peeps", a chorus of which is often described as sounding like sleigh bells.

▼ NORTHERN/WESTERN CHORUS FROG

Scientific name:	*Pseudacris triseriata*
Identification:	Very small, brown or olive-green, dark eye mask and striped back
Length:	$\frac{3}{4}$–$1\frac{1}{2}$ inches
Habitat/Range:	Diverse; woodland, prairies, marshes and farmland throughout most of the eastern US, north into much of central Canada. Also populations in New Mexico and Arizona
Similar species:	Wood Frog has eye mask but is larger

The Northern, or Western Chorus Frog is a member of the treefrog family *Hylidae*, but it is more terrestrial than "true" treefrogs, lacking well-developed toe pads. It may climb amongst vegetation and into low shrubs, but it is far from arboreal. This species also has almost no webbing between its toes, and although it requires at least shallow water for the purposes of reproduction, it exists in some fairly dry habitats. A shy frog, it is seldom seen, but as its common name suggests, it is often heard. This is particularly true during the breeding season. In the south it may breed throughout winter to early spring, later in the north. Its call is quite high-pitched, and described by many as akin to the sound produced by dragging a fingernail along a comb.

NORTHERN CRICKET FROG

Scientific name:	*Acris crepitans*
Identification:	Small, often warty species, variable in color, but stripes on thighs usually prominent
Length:	½–1½ inches
Habitat/Range:	Marshes, ponds and streams from New York along coastal states to east Texas, with subspecies throughout the eastern US into Canada
Similar species:	Southern Cricket Frog (*Acris gryllus*) has a more pointed head

Cricket Frogs are allied to the treefrogs, but do not climb, and the diurnal Northern Cricket Frog seems to prefer areas with more sparse vegetation. Rather than seeking cover during the day, this species enjoys basking in sunlit areas, often on mud or sandbanks, though if alarmed it will bound through grass at the shore or take to water. Breeding takes place from spring to summer, and the distinctive cricket-like chirping of the Northern Cricket Frog may be heard by night and day throughout this period. Unlike most frogs, the female lays around two hundred eggs, depositing them singly, rather than in a large mass.

AMERICAN TOAD

▼

WOODHOUSE'S/COMMON TOAD

Scientific name:	*Bufo americanus*
Identification:	A fairly large toad, brown, gray, or reddish with some dark spots and warty skin. The chest is often heavily mottled. Parotid glands are conspicuous and sometimes joined to the cranial crests with a small spur
Length (including tail):	2 – 4 inches
Habitat/Range:	Moist woodland, meadows, marshes and gardens from Oklahoma and Georgia, north to Quebec and Manitoba
Similar species:	The Southern Toad often closely resembles this species, but has prominent bony ridges on the head

Scientific name:	*Bufo woodhousii*
Identification:	A large toad, variable in color, but usually brown or gray, often blotched, but less distinctly than many species. Light stripe in center of back, prominent parotid glands which touch cranial crest
Length (including tail):	2½–4½ inches
Habitat/Range:	Marshes, grassland, desert streams and suburban areas. Found through the Great Plains and into arid southwestern regions along streams
Similar species:	Fowler's Toad (*Bufo woodhousii fowleri*), once considered a subspecies, is generally smaller, and gray or green with more well defined spots

A large and very common species, the American Toad is usually abundant wherever there is moisture and a good source of invertebrate food. It is mainly nocturnal, preferring to burrow in damp soil or leaf litter during the day, becoming active at twilight, especially on warm, rainy evenings. In spring and fall when it tends to be warmer during the day, the American Toad may be more diurnal. Often found away from water, it is probably the most terrestrial toad, and requires an aquatic habitat only to reproduce. It breeds from spring to summer in shallow pools, ditches or ponds, where males can often be heard producing long, trilling calls. As with other toads, males clasp onto the backs of the females and fertilize their eggs as they are deposited in long strings into the water.

Woodhouse's Toad, also known as the Common Toad, tends to inhabit areas with sandy soils, and may spend much of its time burrowing to avoid extremes of both hot and cold. Alternatively it may be found hiding amongst vegetation. Although it is usually most active at night, particularly in wet or humid weather, it is often also seen abroad on warm days. Insects and worms are its chief food. Woodhouse's Toad has elongated parotid glands, these are the large glands on the head, common to all toads of the family Bufonidae, which produce noxious secretions, and thus make toads unpalatable to many potential predators. These secretions do not cause warts in humans, as is commonly believed, nor are they exceptionally poisonous, but hands should be washed after holding toads, as these substances can cause irritation to the eyes, mouth and nose.

GREAT PLAINS TOAD ▼

Scientific name:	*Bufo cognatus*
Identification:	Often quite large and pale, with large, usually paired, dark blotches. Cranial crest forms a bump or "boss" between eyes
Length (including tail):	2–4 inches
Habitat/Range:	from edge of California, into Arizona and New Mexico, north through the Great Plains to Canada
Similar species:	Paired markings are a distinct feature of this species

As with all toads, the thick, dry skin of the Great Plains Toad means that it is able to live a more terrestrial life than the highly aquatic frogs, and this species inhabits moist open grasslands, spending much of its time burrowing in loose soil. It is often found close to water however, and requires an aquatic habitat in order to breed, though this may take the form of a temporary pool or flooded area. The impulse to reproduce is usually induced by the onset of spring rains, when many individuals will gather at a suitable location. It is at this time that the males are most vocal, emitting an almost metallic call. The vocal sac of the Great Plains Toad differs from most other species in being elongated rather than round, and extending over the snout when inflated. This toad is primarily active at night but is sometimes prompted to emerge during the day by rain or humidity.

EASTERN SPADEFOOT

Scientific name:	*Scaphiopus holbrookii*
Identification:	Usually brown, quite plump, with tiny warts. Often has two broken yellow lines on back
Length (including tail):	2–2½ inches
Habitat/Range:	Forest and open woodlands, typically with sandy soil. Found from Louisiana to Minnesota, east to Florida and New England
Similar species:	The Eastern Spadefoot is the only Spadefoot Toad occurring within its range

Spadefoot Toads belong to the family *Pelobatidae*, and differ from true toads in a number of ways. Perhaps most noticeably, the skin is usually quite smooth, and the parotid glands tend to be small, if indeed they are present at all. They do however produce secretions which may cause an allergic reaction. The pupils of these toads are vertical, and there is a characteristic spade-like projection on each of the hind feet. The Eastern Spadefoot is a secretive toad, spending much of its time buried underground in a burrow of its own making, and in dry conditions it may tunnel to considerable depths, remaining underground for weeks at a time. It is most likely to be encountered close to its burrow or at breeding pools on rainy summer nights. Breeding periods usually only last for one night at a time, but may occur more than once during spring and summer.

Opposite: The Great Plains Toad
Above: The Eastern Spadefoot Toad

SOUTHERN TOAD

Scientific name:	*Bufo terrestris*
Identification:	Brown to black, or reddish, with enlarged cranial crests which provide an almost horned appearance
Length (including tail):	1½–4 inches
Habitat/Range:	Open woodland with sandy soil in coastal areas from Louisiana to Virginia
Similar species:	Large cranial crests should prevent this toad from being confused with other species

The Southern Toad is a common species throughout its range, and particularly abundant in areas with sandy soil which allow for easy burrowing. Primarily nocturnal, this toad has a tendency to remain concealed within its burrow during the day, preferring to forage for food under the cover of darkness. It is however, frequently attracted to house or street lights in suburban areas, where its insect prey is generally plentiful. It breeds from spring through to fall, often gathering *en masse* in temporary pools following heavy rain. The males' call is loud and high-pitched.

NARROW-MOUTHED TOADS

The Narrow-mouthed Toads belong to the family *Microhylidae*, and are unusual, distinctive amphibians, appearing to share certain characteristics of both frogs and toads. Two species occur in North America, the **Eastern Narrow-mouthed Toad** (*Gastrophryne carolinensis*), and the **Great Plains Narrow-mouthed Toad** (*Gastrophryne olivacea*). They are small, about one, to one and a half inches long, are almost triangular in shape, having small pointed heads and wide bodies, but they are generally quite stout, and have short limbs. The skin is smooth and moist, much like that of frogs, but distinguishing features include a fold of skin on the back of the neck and no external eardrum. Colors vary, even amongst individuals, and may change in relation to temperature or surroundings, but these toads are generally reddish-brown or gray, with some spots or blotches. The underside of the Eastern Narrow-mouthed Toad is also mottled. Both species feed at night, mainly on ants, and retreat to moist sheltered areas during the day, usually amongst vegetation or rocks. The Great Plains Narrow-mouthed Toad is also known to share tarantula burrows. They inhabit similar environments, including meadows, marshes and open woodland, but the Great Plains Narrow-mouthed Toad is also found in more arid southwestern regions. The Eastern Narrow-mouthed Toad is found through much of the eastern US, from Texas to New England. Both breed from spring to fall.

ROUGH-SKINNED NEWT ▲

Scientific name:	*Taricha granulosa*
Identification:	Warty, dark brown or gray, with a bright yellow or orange underside. Lower eyelids are dark
Length:	5–8½ inches
Habitat/Range:	Ponds, lakes, streams and surrounding marshes, woodland or meadows. Occurs along the Pacific coast from Alaska to California
Similar species:	The California Newt (*Taricha rivularis*), has light lower eyelids

The Rough-skinned Newt does not go through a terrestrial eft stage, and is highly aquatic, but it may wander from water into adjacent moist habitats, particularly following rain, or when it is humid. Despite the dull-colored back of this species, its warty skin contains many glands which are capable of producing toxic secretions, and it will arch its back and tail to reveal its bright underside to potential predators. Some snakes however, are immune to its poison. Like other newts, it feeds on a variety of smaller amphibians and their spawn, as well as insects and other invertebrates. The female lays her eggs in water, attaching them singly to submerged vegetation.

EASTERN NEWT/ RED-SPOTTED NEWT

Scientific name:	*Notophthalmus viridescens*
Identification:	Adult, olive-green or brown with yellow underside, black speckles and red spots. Eft, bright red or orange with black-edged, red spots
Length:	2½–5 inches
Habitat/Range:	Ponds, lakes, streams, marshes and damp woodland. Occurs from Nova Scotia to the Great Lakes, south to the Gulf of Mexico
Similar species:	Red Salamander is similar to eft stage, but usually larger, with smoother, slimy skin

The Eastern or Red-spotted Newt is unusual amongst newts in that it often goes through a primarily terrestrial stage in its development, when it is referred to as an eft. It begins life as an aquatic larva in spring, transforming into an eft by late summer. At this point it leaves the water and begins to live on land, usually amongst the moist leaf-litter of the woodland floor. During this time it avoids predation by being brightly colored to warn of its toxicity, and it is often abroad in daylight hours. After a period of up to three years, the eft develops duller coloration and returns to water to breed, where it then continues to live an aquatic existence. In some circumstances, particularly in harsher habitats, the land-dwelling stage may not occur.

SPRING SALAMANDER

Scientific name:	*Gyrinophilus porphyriticus*
Identification:	Reddish-brown to pink, with dusky markings. A light-colored line extends from the eye to the nostril
Length:	5–8 inches
Habitat/Range:	Cold springs, streams and adjacent damp forests. Found from southern Quebec and Maine, south to parts of Alabama and Mississippi
Similar species:	The closely related Tennessee Cave Salamander (*Gyrinophilus palleucus*), usually remains in an aquatic larval stage with visible external gills

Like most salamanders, the Spring Salamander is equally at home in both water and surrounding moist habitats. It occurs throughout the Appalachian Mountains where it inhabits cold, clear, mountain streams, and wanders into woodland in search of shelter and invertebrate prey. During the day it is most likely to be found hiding amongst vegetation, or beneath rocks, logs and leaf-litter, emerging under the cover of darkness to feed at night. The juveniles of this species tend to be more brightly colored and distinctively marked, with the adults often having a darker, cloudier appearance.

(NORTHERN) RED SALAMANDER ▼

Scientific name:	*Pseudotriton ruber*
Identification:	Quite stout-bodied, bright red with black speckles, yellow eyes and a short tail
Length:	4–7 inches
Habitat/Range:	Mountain springs, woodland, lowland streams and meadows, from New York and Indiana to Florida and Louisiana
Similar species:	The eft stage of the Eastern Newt is almost identical, but generally smaller

The Red Salamander typically breeds in cold woodland streams, often at fairly high altitudes, but it is also found close to water in lowland meadows. The young hatch in fall or winter and remain in an aquatic larval state for around two years before becoming more terrestrial. As a defense against predation this species closely mimics the highly poisonous, land-dwelling eft of the Eastern Red Newt, but adults typically darken with age to a more purplish color, with their markings becoming more blotchy and less well defined. The Red Salamander can also be distinguished from the red eft by its larger size, smooth, slimy skin and in having characteristic costal grooves along its sides.

TIGER SALAMANDER

Scientific name:	*Ambystoma tigrinum*
Identification:	Large, with a broad, rounded head and heavy body. Color and markings vary, but typically consist of olive and brown marbling spots or stripes
Length:	6–13 inches
Habitat/Range:	Ponds and surrounding areas in woodland, prairie and sagebrush habitats. Occurs from southern Canada through much of the US, but absent from many western and north eastern regions
Similar species:	The Marbled Salamander is smaller and patterned in black and white or gray

Along with the Pacific Giant Salamander (*Dicamptodon ensatus*), the Tiger Salamander attains the largest size of the terrestrial salamanders, being heavy-bodied and reaching over one foot in length. It is seldom seen, however, living a subterranean existence for much of the time. It belongs to the family of mole salamanders or *Ambystomatidae*, members of which reside in burrows, leaf-litter, or under rocks and logs, occasionally venturing out to feed, particularly on rainy nights. In late winter and spring however, Tiger Salamanders undertake migrations to breeding pools, where they may congregate in quite large numbers. This species preys upon smaller amphibians, large insects and other invertebrates. It is in turn eaten by many large fish, a fact which has led to this species being widely used by anglers as bait, and subsequently being introduced to areas outside of its natural range.

MARBLED SALAMANDER ▲

Scientific name:	*Ambystoma opacum*
Identification:	Short but stocky salamander, black, with silvery gray or white bands which may run together
Length:	3½–5 inches
Habitat/Range:	Near ponds or temporary pools in marshes, woodland and hilly grasslands. Found from New England and the Great Lakes, south to parts of Florida and Texas
Similar species:	The larger Tiger Salamander is usually olive or yellowish in color, with dark markings

A mole species, the Marbled Salamander generally lives in an underground burrow or similar hiding place, and is rarely seen in the open. As with other salamanders however, it may sometimes be observed on wet nights. Unlike most salamanders, it does not travel to water to breed, but lays its eggs in a sheltered hollow or burrow on land. Breeding normally takes place in fall, and the female Marbled Salamander may produce up to two hundred eggs at a time. However, they are deposited singly rather than in a mass. She will then often remain with them until the nest fills with rainwater.

NORTHERN DUSKY SALAMANDER

Scientific name:	*Desmognathus fuscus*
Identification:	Yellowish to dark brown, with large, dark blotches or mottling. A light line is present from the eye to the mouth and the tail is keeled
Length:	2½–5½ inches
Habitat/Range:	Sheltered woodland streams, springs and marshes from Quebec, south to Georgia and Louisiana
Similar species:	The Mountain Dusky Salamander (*Desmognathus orchrophaeus*), has a rounded, tapering tail

Like the Red and Spring Salamanders, this abundant species is lungless and has a naso-labial groove on the snout. It breathes through its skin and through the lining of the mouth. Most common in the Appalachian Mountains, the Northern Dusky Salamander lives in a variety of habitats, and is largely terrestrial, but it is rarely found far from water. It is active at night, hiding amongst rocks, leaf-litter and other debris during the day, and if disturbed, or threatened by a predator it is capable of jumping some distance to safety. The females lay their eggs close to ponds or streams, but the larvae may spend some time on land before entering water.

HELLBENDER ▲ LESSER SIREN

Scientific name:	*Cryptobranchus alleganiensis*
Identification:	Large, gray or brown and often spotted, with a paler underside. Head and body are flattened and the skin is wrinkled
Length:	1–2 feet +
Habitat/Range:	Large, clear streams and rivers, from New York and Illinois to Georgia and Alabama
Similar species:	The Mudpuppy has external gills throughout its life

Scientific name:	*Siren intermedia*
Identification:	Dark, eel-like body, small front limbs, no hind limbs. External gills visible
Length:	7–26 inches
Habitat/Range:	Ditches, ponds, lakes and swamps. Occurs from North Carolina to Florida and the Gulf coast, north to Illinois and Indiana
Similar species:	The Greater Siren (*Siren Lacertina*), may grow to three feet in length

Known to reach lengths of almost two and a half feet, the Hellbender is one of the largest of all salamanders. Like the Mudpuppy and sirens, it is entirely aquatic, but it does not retain its gills throughout its life as some species do. It usually lives in larger bodies of water, but often inhabits the shallows, where it may be found hiding under logs or large rocks. The Hellbender feeds on crustaceans, mollusks, worms and insects. Mating takes place in late summer or fall. The female lays her eggs in long strings, securing them beneath stones or logs, and they are guarded by the male until hatching.

The Lesser Siren is a neotenic species, retaining its gills into adulthood. It is solely aquatic and is usually found in weedy shallows, where it spends the day concealed amongst vegetation or burrowed into the mud at the bottom. It becomes active at night, feeding on fish, invertebrates and plant material. The Lesser Siren often lives in temporary pools, and has developed a means to avoid dehydration if its water supply dries up. It burrows deep into the mud of the pond or lake bed, cocooning itself within a protective coating secreted from its skin. It can remain in this state for some months if necessary, waiting until rainfall replenishes its habitat.

MUDPUPPY

Scientific name:	*Necturus maculosus*
Identification:	Large, gray to brown or black, with dark red, feathery gills and a stripe through each eye
Length:	8–18 inches
Habitat/Range:	Lakes, streams and rivers, from southern Manitoba to Quebec, south to Louisiana and Georgia, but absent from most coastal areas
Similar species:	Adult Hellbender has flat head and lacks external gills

The Mudpuppy is completely aquatic and neotenic, that is, it retains larval characteristics, such as gills, throughout its adult life. However, it may grow to a considerable size. The Mudpuppy is found in a range of environments, including deep, muddy or densely vegetated waters, and in such conditions it may be active during the day. In general however, this species is nocturnal. It feeds on small fish, amphibians and invertebrates. Mating occurs in spring, following which the female may lay over one hundred eggs. They are deposited under submerged rocks or logs, and guarded until they hatch.

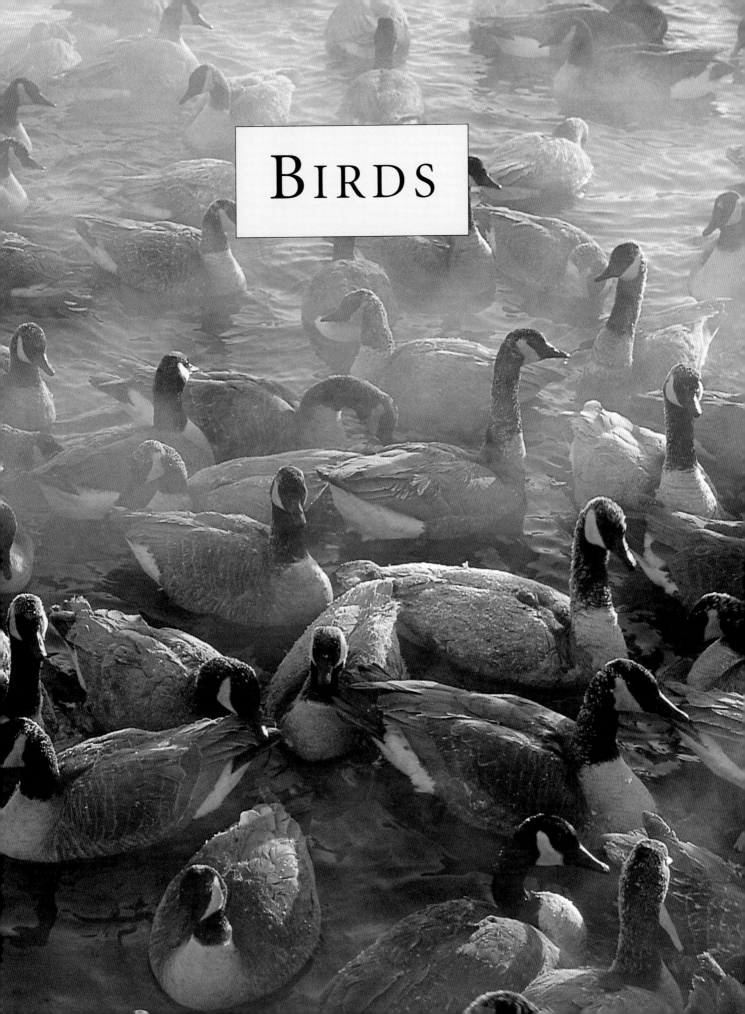

BIRDS

COMMON LOON

Scientific name:	*Gavia immer*
Length:	2½ feet
Habitat/Range:	Forest lakes and coastal areas in Canada and the northern US
Identification:	Thick neck and bill, dark plumage, white checker-pattern to back in summer
Similar species:	Winter plumage similar to the larger Yellow-billed Loon (*Gavia adamsii*) which is rarely seen south of Canada

A large loon, with a thick bill that has a slightly curved upper edge. During the breeding season, the adult has a distinctive black back with a white checker-pattern, black head and bill and a black-and-white, striped collar with a small "chin-strap". In winter the back is much darker, and the throat is plain white. Breeding takes place on large lakes, and this species is still fairly common across Canada and the northern US in summer, although due to pollution and habitat destruction, its population is declining. It migrates both overland and along the coast, and generally flies much higher than other loons. The Common Loon winters around both coastlines on any large inland lake that remains free of ice. It can dive down to more than 150 feet in search of fish, and stay below the surface for long periods.

PIED-BILLED GREBE

Scientific name:	*Podilymbus podiceps*
Length:	13½ inches
Habitat/Range:	Freshwater ponds, marshes and lakes throughout North America
Identification:	Diving waterbird. Drab brown plumage, black bill ring and throat in summer
Similar species:	Sometimes seen with other waterfowl, but its black striped bill in the summer months makes it unmistakable

Over much of its range the Pied-billed Grebe is a permanent resident and is very common, although it is usually seen on its own or in pairs rather than in flocks. It occasionally mixes with other waterfowl, but in general is somewhat secretive and elusive. The Pied-billed Grebe is rarely seen on land or in flight, preferring to spend most of its time on water. When threatened, it may sink below the surface of the water leaving its head exposed, or completely submerge. It nests on a floating raft of vegetation, anchored to reeds or bushes in the water, and young hatchlings are carried and fed on their parent's back. Although this species breeds across North America, in northern areas it migrates south to spend the winter on open water free of ice. Like other grebes, the Pied-billed feeds on fish, crustaceans and insects.

WESTERN GREBE

Scientific name:	*Aechmophorus occidentalis*
Length:	2 feet
Habitat/Range:	Freshwater lakes and inshore coastal areas, mainly in western parts of North America
Identification:	Large long-necked grebe. Black above, white below, long thin yellow bill
Similar species:	Once considered to be the same species as Clark's Grebe *(Aechmophorus clarkii)*. Can be told apart only by its yellow-green bill and black cap that extends around the eyes

The Western Grebe is North America's largest grebe, and is an elegant bird, seen on freshwater lakes in the western US. It winters around the west coast on sheltered bays and open inland waters, being most numerous in the north. During the breeding season, mating pairs perform a spectacular courtship dance, with each pair racing across the water, diving and then rearing up in a mirror image of each other; several hundred birds may display together. It migrates in loose flocks, that spread out to feed during the day. When leaving the floating nest to reach the feeding grounds, the adult birds swim underwater to avoid the territories of other nesting pairs. Both parents care for the eggs and feed the chicks.

AMERICAN WHITE PELICAN

Scientific name:	*Pelecanus erythrorhynchos*
Length:	5 feet
Wingspan:	9 feet
Habitat/Range:	Seawater and large lakes along the Pacific coast and Gulf of Mexico
Identification:	Large waterbird. White plumage, black on trailing edge of wings, large yellow pouched bill
Similar species:	Its huge bill and body-shape make it unmistakable

The American White Pelican is a massive bird, which can be seen in many areas of North America at different times of the year. It is sociable, and often found in flocks. It nests near water, building a large nest mound to hold its two eggs, and during the breeding season, the adult develops a fibrous plate on the upper mandible, and a yellow crest, both of which are shed after the eggs are laid. The pelican is rather ungainly on land but is handsome in flight, often flying in large groups, soaring high in unison. It eats fish, which it scoops up in its bill, filling its huge throat pouch as it swims along the water. The bill and throat pouch can hold nearly 3 gallons of water – which is more than twice the capacity of its stomach. Flocks may also hunt together, lining up in a row to drive fish into the shallows where they cannot escape.

Brown Pelican

Scientific name:	*Pelecanus occidentalis*
Length:	4 feet
Wingspan:	7 feet
Habitat/Range:	Coastal areas along both the Pacific and Atlantic, mainly in the southern US
Identification:	Large, with gray-brown plumage, white head, large, gray, pouched bill
Similar species:	The shape and coloring of the Brown Pelican, and its huge bill, make it unmistakable

Unlike the American White Pelican, the Brown Pelican is almost exclusively found in marine habitats, rarely finding its way inland. A sociable bird, it tends to stay in flocks and may be seen flying in single file over water. It builds a bulky nest of sticks lined with fresh green plants near water, to hold its 2–3 eggs. During the breeding season, which takes place from December to August, the throat-pouches of Brown Pelicans found on the Pacific coast often turn bright red. In flight, the Brown Pelican alternately flaps and glides with its broad, powerful wings. It eats fish, which it catches by making a spectacular plunge of up to 30 feet into the sea, grabbing fish in its bill. It comes to the surface to eat, tossing the fish into the air to swallow it headfirst. Once severely threatened by pesticides, the Brown Pelican has made a comeback since DDT was banned.

ANHINGA

Scientific name:	*Anhinga anhinga*
Length:	3 feet
Wingspan:	3½ feet
Habitat/Range:	Swamps and marshes in coastal areas, from the Carolinas to Texas. Also north along the Mississippi
Identification:	Black plumage, with white spots and streaks on wings and upper back, long slim neck, Female's neck buff-colored
Similar species:	May be confused with a cormorant, but can be distinguished by the white markings on the upper part of wings, thin, narrow, pointed bill and fan-shaped tail

The Anhinga is a tropical bird, so those found in the southern swamps of North America are at the northern edge of their range. They nest in colonies, along with egrets and other birds, building a small mass of twigs and sticks lined with green leaves up to 40 feet above the ground, either in trees or bushes - they sometimes take over an old heron's nest. They lay 1–5 eggs, which are incubated for 25–28 days by both parent birds. The Anhinga often swims with only its head and neck above the surface of the water, earning itself the nickname of "snakebird". It spears fish, frogs and small crustaceans with its dagger-like bill, before surfacing fully to toss them up in the air and swallow them headfirst. It can often be seen perched on stumps or branches with its wings spread out to dry. When flying it can soar to great heights, gliding on warm air currents for hours on end.

DOUBLE-CRESTED CORMORANT

Scientific name:	*Phalacrocorax auritus*
Length:	2½ feet
Wingspan:	4 feet
Habitat/Range:	Seawater, inland lakes and rivers. Found throughout North America
Identification:	Hooked bill, black plumage, orange throat pouch. Small tufts on head when breeding
Similar species:	The Great Cormorant (*Phalacrocorax carbo*) has very similar plumage, but is larger

This is the most widespread cormorant in North America, common in many areas, especially inland. It often nests in colonies near large areas of deep water, either high up in trees, on cliff edges or on the ground on an island. The nest is a mass of sticks or seaweed and the 2–9 eggs are incubated for around three weeks, by both adult birds. During the breeding season it develops small tufts on each side of the head that are black in southeastern birds and whitish in northern and western individuals. The Double-crested Cormorant tends to fly in long lines or in a V-formation, and holds its neck with a slight kink just behind the head. When foraging, it dives and swims underwater for fish.

GREAT BLUE HERON

Scientific name:	*Ardea herodias*
Length:	4 feet
Wingspan:	6 feet
Habitat/Range:	Ponds, lakes and marshes, throughout much of North America
Identification:	Large, long-legged, long-necked wading bird Blue-gray plumage, white head with black stripe and black plumes behind eye
Similar species:	The Green Heron (*Butorides virescens*) attains a length of only 1½ feet

The most widespread and familiar heron across much of the country, the Great Blue is also the largest heron in North America. It is generally solitary, although it tends to nest in colonies that can contain hundreds of birds. The nest is an untidy-looking platform of sticks, positioned in trees, bushes, or on cliffs, and is built up to 100 feet above the ground. The 3–7 eggs are incubated for around 28 days, by both adult birds. The chicks leave the nest about 8 weeks after they hatch. The Great Blue Heron may fly 10–15 miles in order to find a plentiful supply of fish, and will then stand patiently in the water or on the bank waiting to spear a catch. They also sometimes eat frogs, snakes and small mammals. In Florida, all-white individuals occur, which were previously thought to be a separate species known as the Great White Heron.

GREAT EGRET

Scientific name:	*Ardea alba*
Length:	3 feet
Wingspan:	4 feet
Habitat/Range:	Lakes, marshes and wetlands. Occurs in most of the US, but largely absent from the Rocky Mountains
Identification:	Large, long-legged, long-necked wading bird. White plumage, long thin yellow bill, black legs
Similar species:	Its large size distinguishes this species from other egrets, and its black legs set it apart from the all-white version of the Great Blue Heron

The Great Egret is the largest and the most widespread egret in North America. Most egrets are white, and their population was endangered in the late 19th century by hunters killing them for their feathers, which were highly prized in the millinery industry. Today however, the birds are in danger from the draining of their habitats. The Great Egret is a sociable bird and nests in large colonies, either in reeds or more usually in trees. It builds a large, sturdy platform of sticks, often repairing and reusing old nests, where it lays 3–5 eggs. These are incubated for around a month, and the chicks remain in the nest for 6–7 weeks after hatching. Breeding birds have long lacy white plumes extending from their back, reaching further than the end of the tail. The Great Egret wades elegantly through shallow water, stalking its prey slowly and methodically. It eats fish, frogs, water snakes and insects.

MUTE SWAN

Scientific name:	*Cygnus olor*
Length:	5 feet
Habitat/Range:	Ponds, lakes and parks. Found mainly on the east coast and around the Great Lakes
Identification:	Very large, long-necked waterfowl. White plumage, orange bill with black knob at base. Tends to hold neck in S-curve
Similar species:	The juvenile Mute Swan looks very similar to the juvenile Trumpeter, but tends to hold its neck in more of a curve

The Mute Swan is an Old World species that was introduced into North America, and as populations increase, displacing native birds, they are being removed in some areas. Like other swans it breeds near water, building a large mass of plant material in which it lays 4–6 eggs. Incubation is performed by the female bird, and takes around 34–38 days. The young birds leave the nest very soon after hatching, but stay with the parent birds for a further 4 months. The Mute Swan eats aquatic plants, which it dislodges with its powerful bill. It is often silent, although it sometimes hisses or grunts, and when flying its wingbeats produce a loud rhythmic hum.

Trumpeter Swan

Scientific name:	*Cygnus buccinator*
Length:	5 feet
Habitat/ Range:	Wooded ponds and rivers, mainly in the northwest, but introduced elsewhere
Identification:	Very large, long-necked waterfowl. White plumage, black bill. Tends to hold neck straight upward
Similar species:	Very similar to Tundra Swan, but larger, with a longer bill that lacks a yellow spot

At the beginning of the twentieth century, this species had almost died out, after hunters slaughtered it for its down and skin, and swans' eggs had become sought-after by gourmets. After protection was introduced, the population rose and is still slowly increasing. The Trumpeter Swan breeds near water, building a large mound of plant material in which it lays 2–13 eggs, which hatch after around 33 days. The young birds leave the nest very soon after hatching, but stay with the parent birds until the following spring. This species eats aquatic plants and insects, using its long neck to reach food on the bottom.

Tundra Swan

Scientific name:	*Cygnus columbianus*
Length:	4½ feet
Habitat/ Range:	Shallow ponds, lakes, marshes and rivers, from Alaska and Canada, south to the Rocky Mountains and along both coasts
Identification:	White plumage, black bill with yellow spot in front of eye. Tends to hold neck straight upward
Similar species:	Smaller than the Trumpeter Swan, with a shorter bill. Mute Swan is also larger, and has an orange beak

Formerly known as the Whistling Swan, the Tundra Swan is found in summer on Arctic tundra but migrates further south in the winter. It tends to return to old haunts and is usually seen in flocks. It breeds near tundra ponds, building a large mound of leaves and grass in which it lays 2–7 eggs, and incubation takes around a month. The Tundra Swan is the smallest American swan, and is also notable for its rather musical call. This species feeds on both land and water, eating vegetation, small mollusks and other invertebrates.

CANADA GOOSE

Scientific name:	*Branta canadensis*
Length:	2–3½ feet
Habitat/Range:	Ponds, marshes, grassland and open farmland throughout North America
Identification:	Black head and neck, white "chin strap" and breast, dark back, white undertail coverts
Similar species:	Brant Goose (*Branta bernicla*) is usually smaller, and has a dark front and belly

The most common and distinctive goose in America, which can be found across the entire country at different times of the year. Its nest is a large hollow lined with plant matter and soft down, in relatively open areas near water. It lays 2–12 white eggs, which are incubated by the female for around 25–30 days. The male defends his mate and offspring fiercely, warning intruders away at first, but it will not hesitate to attack a perceived enemy, even those larger than itself. The young birds are downy and leave the nest soon after hatching, but stay with the parents until the following spring. The Canada Goose flies in V-formation when migrating, stopping often to feed. It eats aquatic plants, grain, grass and small aquatic animals. This species is currently spreading into city parks and golf courses and populations are increasing.

SNOW GOOSE

Scientific name:	*Chen caerulescens*
Length:	2–2½ feet
Habitat/Range:	Grassland, grainfields and coastal wetlands, from the Arctic, south through much of the US
Identification:	White with black wingtips, pinky-orange bill with black "grin patch"
Similar species:	Ross's Goose *(Chen Rossii)* is smaller, has shorter neck and rounder head, bill lacks black "grin patch"

A very common bird in some parts of the south in winter, and seen in large flocks of hundreds of birds when migrating from its breeding grounds on Arctic tundra. It nests in colonies near water, making a shallow depression lined with grass, plant stems and down in which it lays 3–8 eggs. Incubation takes around three weeks. The young birds leave the nest soon after hatching, but stay with the parent birds until the following spring. The Snow Goose eats aquatic plants, grain and insects and can often be seen in winter grazing in fields. This species also occurs in a form known as the Blue Goose, which has a mostly white head, a gray-brown back, variable amounts of white underneath and more black on the wings.

MALLARD

Scientific name:	*Anas platyrhynchos*
Length:	2 feet
Habitat/Range:	Freshwater shallows and tidal marshes throughout most of North America
Identification:	Male has green head, white collar, yellow bill, gray body. Female is sandy brown, with an orange bill marked with black. Wings have bright blue patch on upper side, bordered with white
Similar species:	Male easily identified by its metallic green head and neck, female by orange and black beak

The Mallard is probably the most abundant and familiar wild duck in the Northern Hemisphere, and is the ancestor of most domestic ducks. It is common across much of America, not only in the wild but also in a semi-wild state around cities and in parks. It nests near water in vegetation, lining a hollow with grass, stems and down, which holds 5–14 eggs. The young are able to fly around eight weeks after hatching. This species dabbles in shallow water, tipping tail-up to forage for aquatic plants, snails, insects and small fish.

AMERICAN BLACK DUCK

Scientific name:	*Anas rubripes*
Length:	2 feet
Habitat/Range:	Woodland lakes and streams, freshwater and tidal marshes, east of the Rocky Mountains
Identification:	Sooty-brown, with a yellow bill. Wings have violet patch on upper side, and white linings
Similar species:	Both sexes look similar to the female Mallard, but have a darker body and gray head

The American Black Duck is common in the northeast, but its population is declining inland to the west, where it is being replaced by the Mallard. These two species also interbreed, so hybrids are often seen. The American Black Duck prefers woodland ponds and coastal salt marshes and is a very wary bird, flying away instantly and at great speed if disturbed. It nests in vegetation near water, lining a hollow with grass and stems to hold 5–17 eggs. The downy young leave the nest soon after hatching, and are able to fly around 9 weeks later. This species feeds on submerged plants, worms, snails, frogs and seeds.

NORTHERN PINTAIL

Scientific name:	*Anas acuta*
Length:	1½–2 feet
Habitat/Range:	Marshes, open ponds and lakes. Found across North America
Identification:	Male has white breast with thin white stripe to brown head, gray body, long black tail feathers. Female is buff-brown, long tail, grayish bill. Both sexes have metallic brown-green patch on upper wing and white band on trailing edge
Similar species:	Male is unmistakable because of its coloring and long thin tail. Female is similar to many other female ducks, but is larger than most

A lean, elegant species, the Northern Pintail is found across much of America, breeding in the north and wintering in the south. It prefers open areas and is more common in the west than in the east. Its nest is a hollow of plant material, lined with down and holding 6–12 eggs. These are incubated for around 26 days by the female, and the young chicks leave the nest soon after hatching and fly at about 7 weeks. The Northern Pintail prefers shallow water as it dabbles for food, foraging on the bottom for snails, small fish and crustaceans and also eats insects and seeds. Like other dabblers, it does not need to run across the water to get airborne, but can simply leap up from the surface into flight.

BARROW'S GOLDENEYE

Scientific name:	*Bucephala islandica*
Length:	1½ feet
Habitat/Range:	Lakes, ponds, rivers and coastal waters. Mainly found from southern Alaska into the northwestern US
Identification:	Male has white crescent before yellow eye, purple-black head, black back and sides, white chest, row of white spots on side. Female has chocolate-brown head and gray body
Similar species:	Common Goldeneye has larger bill and sloping forehead, male has white spot instead of crescent before eye

A diving duck which prefers cold water, Barrow's Goldeneye is found across western America, with a few also in the northeast. It is much rarer than the Common Goldeneye but they are sometimes seen together in small flocks. Barrow's breeds around open lakes and small ponds, spending the winter in coastal areas or on inland lakes and rivers. Like the Common Goldeneye, it nests in trees, and utilizes old woodpecker nests. It feeds mainly on aquatic insects, mollusks and crustaceans.

COMMON GOLDENEYE

Scientific name:	*Bucephala clangula*
Length:	1½ feet
Habitat/Range:	Lakes, rivers and coastal waters. Widespread in North America
Identification:	Medium-sized diving duck. Male has white spot before yellow eye, green-black head and back, white chest and sides. Female has chocolate brown head, gray body
Similar species:	Barrow's Goldeneye has smaller bill, steeper forehead, male has white crescent instead of spot before eye, more black on back

The Common Goldeneye breeds around lakes and bogs near coniferous forests, spending the winter in coastal areas or on inland lakes and rivers. It tends to nest high up in trees, often taking over an abandoned woodpecker's nest, sometimes quite far from water. The cavity is lined with down and holds 6–15 greenish eggs. Incubation takes 27–32 days and the chicks leave the nest soon after hatching, dropping up to 60 feet to the ground since they cannot fly until they are around 8 or 9 weeks old. In flight, the wings make a whistling sound, giving rise to this species' nickname of "Whistler". The Common Goldeneye mainly eats aquatic plants and insects, mollusks and crustaceans.

RUDDY DUCK

Scientific name:	*Oxyura jamaicensis*
Length:	15 inches
Habitat/Range:	Freshwater wetlands, lakes, bays and salt marshes. Breeds in the western US and Canada, migrating to the south and east for the winter
Identification:	Small diving duck, with long stiff tail feathers. Male has chestnut-brown body, dark cap, white cheeks. Bill is bright blue in breeding season. Female brownish with pale cheeks crossed by single dark line
Similar species:	Coloring and stiff tail feathers make this species distinctive

The Ruddy Duck is a small diving bird that is common in many areas across America and is often seen in large flocks. It breeds in freshwater wetlands, spending the winter on lakes, bays and salt marshes. Its nest is a floating woven mass of vegetation anchored in dense reeds and lined with feathers and down, which holds 5-17 large whitish eggs. The female incubates the eggs for 24 days, but both parent birds care for the ducklings. The stiff tail feathers of the adults are often carried on or below the water surface, but can be raised in display. The Ruddy Duck flies close to the water, with rapid beats of its rather short wings. It is a deep water diver, mainly eating the seeds and foliage of aquatic plants. Even the hatchlings dive to feed, unlike other species which start by picking off food at the surface.

BUFFLEHEAD ▼

Scientific name:	*Bucephala albeola*
Length:	1 foot
Habitat/Range:	Woodland lakes, ponds, sheltered bays and rivers. Common across much of America at different times of the year
Identification:	Male has a white patch on black head, black back, white chest and sides. Female has gray head with white ear spot, gray back, white chest and belly
Similar species:	Has similar coloring to Goldeneye, but is smaller. Hooded Merganser has similar head pattern, but different body coloring

The smallest of the diving ducks, the Bufflehead is often seen in small flocks. It breeds around lakes and shallow ponds, spending the winter in coastal areas or on inland lakes and rivers. It typically nests in tree cavities. The hole is lined with feathers and down and holds 6–12 buff eggs, which hatch after about a month. The young drop to the ground, and are cared for by the female until they can fly with her to join the males. The Bufflehead flies fast and usually close to the water; and if disturbed a flock often rises, but settles back into its original place. This species dives to forage for aquatic insects and plants, snails and crustaceans.

COMMON MERGANSER

Scientific name:	*Mergus merganser*
Length:	2 feet
Habitat/Range:	Woodland lakes and rivers across Canada, wintering throughout much of the US
Identification:	Male is mostly white, with a black back and green head. Female is gray with a rusty-red head and white throat
Similar species:	The male Mallard has a green head, but different shape and body coloring. Female is like female Red-breasted Merganser *(Mergus serrator)* but contrast between head and neck coloring is sharper

The largest of the North American mergansers, the Common Merganser can be found in quite large flocks, favoring wooded lakes and rivers in the breeding season. It nests in a tree cavity, hollow log, or among rocks, lining its chosen spot with a mass of down. The female lays 6–12 pale buff eggs, which she incubates for 28–32 days. The chicks begin to fly around 9–10 weeks after hatching. The adult bird has a long body and sits low in the water, and like other mergansers, this species has a long, narrow bill with serrated edges and a hooked upper mandible. Hence, they are sometimes referred to as "sawbills", particularly by hunters. The Common Merganser dives to pursue its prey underwater; it eats aquatic invertebrates, small frogs, newts and small fish.

HOODED MERGANSER

Scientific name:	*Lophodytes cucullatus*
Length:	1½ feet
Habitat/Range:	Woodland ponds, rivers and backwaters, mainly in eastern areas
Identification:	Male has white crest with black border that can open up like a fan, black back, white below, and cinnamon sides. Female is brownish with paler crest
Similar species:	Similar head pattern to male Bufflehead, but different body coloring

The smallest of the North American mergansers, the Hooded is common in the east but uncommon in the west. It prefers fresh water near the coast in the winter and in the breeding season is found on woodland ponds, rivers or backwaters in small flocks. It makes its nest in a tree cavity or old log, into which 8-12 white eggs are laid. The female incubates these for 28-32 days. At the start of the breeding season, the male performs an exciting courtship dance, then swims round and round the chosen female in a further display. The Hooded Merganser flies with rapid wingbeats and both sexes show a small white patch on the inner wing. It eats aquatic invertebrates, small frogs, newts and small fish.

OSPREY

Scientific name:	*Pandion haliaetus*
Length:	2 feet
Wingspan:	5 feet
Habitat/ Range:	Coastal areas and freshwater habitats throughout North America
Identification:	Large hawk. Long narrow wings, plumage dark brown above, white below, white head with dark eye stripe
Similar species:	Unlikely to be confused with other predatory birds, as behavior, shape and coloring are distinctive

Sometimes known as the "fish hawk" or "fish eagle", the Osprey is fairly common in coastal areas and is sometimes seen along rivers and over inland lakes. It was once threatened by the use of DDT, but since this and other pesticides have been banned, populations have recovered. Its nest is a large construction of sticks in a tall tree, rock pinnacle or any tall structure near water, and is reused year after year. It holds 2–4 buff-colored eggs, blotched with brown, which are usually incubated by the female for around a month. The young are downy white, and leave the nest around 2 months after hatching. The adult bird has long narrow wings, held above horizontal and slightly arched in flight, with a distinct bend at the wrist. Unlike other hawks, the Osprey feeds almost exclusively on fish, which it catches by soaring over the water and diving, talons first.

Bald Eagle

Scientific name:	*Haliaeetus leucocephalus*
Length:	3 feet
Wingspan:	6½ feet
Habitat/Range:	Rivers, lakes, and coastal areas throughout much of North America
Identification:	Large bird of prey. White head, neck and tail, brown-black body, yellow bill
Similar species:	Adult is unmistakable, juvenile may be mistaken for juvenile Golden Eagle but has larger head, shorter tail and blotchy, less defined patterning under wings and on tail

The magnificent Bald Eagle has been the national symbol of the United States since 1782. It is seen across much of North America, particularly near water, but is most common in Alaska, parts of Florida, and during the winter in the midwest. It was endangered in the 1970s, but conservation programs and the banning of pesticides have led to a gradual comeback in many areas. Its eyrie is a large pile of sticks up to 150 feet above the ground, usually in a tall tree near water, and it is renovated and added to every year – increasing in size until either its own weight or a winter storm brings it down. The 1-3 dull, whitish eggs are incubated by both parents for up to 35 days, and the chicks leave the nest around 10 weeks after they have hatched. Juveniles are mostly dark brown, except for blotchy white underneath and on the wing linings, but achieve a little more white at each molt, taking four to five years to reach the full adult plumage. Although it is a very skilled hunter, the Bald Eagle often eats carrion or will steal fish from the smaller and weaker Osprey. Large numbers of Bald Eagles will often congregate where pickings are easy, particularly at spawning runs.

GOLDEN EAGLE

Scientific name:	*Aquila chrysaetos*
Length:	2½–3 feet
Wingspan:	6½ feet
Habitat/Range:	Mountains, plains, open country, widespread, but more common in the west
Identification:	Large bird of prey. Dark brown plumage overall, with golden nape
Similar species:	Adult is unmistakable, juvenile may be mistaken for juvenile Bald Eagle but has smaller head, longer tail and defined white markings under wings and on tail

The majestic Golden Eagle is a solitary bird, sometimes seen in pairs but rarely gathering in groups. It prefers wilderness areas away from humans and is fairly numerous in the west but not so often seen in the east. Its eyrie is a large mass of sticks in a tall tree or on a cliff, and a pair may alternate between several sites in different years. The 2 whitish, brown-blotched eggs are incubated by both parents for up to 44 days, and the chicks leave the nest around 10 weeks after hatching. The Golden Eagle soars with long, broad wings held flat or slightly uplifted. Despite rumors of them taking lambs, they rarely do; they normally feed on small mammals such as rabbits, birds, snakes and carrion, although they are capable of taking animals the size of a deer.

Sharp-shinned Hawk

Scientific name:	*Accipiter striatus*
Length:	9–14 inches
Wingspan:	1½–2½ feet
Habitat/Range:	Dense woodland and suburbs across much of North America
Identification:	Short-winged, long-tailed hawk. Square, barred tail, often notched, blue-gray plumage above, white below with rusty barring. Female is similar, but larger
Similar species:	Coloring similar to Cooper's Hawk (*Accipiter cooperi*) but Sharp-shinned is smaller with a shorter, squarer tail and thin legs

The Sharp-shinned Hawk is the smallest of the North American accipiters, a family of hawks distinguished by short, broad wings that are adapted for fast flight in wooded country. It is fairly common over much of its range, particularly in the east, and is usually found in mixed woods and forests. Its nest is a platform of sticks and twigs, generally 10–60 feet above ground in a dense conifer or other woodland tree. It lays 4–5 bluish, spotted eggs which are incubated for about 35 days by both adult birds. The young leave the nest around 2 months after they have hatched. Although it normally hunts small birds, rodents and insects in thick woodland, the Sharp-shinned Hawk will also come into the suburbs to take small birds near feeders.

Red-tailed Hawk

Scientific name:	*Buteo jamaicensis*
Length:	2 feet
Wingspan:	4 feet
Habitat/Range:	Woods, plains and prairies throughout most of Canada and the US
Identification:	Large broad-winged, short-tailed hawk. Usually dark brown back with pale mottling, white underneath with belly band of dark streaks, but color varies according to range. Most adults have reddish tail above, whitish beneath, heavy bill
Similar species:	Rough-legged Hawk (*Buteo lagopus*) has long white tail

One of the most common American hawks, the Red-tailed is seen across much of North America and in summer up into Canada. It can be spotted soaring over open country, particularly if there are nearby woods offering seclusion for nesting. It builds a large and solid nest, in a tree or on a cliff, with a small cup in the center lined with fine green shoots. The female lays between 1 and 4 whitish eggs, which are incubated for 27–33 days. The Red-tailed Hawk sits for hours on a telegraph pole or fence post, before gliding off to catch its prey; it mainly eats rodents, which makes it very popular with farmers.

AMERICAN KESTREL

Scientific name:	*Falco sparverius*
Length:	10½ inches
Wingspan:	2 feet
Habitat/Range:	Open country, deserts and urban areas. Found from Alaska, and northern Canada, south throughout the US and beyond
Identification:	Small falcon with a russet crown, back and tail, double black stripes on white face, hooked bill. Male has blue-gray wings, buff breast and white underparts with dark spots
Similar species:	Male is similar to male Merlin (*Falco columbarius*) but russet back and tail are distinctive

The smallest and most common American falcon, the American Kestrel is found in open country and in cities across the country, with birds in the far north migrating south for the winter. It was formerly known as the "Sparrow Hawk". It does not build a nest, but lays 3–6 buffy-pink to grayish-white eggs in a tree hole, crevice of a building or an old magpie nest. The eggs are incubated for around 30 days, mainly by the female although the male may also help, and the chicks are ready to leave the nest around one month after hatching. When hunting, the Kestrel either hovers over the ground or sits on a convenient tree or telephone wire, plunging to catch mice, insects, and in winter, small birds.

RED-SHOULDERED HAWK

Scientific name:	*Buteo lineatus*
Length:	1½ feet
Wingspan:	3 feet
Habitat/Range:	Mixed woodland near water. Found in Canada, much of the eastern US and along parts of the Pacific coast
Identification:	Small, long-tailed, long-legged woodland hawk. Rusty-red shoulder patch, body and underwing. Black and white bands on tail and wings
Similar species:	Juvenile can be confused with juvenile Broad-winged Hawk (*Buteo platypterus*) but is usually larger

A forest bird, the Red-shouldered Hawk is fairly common in Florida and California, and is often seen in the southeast although it is rare elsewhere. Its nest is a large, flat construction of twigs and sticks, built high up in a tall woodland tree near moving water. It uses the same nest year after year, adding fresh, green sprigs upon its return. It lays 2–5 whitish eggs. The Red-shouldered Hawk flies with several quick wingbeats followed by a glide and defends its territory at nesting time by soaring in spectacular displays. It eats reptiles, small birds and mammals, frogs and crayfish.

NORTHERN HARRIER

Scientific name:	*Circus cyaneus*
Length:	1½–2 feet
Wingspan:	3½ feet
Habitat/Range:	Wetlands, marshes and open fields throughout North America
Identification:	Long-winged, long-tailed hawk. Male light gray above, white rump, white beneath with reddish spots; in flight black wingtips, barred tail. Female brown above, white rump, brown streaks below
Similar species:	Shape and coloring make this species distinctive

A slim bird, with an owl-like face, the Northern Harrier is common across much of North America, spending summer in the north, then migrating south in winter. It prefers wetlands and open fields, and was previously known as the Marsh Hawk. It nests on the ground on a platform of reeds and grasses, where 4–6 white eggs are laid. The chicks stay in the nest for up to 5 weeks following hatching, during which time the male bird brings food to the female, who then feeds the chicks. Harriers are usually seen flying low and gliding with their wings raised in a shallow V, as they hunt for small birds, rodents, frogs and reptiles. They rarely soar, except when migrating or during their acrobatic courtship display.

PEREGRINE FALCON

Scientific name:	*Falco peregrinus*
Length:	17–20 inches
Wingspan:	3 feet
Habitat/Range:	Open wetlands, cliffs and cities. Distribution patchy, but widespread
Identification:	Large short-tailed falcon. Male slate-gray above, black on head like helmet, whitish neck, buff beneath, lightly barred breast. Female browner
Similar species:	Prairie Falcon lacks the well-defined, black helmet

The Peregrine Falcon was once found across North America, but DDT and other pesticides helped eliminate the eastern population and brought it close to extinction. The banning of such pesticides has led to a slow recovery and captive-breeding programs have reintroduced birds to some areas. The Peregrine does not build a nest, but lays 2–4 reddish, darker flecked eggs in a hollow on a cliff, bare rocky outcrop or on the ledges of tall city buildings. The adult bird is sleek and powerful, with pointed wings and a short tail; the tips of its wings almost reach the end of the tail when it is perched. When hunting, the Peregrine Falcon flies very fast and makes dramatic swoops to catch small birds in midair. It also eats large insects and small mammals.

PRAIRIE FALCON

Scientific name:	*Falco mexicanus*
Length:	17½ inches
Wingspan:	3 feet
Habitat/Range:	Dry grassland, desert and prairie, in the western US and Canada
Identification:	Large long-tailed falcon. Adult sandy-brown above with pale barring, white patch behind eye, creamy below with darker spotting. In flight shows long dark patch under wing
Similar species:	Peregrine Falcon is similarly colored, but has distinctive black helmet. Also resembles female and juvenile Merlin *(Falco columbarius)* but is larger and lacks strongly marked tail bands

A similar size and shape to the Peregrine Falcon, the Prairie Falcon is much more common and is found over grassland and dry country in the west of America throughout the year. It rarely builds its own nest, laying 3–6 reddish, dark-spotted eggs on a ledge or in the old nest of another bird. The eggs are incubated for around a month and the chicks fly about 6 weeks after hatching. When hunting, the Prairie Falcon does not dive from the sky but pursues its prey flying fast and low over the ground, twisting and turning and outmaneuvering birds, ground squirrels and other rodents.

BLACK VULTURE

Scientific name:	*Coragyps atratus*
Length:	2 feet
Wingspan:	5 feet
Habita /Range:	Open country, swamps and suburban areas in the southern US
Identification:	Stocky, with black plumage, white patch near wing tips, large dark gray head and white feet.
Similar species:	Turkey Vulture has red head, long tail, long black wings edged in gray, and a relatively small head

New World vultures are now considered to be related to storks, but they look like birds of prey. The Black Vulture is very common all year round in much of the south, but is rarely seen further north. It soars for hours hunting for food, gliding with its wings held flat, punctuated with several rapid flaps. It often flies in groups, and when one bird spots carrion they all converge on it. It sometimes steals from the Turkey Vulture, which is much more efficient at scenting food. In the tropics, the Black Vulture is often seen around cities and towns, where it performs a useful function by cleaning away carrion and garbage. It does not build a nest, but lays 1–2 blotchy, whitish eggs on bare ground, or sheltered under a rock, on a ledge or in a cave. Incubation takes around 40 days but the young do not leave until 10–11 weeks later.

TURKEY VULTURE ▶

Scientific name:	*Cathartes aura*
Length:	2 feet
Wingspan:	5–5$\frac{1}{2}$ feet
Habitat/Range:	Open country, woodland and farms, from southern Canada, south through the US
Identification:	Large carrion-feeder. Black-gray plumage, gray edging to wings, bare red head and yellow feet.
Similar species:	Black Vulture has gray head, short tail and black, white-tipped wings

The Turkey Vulture is much more widespread than the Black Vulture, being found as far north as southern Canada. It glides all day over open country, looking for food which it finds by scent. It often roosts in flocks, and many birds will converge to feed at a carcass. It prefers the meat to be quite ripe, which makes it easier to strip off the bones, hence its bare head. It does not build a nest, but lays 1–3 eggs on bare ground, or in an old building, cave or hollow log. The Turkey Vulture glides for hours with its wings held in a shallow V, and in the right conditions it rarely has to flap its wings to stay aloft.

RUFFED GROUSE

Scientific name:	*Bonasa umbellus*
Length:	17 inches
Habitat/Range:	Deciduous and mixed woodlands in Canada and the northern US
Identification:	Long neck and tail. Male brownish with buff streaks above, gray-brown cross-barring on flanks, dark cross-bars and broad black tip on tail.
Similar species:	Female Spruce Grouse (*Dendragapus canadensis*) is similar, but has a shorter tail and barred underside

Fairly common across its range, the Ruffed Grouse is found on the ground in mixed woodland, but may also be seen high in trees. In spring, the male attempts to attract a mate by standing on a fallen log or simiar perch, with its tail spread in a fan and its neck ruff puffed up , drumming the air with its wings. The female lays her eggs in a leaf-lined scrape, under a tree, bush, rock or log. The chicks hatch around three weeks later, and although capable of flight around a week after hatching, they remain with the mother for around 12 weeks. The Ruffed Grouse eats buds, catkins and twigs in winter, but will also feed on seeds, berries and fruits in summer.

BLUE GROUSE

Scientific name:	*Dendragapus obscurus*
Length:	20 inches
Habitat/Range:	Open coniferous or mixed woodland, brushy lowland, mountain slopes. Found from western Canada, south to California
Identification:	Quite large, with a short bill and long tail. Male blue-gray, with an orange-yellow comb above each eye. Tail is dark with gray tip. Female mottled gray-brown overall
Similar species:	Female very like female Spruce Grouse, but larger with a longer tail. Also lacks barring beneath

The Blue Grouse is found in open lowland woods in the west, but moves up to higher altitudes in the winter; it is usually seen singly and prefers areas near large clearings. In spring, the male stands high up, often in a tree, spreading its tail in a fan and inflating its yellow or purplish neck sacs, which are surrounded by white-based feathers. It also flies down to strut with its tail fanned, dragging its wings. The female lays 6–10 creamy, brown-speckled eggs, in a scrape lined with pine needles and grass and sheltered under a tree, rock or log. The Blue Grouse eats pine needles in winter, but also seeds, berries and insects in summer.

RING-NECKED PHEASANT

Scientific name:	*Phasianus colchicus*
Length:	21–33 inches (male larger than female)
Habitat/Range:	Open country, farmland and woodland edges in much of North America
Identification:	Male iridescent bronze, mottled with brown, black and green. Glossy, green-black head, red eye patches, white collar. Female buffy overall
Similar species:	Male unmistakable. Female very like female Sharp-tailed Grouse (*Tympanuchus phasianellus*) but larger, with longer tail

A native of Asia, the Ring-necked Pheasant was introduced to America in the late 19th century as a game bird and has since become well established. In many areas it is quite common, although populations are smaller in the east. Other sub-species have also been introduced and have interbred, so there are variations in some areas, such as the white-winged birds found in parts of the west and the Japanese Green Pheasant in Virginia and Delaware. The Ring-necked Pheasant is a fast runner, but rises up noisily when flushed. It eats seeds, nuts, berries and insects. During the breeding season, each male attracts a number of females, who do not build a nest, but lay their eggs in a grass-lined scrape, concealed amongst vegetation.

COMMON MOORHEN

Scientific name:	*Gallinula chloropus*
Length:	14 inches
Habitat/Range:	Ponds, freshwater marshes and slow-moving rivers. Most numerous in the eastern US and southern Canada
Identification:	Marsh bird, long legs, large feet. Black-gray head and neck, red forehead shield, red bill with yellow tip, brownish-olive back, slate underparts, white streak on flanks, yellow legs and feet
Similar species:	Distinguished from Purple Gallinule (*Porphyrula martinica*), and American Coot by white line and red facial shield

Related to the Purple Gallinule, the Common Moorhen was once known in North America as the Common Gallinule. It is fairly widespread and common in freshwater marshes, ponds and slow-moving rivers across much of the country, able to subsist even in small patches of cattails or reeds. Its nest is built of grass stems and reeds, in marsh vegetation a foot or so above the water level, often with a ramp of compressed vegetation leading down to the water. Like the Purple Gallinule, the Common Moorhen has long legs and very large feet to allow it to walk across lily pads and floating marsh vegetation. It has a very wide diet, feeding on mosquitoes, spiders, tadpoles, insect larvae, fruits and seeds.

AMERICAN COOT

Scientific name:	*Fulica americana*
Length:	15½ inches
Habitat/Range:	Freshwater marshes, wetlands and salt marshes. Found from southern Canada, south into much of the US
Identification:	Stocky, with large, lobed feet. Gray body, black head and neck, ivory-colored forehead shield with reddish upper edge, whitish bill with dark band near tip
Similar species:	Common Moorhen has white line and red facial shield

The American Coot is fairly widespread and common on lakes, ponds and marshes across most of North America. It is seen in flocks of hundreds of birds and often becomes quite tame in urban areas, where it lives in parks and on golf courses. Its nest is a platform of reeds and marsh vegetation, usually on the edge of open water, and old nests are used throughout the year for resting and preening. It lays 8–20 buff or pinkish, brown-spotted eggs, which are incubated for around 25 days by both adult birds. The downy chicks have a red and blue frontal shield, which seems to trigger a feeding impulse in the adult; they leave the nest soon after hatching and are independent within 7–8 weeks. The adult is stocky, with big lobed feet that enable it to walk across floating vegetation, and are useful for swimming. Coots nod their heads as they swim, and in flight the white trailing edge along most of the wing is distinctive. They dive to the bottom to catch fish and mollusks, but also dabble on the surface for insects and pond weed and forage on lawns in urban areas.

KILLDEER

Scientific name:	*Charadrius vociferus*
Length:	10½ inches
Habitat/Range:	Grassy fields, lake and river shores, throughout North America
Identification:	Lanky, long-tailed, open-country bird with slender wings. Gray-brown above, underparts white, two black breast bands, pale gray legs and feet, long thin dark bill. Red-orange rump in flight
Similar species:	Double breast band is distinctive

A common bird across much of North America, the Killdeer is found across the south throughout the year and spreads north in summer. It lives both inland and on the coast, and nests on open ground, usually laying four eggs in a scrape in gravel or bare soil, which is sometimes lined with a few grass stems. The downy chicks leave the nest soon after hatching and fly within a month. If danger threatens the nest or the chicks, the Killdeer performs a convincing impression of having a broken wing, leading predators away. The Killdeer feeds in loose flocks, mainly eating earthworms, snails and insects.

LEAST SANDPIPER

▲

SPOTTED SANDPIPER

Scientific name:	*Calidris minutilla*
Length:	6 inches
Habitat/Range:	Rivers, ponds and marshes, south from the Arctic
Identification:	Small, yellow-legged bird. Breeding adult has mottled warm brown-gray on back, head and upper breast sometimes tinged rufous, white belly. Winter birds gray above, white below
Similar species:	Easily confused with Semipalmated Sandpiper (*Calidris pusilla*) but has yellow legs and is darker above

Scientific name:	*Actitis macularia*
Length:	7½ inches
Habitat/Range:	Streams, ponds, lakes and marshes. Breeds throughout North America and overwinters in the southern US
Identification:	Short-necked, long-tailed wading bird. Olive-brown back and wash on sides of breast, light eye stripe, white eye ring, white below, flesh-colored legs. Breeding bird has large black spots below
Similar species:	Bobbing walk is unmistakeable and breeding plumage is distinctive. Winter plumage of Solitary Sandpiper (*Tringa solitaria*) is darker, with a more distinct eye ring

The Least Sandpiper is widespread, and is most often seen inland in spring and fall across much of North America, as it migrates from its breeding grounds in the north to spend the winter in the south or in South America. It spends the summer across Arctic tundra, where it lays 4 pale buff, brown-marked eggs in a depression scantily lined with leaves or grass, or in a scrape in boggy tundra. The Least Sandpiper frequently forages for marine animals and aquatic insects with the Semipalmated Sandpiper, and it is very difficult to tell them apart at a distance. Sandpipers in general are commonly known as "peeps".

The Spotted Sandpiper is a common bird, widespread across much of North America in summer, spending the winter in the far south and down into South America. It is usually seen singly rather than in flocks, on the edges of coastal mud flats, in marshes and along streams and ponds. When moving across the ground, it has a distinctive bobbing, teetering walk. It lays up to 4 greeny or buffy eggs in a depression in the ground near water. These are incubated for around 21–24 days, often by the male bird. The Spotted Sandpiper flies with stiff, shallow wingbeats and shows a short white stripe on the upper wing. It eats insects, small fish and crustaceans.

COMMON SNIPE

Scientific name:	*Gallinago gallinago*
Length:	10½ inches
Habitat/Range:	Marshes, damp fields and muddy pond edges. Occurs through most of North America, but largely absent from the Rocky Mountains
Identification:	Very stocky, with a long bill, short legs and wings, a striped head, brown mottled back, and barred flanks.
Similar species:	Shape, plumage and bill distinctive

A very solitary and secretive bird, the Common Snipe may be seen in flight after it has been disturbed, but can be difficult to spot on the ground. It was previously known as Wilson's Snipe and is found across much of North America in bogs and marshy areas with enough vegetation to provide cover. It spends the summer in the northern half of the continent, where it typically breeds, laying 4 olive-brown eggs in a grass-lined depression in the ground. In winter it moves further south. Its rapid, sharply zig-zagging flight when flushed is distinctive, and during its swooping display flight it vibrates its tail feathers to make a hooting sound. The Common Snipe probes with its long bill in a rhythmic, jerky motion, penetrating deeply into mud to catch crustaceans, insects and other small animals.

SEMIPALMATED PLOVER

Scientific name:	*Charadrius semipalmatus*
Length:	7½ inches
Habitat/Range:	Beaches, lake and tidal flats throughout North America, migrating between the Arctic and southern coastal regions
Identification:	Small, with long legs and wings. Dark sandy brown above, white underparts, forehead and eyebrow, black breast band and eye stripe. Legs, feet, and bill yellow. Bill has black tip
Similar species:	Snowy Plover (*Charadrius alexandrinus*) has paler plumage, thin black bill and gray legs

The Semipalmated Plover is the most common of the small plovers and can usually be distinguished by its yellow-orange legs and dark yellow bill with black tip. It is found all across America during spring and fall migration and spends the winter on southern beaches along both coasts. It breeds in the far north, making a scrape in the ground or among beach pebbles, in which it lays 4 buff or whitish eggs that are tended by both adults for around 24 days. The downy chicks leave the nest soon after hatching and are independent within a month. The Semipalmated Plover forages by running quickly, stopping suddenly and making a swift jab to catch a crustacean or insect.

GREATER YELLOWLEGS

Scientific name:	*Tringa melanoleuca*
Length:	14 inches
Habitat/Range:	Shallow coastal waters, woodland, lakes and swamps. Found across Canada and in southern coastal areas
Identification:	Tall and slender with a long neck. Gray-brown overall, black and white mottling above, white below, white rump, barred tail. Long, bright yellow legs and long, slightly upturned bill
Similar species:	Almost identical to Lesser Yellowlegs (*Tringa flavipes*) but larger

A large sandpiper, the Greater Yellowlegs is fairly common across its range. It winters in the south and summers in the north, migrating between the two in spring and fall. It breeds in northern swamps, the taiga and damp boreal forests, laying up to 4 eggs in a shallow scrape in woodland, often quite far from water. In winter, Greater Yellowlegs are found in flocks with other wading birds around the southern coasts and on the muddy shores of inland lakes. It wades into deeper water than some others, sweeping the water with its bill to catch invertebrates or stabbing small fish. It also eats aquatic insects and their larvae, and water snails.

DUNLIN

Scientific name:	*Calidris alpina*
Length:	8½ inches
Habitat/Range:	Mud flats, tundra, marshes and coastal areas in the Arctic
Identification:	Gray-brown above, rufous back, white belly and flanks with black belly patch. Winter birds brown-gray above, whitish below
Similar species:	Easily confused with Rock Sandpiper (*Calidris ptilocnemis*) but has a black belly patch rather than dark gray lower breast patch, and darker legs

Large flocks of Dunlins can be seen on mud flats along both North American coasts from fall through to spring. When disturbed, hundreds of birds rise in a tightly-packed swirling mass, flying in perfect formation. The Dunlin spends the summer on Arctic tundra in the far north, where it breeds and lays 4 buff greenish, brown-spotted eggs in a small scrape in the ground lined with grass. The Dunlin wades slowly through shallow water, probing with its bill to find mollusks, aquatic insects and small crustaceans.

WILLET

Scientific name:	*Catoptrophorus semipalmatus*
Length:	15 inches
Habitat/Range:	Wetlands, beaches and marshes. Found in western prairies, from Canada to Nevada, wintering in California. Also occurs along the Atlantic coast
Identification:	Bulky, with long legs and bill. Sand-gray back, white below, gray legs. Breeding adult heavily mottled. In flight has striking black and white wings
Similar species:	Larger and stockier than most other sandpipers

Found in many habitats, the Willet is a noisy bird that is seen in small flocks or singly on beaches. It winters in the south along both North American coasts, but spends the summer further north. It breeds in wetlands, laying 3 or 4 spotted buffy eggs in a cup made of grass or in an unlined scrape in the ground. In flight, it has very striking wings, with a black patch and trailing edge, separated by a broad white band. When disturbed, it flashes these wings at predators to startle them. The Willet feeds in small flocks, but the birds are quite widely spaced. It eats insects, small marine animals and seeds.

GREAT BLACK-BACKED GULL

Scientific name:	*Larus marinus*
Length:	2½ feet
Wingspan:	5 feet
Habitat/Range:	Breeds in coastal areas from Greenland and Labrador, south to North Carolina, with a small population in the Great Lakes
Identification:	Large, long-winged seabird with big yellow bill. Mature bird has large white head, black upperparts, white underparts, pink legs
Similar species:	Size is distinctive, but year-old juveniles may resemble those of Herring Gull in winter

A very common gull along the northeast coast, the Great Black-backed Gull is also found some way inland and on the eastern Great Lakes and is expanding further south, although it is still very rare around the Gulf. It nests in colonies, sometimes with other seabirds, building a cup of seaweed, grass and moss to hold 2-3 olive-brown, spotted eggs. The Great Black-backed Gull takes 4 years to reach its mature plumage. The 1st winter bird is checkered gray-brown with lighter head and underparts and a large black bill. By the 2nd winter, it has much whiter underparts and head and the back is darker gray. In the 3rd winter the plumage is more like the adult, with a white head and underparts and a mainly yellow bill, although there is still some brown in the wings. The Great Black-backed Gull eats fish, the eggs and young of other seabirds, and carrion. It also scavenges in garbage dumps.

HERRING GULL

Scientific name:	*Larus argentatus*
Length:	2 feet
Wingspan:	4½ feet
Habitat/Range:	Coastal areas, large lakes, landfills and docks. Most common in the eastern US for much of the year. Breeds across northern Canada, south to the Great Lakes
Identification:	Large, with heavy yellow bill marked in red. White head and neck in summer, neck extensively streaked brown in winter. Typical coloration includes gray back, white underparts and black wing tips spotted with white. Legs and feet pink
Similar species:	Plumage is variable at all ages, so it can be mistaken for several other large gulls

Since the Herring Gull will eat almost anything, its population is expanding in many areas and driving out weaker species. It breeds in large colonies on islets or cliffs, building a nest of seaweed or grass on the ground. The juvenile bird takes 4 years to develop its mature plumage, but all stages are quite variable so it can be difficult to identify. By its 1st winter it has a pale face and throat, dark patterning on its back, and a black bill with pink at the base. By the 2nd winter its back is pale gray, wings brown, and the bill is pinkish with a black tip. The 3rd winter bird is much like the adult, but the yellow bill has a black patch. The Herring Gull scavenges on garbage dumps and in harbors, but also catches fish and small crustaceans.

RING-BILLED GULL

Scientific name:	*Larus delawarensis*
Length:	17½ inches, wingspan 48 inches
Habitat/Range:	Beaches and inland waters from northern California, northeast to Newfoundland
Identification:	White head and neck in summer, nape washed brown in winter. Pale gray back, white underparts, black wing tips with white spot, yellow legs and feet. Yellow, black-ringed beak
Similar species:	Herring Gull may have pale bill-ring in winter, but has pinkish legs and heavier streaking on neck

An abundant and widespread gull, the Ring-billed breeds in large colonies, often with the California Gull (*Larus californicus*), building a nest of grass and stems on the ground to hold 3 buff, dark-splotched eggs. The juvenile takes 3 years to reach mature plumage, but by its 1st winter has a gray back and is white beneath, spotted with brown, with a brown streaked head and a pink, black-tipped bill. Its wings are brown with dark tips and pale linings. By the 2nd winter it is much like the adult, but the tip of the tail is spotted in black and its bill ring is wider. The Ring-billed Gull eats worms, mollusks, insects and grasshoppers; it also scavenges near urban areas.

LAUGHING GULL

Scientific name:	*Larus atricilla*
Length:	16½ inches
Wingspan:	3 feet
Habitat/Range:	Offshore, and in salt marshes, along the coast from Nova Scotia and the Great Lakes, south to Texas. Scattered populations in the west
Identification:	Mature bird has black head in summer, gray streaked in winter, white neck and underparts, dark-gray back, black wing tips and a reddish bill
Similar species:	Adult Franklin's Gull (*Larus pipixcan*) has very similar summer coloring, but has more white around eye

Common along the southern Atlantic and Gulf coasts, the Laughing Gull ranges north to New England in summer, but is only found inland around the Salton Sea. It breeds in colonies on salt marshes, building a nest of reeds and grass to hold 3-4 olive, brown-spotted eggs that are incubated by both adults. The juvenile bird takes 3 years to reach mature plumage. In summer, the adult has a black-hooded head with narrow white crescents around the eyes. In winter, the black hood fades to leave gray streaking to the rear of a white head. The Laughing Gull eats fish, worms and insects and scavenges garbage from ships.

BLACK TERN

Scientific name:	*Chlidonias niger*
Length:	9½ inches
Wingspan:	24 inches
Habitat/Range:	Breeds on lake shores and freshwater marshes from western prairies to New England and southeastern Canada. Winters in the south
Identification:	Small, short-tailed water bird. Breeding adult mostly black, with dark gray back, wings and tail, white undertail coverts, short black bill, dark legs and feet
Similar species:	Size and plumage distinctive

Only slightly larger than the Least, the Black Tern is also only seen in summer but is more of an inland bird. It is very rarely seen on the west coast, and only on a small part of the east, and spends the winter in the Southern Hemisphere. It breeds in small, dense colonies on lake shores and in freshwater marshes, laying 2–3 buff eggs, blotched with brown, in a floating nest constructed of marsh vegetation. The Black Tern circles and hovers buoyantly above water, dipping to catch flying insects, small fish and crustaceans. Populations have declined in many areas, probably due to loss of habitat.

COMMON TERN

Scientific name:	*Sterna hirundo*
Length:	14½ inches
Wingspan:	2½ feet
Habitat/Range:	Beaches and islands, in Canada and the northern US, south in winter
Identification:	Medium-size short-legged water bird, with a long forked tail. Breeding adult has black cap, red bill with black tip and gray body, paler beneath. Wings are long, with dark wedge at tip
Similar species:	Arctic Tern (*Sterna paradisaea*), has shorter legs, a longer tail and all-red bill

The most widespread and numerous of the North American terns, the Common Tern breeds across much of Canada and northern America and winters in the Southern Hemisphere. It nests in large colonies on sandbars, beaches or islands, laying 2–3 green to buff eggs with brown markings, in a scrape on open ground. These are incubated by both male and female for around 24 days, and the young chicks fly around 4 weeks later. The Common Tern flies slowly over water, diving to catch fish or other aquatic prey.

BLACK SKIMMER

Scientific name:	*Rynchops niger*
Length:	1½ feet
Wingspan:	3½ feet
Habitat/Range:	Offshore and on beaches, mainly in the southern US, north to New England in summer
Identification:	Large, long-winged sea bird with lower bill longer than upper. Black back and crown, white below, white nape turns black in summer, red legs and black-tipped, red beak
Similar species:	No other bird has the lower bill longer than the upper

A coastal bird, the Black Skimmer is found around the southern Atlantic and Pacific throughout most of the year, but ranges northwards as far as New Hampshire in summer. It rarely moves inland, except when coastal waters are too rough, but it is sometimes seen over quiet, shallow water. A relative of the tern, it breeds on sandy beaches, nesting in colonies and laying up to 5 eggs in a scrape in the sand. The young stay near the nest for some time after hatching. The Black Skimmer flies gracefully and buoyantly, with long, slow beats, holding its head lower than its tail and showing white wing linings with darker tips. When feeding, usually at night, it flies just above the surface of the water, with its long lower mandible slicing the surface, until it finds a small fish or crustacean, which it catches by snapping shut the upper bill.

ATLANTIC PUFFIN

Scientific name:	*Fratercula arctica*
Length:	12½ inches
Habitat / range:	Atlantic coast, offshore and on islands, from Canada to New England, sometimes further south
Identification:	Black above, white beneath, white face, large, brightly-colored, parrot-like bill. Winter adult has gray face and duller bill
Similar species:	The only puffin seen on the east coast

The Atlantic Puffin is the only puffin found on the Atlantic coast of North America, although it tends to stay in the north and only comes as far south as Virginia in winter, when it is usually well offshore. In summer it comes to land to nest in large colonies on offshore islands, where it is often seen sitting upright. It lays 1 white egg, sometimes spotted brown, usually at the end of a burrow in soft earth but sometimes in rock crevices. The female incubates the egg alone for 5–6 weeks, and the chicks are ready to leave the nest some 7 weeks later. The juvenile resembles the winter adult, but has a darker face and its bill is small and brownish. The Atlantic Puffin dives for fish, and also eats mollusks and crustaceans, "flying" gracefully underwater.

BARN OWL

Scientific name:	*Tyto alba*
Length:	1½ feet
Habitat / Range:	Barns, old buildings, cliffs and trees. Found from southern Canada to Mexico, but largely absent from the southeastern US
Identification:	White, heart-shaped face and dark eyes. Face edged with tan, light tan back with fine pale gray streaks. Underside white to cinnamon
Similar species:	Snowy Owl usually whiter, has small head and yellow eyes

Although it is widespread across much of North America, the Barn Owl is quite rare and its population is declining. It hunts over farmland, woodland and suburbs at night, catching rodents such as mice and rats. During the day, it usually roosts in the dark corners of farm and city buildings, or sometimes on cliffs or trees, but it may also hunt in the daylight hours, particularly if the weather is overcast. It does not build a nest when breeding, but lays 5-11 white eggs on a bare surface in a cavity such as a cave, or corner of a barn or attic.

EASTERN SCREECH-OWL

Scientific name:	*Otus asio*
Length:	8½ inches
Habitat/Range:	Large trees in woodland and suburban parks, east of the Rocky Mountains
Identification:	Small, yellow-eyed owl with ear tufts. Colour ranges from gray to rusty-brown, with vertically streaked underparts crossed with dark bars. Bill is yellow-green with a white tip
Similar species:	The Western Screech Owl (*Otus kennicottii*) is generally gray and has a dark bill

The Eastern Screech-Owl is very common in most areas across its extensive range, but because of its nocturnal habits, small size and good camouflage it is often not noticed. It likes large mature trees, and lives undetected in many parks and suburban gardens. It nests in tree cavities, often in an old woodpecker hole, or will inhabit a nesting box. It lays 4–6 white eggs that are mainly incubated by the female for up to 4 weeks, while the male hunts for food and protects the nest. The chicks are downy and stay in the nest for around 4 weeks after hatching. The Eastern Screech-Owl hunts at night for mice and insects, and sometimes dives for fish.

SNOWY OWL ▶

Scientific name:	*Nyctea scandiaca*
Length:	2 feet
Habitat / Range:	Tundra and other open habitats in Canada and the northern US. Sometimes found further south
Identification:	Large, stocky owl with small head and yellow eyes. Mature adult male white, younger birds white with variable black barring
Similar species:	The Barn Owl can be very pale, but has heart-shaped face and dark eyes. Downy young of other owl species also often white

The Snowy Owl is an Arctic bird, but since it depends on the lemming, a small rodent, as its major food it migrates south whenever the lemming population decreases. When breeding on the Arctic tundra, it lays around 5-9 white eggs, sometimes more, in a shallow, moss and grass-lined depression in the ground. The eggs are usually incubated by the female alone for around 4-5 weeks, and the chicks are ready to leave the nest about 6 weeks after they have hatched. The Snowy Owl will hunt by both day and night, since daylight hours are so much longer above the Arctic circle during the summer months. As well as lemmings, it also eats birds, various other small mammals and carrion.

GREAT HORNED OWL

Scientific name:	*Bubo virginianus*
Length:	2–2½ feet
Habitat/Range:	Forest, open desert and urban areas throughout North America
Identification:	Large, bulky owl with wide-spaced ear tufts. Mottled gray-brown above, white throat, fine dark gray horizontal barring beneath
Similar species:	Long-eared Owl (*Asio otus*) is smaller and more slender, lacks white throat and has vertical streaking beneath

The most widespread and best-known owl in North America, the Great Horned Owl is found in a great variety of habitats and may often be seen perching high up at dusk. It does not build its own nest, but lays 2–4 white eggs in the abandoned nest of a hawk, heron or crow, in a rocky crevice, tree or cliff. The eggs are incubated by the female for about 7 weeks, but the downy whitish chicks are fed by both parents and are ready to leave the nest around 10 weeks after hatching. The Great Horned Owl is a skilled and voracious predator with powerful talons and a sharp, hooked bill. It is capable of tackling quite large prey such as rabbits, squirrels, geese, skunks and snakes. It hunts mainly at night, but is sometimes seen in the day, when it is often mobbed by smaller birds.

BURROWING OWL ▲

Scientific name:	*Speotyto cunicularia*
Length:	9½ inches
Habitat/Range:	Open country and urban areas in the Great Plains region and Rocky Mountains, from southern Canada to Mexico. Also found in Florida
Identification:	Small, long-legged, short-tailed owl with flat head. Brown spotted with white above and on upper breast, barred brown and white below. White throat and yellow eyes
Similar species:	Long legs distinctive

The Burrowing Owl was once well-known and common, but its numbers have declined over recent years. It inhabits open areas, including airports and golf courses in urban areas. It does not build a nest, but takes over the abandoned burrow of a ground squirrel or prairie dog, or a gopher tortoise in Florida. Here it lays 5–7 white eggs. These are incubated for around 4 weeks and the chicks appear from the burrow soon after hatching, although little is known about their exact nestling period. The Burrowing Owl stands upright on the ground or on fence posts and feeds mainly on large insects and small rodents, but will also take small birds. Although it normally hunts in the day, the male hunts both day and night when it is providing food for the young.

MOURNING DOVE

Scientific name:	*Zenaida macroura*
Length:	1 foot
Habitat:	Open brush and urban areas, from southern Canada to Mexico
Identification:	Slender dove with long, pointed, tapering tail. Pale gray-brown above with large black spots on wings, buff below. Male pinkish on chest and iridescent blue-gray on crown
Similar species:	Juvenile may be mistaken for Common Ground-Dove (*Columbina passerina*), but lacks rufous wings

Very common across much of America, the Mourning Dove also spreads north into Canada in the summer. It likes a variety of habitats, except for deep woods, and is seen both alone and in flocks, either perched prominently on poles or wires or walking on the ground. At the start of the breeding season, it builds a rather loose nest of twigs and sticks in a bush or a tree, in which it lays 2 white eggs. These are incubated for around 2 weeks by both birds alternately, and the chicks stay in the nest for around 16 days. There may be 2–4 broods in one season. The Mourning Dove makes a whistling noise with its wings as it takes flight, but the bird's name comes from the male's mournful cry, which sounds a little like an owl. It mainly eats seeds and grain.

ROCK DOVE

Scientific name:	*Columba livia*
Length:	1 foot
Habitat:	Urban areas and rocky habitats throughout North America
Identification:	Long-winged domestic pigeon, small round head, short straight bill, variable colors
Similar species:	The feral Rock Doves come in such a wide variety of colors that it can look similar to several of the wild native species

The Rock Dove was introduced from Europe, where it was originally found on rocky cliffs around the Mediterranean coasts, but they were domesticated, and raised for meat, and also used to carry messages. During centuries of breeding, multicolored birds were developed and descendants of escaped birds now form feral flocks in most areas, except for the taiga and tundra region. The Rock Dove builds a haphazard nest of sticks and grass on the sheltered ledge of a building, bridge, cliff or sometimes in a tree, in which it lays 1–2 white eggs. The adults nest throughout the year and there may be several broods in a season. The Rock Dove eats grain and seeds, but will also feed on fruit and scraps of bread.

YELLOW-BILLED CUCKOO

Scientific name:	*Coccyzus americanus*
Length:	1 foot
Habitat:	Open woods, and in trees along lowland rivers. Widespread in North America, often winters south into Central America
Identification:	Gray-brown above, white beneath. Yellow, curved bill, yellow eye ring, undertail black with large white spots, rufous wing patches in flight
Similar species:	Yellow bill and rufous patches on wings in flight are distinctive in adult, but juvenile similar to Black-billed Cuckoo (*Coccyzus erythropthalmus*)

The Yellow-billed Cuckoo is fairly common in woodland in summer, but hides in dense foliage so can be easily overlooked. It usually builds a frail platform of twigs, up to 10 feet above the ground in a small tree or dense bush, in which it lays 2–4 greeny-blue eggs. These are incubated for about 2 weeks by both birds, and the chicks leave the nest around 2 weeks after hatching. This species eats insects and berries, and particularly likes hairy caterpillars, which few other birds will touch. Its population is decreasing with the loss of its natural breeding habitat.

GREATER ROADRUNNER

Scientific name:	*Geococcyx californianus*
Length:	2 feet
Habitat/Range:	Scrub desert and mesquite groves from southern California to Arkansas
Identification:	Large, brown with green sheen, streaked black and white above, buff below with brown streaks breast. Distinctive crest and heavy bill.
Similar species:	Unmistakable

Famous for its odd behavior, the Greater Roadrunner is a member of the cuckoo family that prefers to run along the ground on its strong feet, although it can fly if it has to. Its range extends across much of the southern US, but it is most common in the desert of the southwest, where it darts away to cover at speeds of up to 15 miles per hour if surprised in the open. It sometimes flicks its tail up or raises its shaggy crest, and may adopt unusual postures when resting on a fence post or rock. It runs in fast bursts to catch a wide variety of food, including large insects, scorpions, lizards, snakes, small birds and rodents. It builds its small, neat nest in mesquite, a large cactus or shrub, in which it lays 3–6 white eggs. These are incubated for up to 3 weeks, with the young chicks hatching at intervals and staying in the nest for a further 2–3 weeks, fed by both parent birds.

WHIP-POOR-WILL

Scientific name:	*Caprimulgus vociferus*
Length:	9¾ inches
Habitat/Range:	Open coniferous woods, mixed woods and wooded canyons. Found mainly in eastern North America, south from Canada, wintering in Florida and around the Gulf Coast
Identification:	Medium-size, round-winged nightjar with long rounded tail. Mottled gray-brown-black, black throat with white necklace, outer tail feathers of male mostly white, those of female tipped buff
Similar species:	Chuck-will's-widow *(Caprimulgus carolinensis)* is larger and redder, with whitish band above black breast

Found mainly in northeast America, the Whip-poor-will prefers mixed woodland and open conifer woods. Some birds spend the winter in southern Florida, others move down into Mexico and further south. If it is discovered during the day it may well appear tame, sitting still when approached and relying on its camouflage for protection. It lays its eggs directly amongst leaves on the forest floor. The eggs are incubated by the female for about 3 weeks, and the young leave about 2–3 weeks after hatching. The Whip-poor-will glides at night not far above the ground, with mouth gaping widely to catch beetles, moths and other large insects. Nightjars and nighthawks were once known as goatsuckers, because they swarm round animals at night to feed off the insects surrounding them, which led to a belief that they sucked the milk from goats' udders.

COMMON NIGHTHAWK ▲

Scientific name:	*Chordeiles minor*
Length:	9½ inches
Habitat/Range:	Woodland, farmland and suburbs in much of North America
Identification:	Slender, very long-winged bird. Mottled brown-black above, paler beneath with bold dusky barring and a white bar across wing near base of primaries, male also has a white throat and white tail band
Similar species:	Lesser Nighthawk *(Chordeiles acutipennis)* is paler, and has more rounded wings. White wing bar is nearer tip

The Common Nighthawk is found all across North America in summer in a variety of habitats including city suburbs, but not in dry desert areas and tundra. It spends the winter in sub-tropical areas of Mexico and South America. It lays its 2 creamy or greenish-gray eggs, which are often densely speckled, directly on the ground or a flat roof. They are incubated by the female bird for around 20 days, but both parents feed the chicks until they are ready to leave, about 3 weeks later. The Common Nighthawk flies and glides high above the ground, bounding along with fluttery, rather erratic wingbeats, catching insects on the wing. It is common across much of its range, although numbers are declining.

CHIMNEY SWIFT

Scientific name:	*Chaetura pelagica*
Length:	5¼ inches
Habitat/Range:	Urban areas, woodland and clifs, east of the Rocky Mountains
Identification:	Small, short-tailed bird with slim body and long, narrow, curved wings. Sooty brown overall with paler throat
Similar species:	Vaux's Swift (*Chaetura vauxi*) is slightly smaller, and usually paler on breast and rump

The Chimney Swift has often been described as looking like a "cigar on wings", with its short, almost cylindrical body. It is found all over eastern North America in summer, but migrates to the rainforests of South America to spend the winter. It flies fast with quick wingbeats, or sails with wings held stiff. It may nest in a hole or hollow of a tree, but often builds a half-cup of twigs glued together with saliva inside a chimney or barn, in which it lays 4 or 5 white eggs. These are incubated for up to 3 weeks by both adult birds, and the young leave the nest around 4 weeks after they have hatched. The Chimney Swift does not perch but clings to a vertical surface when roosting at night. During the day it is always on the wing, sweeping through the air to catch insects.

BELTED KINGFISHER

Scientific name:	*Ceryle alcyon*
Length:	1 foot
Habitat/Range:	Rivers, streams, ponds, lakes and estuaries in much of North America
Identification:	Blue-gray above and on head, with shaggy crest, heavy bill and white collar. Male has blue-gray breast band and white belly. Female has blue-gray breast band, and rust-red band across white belly
Similar species:	Male unmistakable. Female Ringed Kingfisher (*Ceryle torquata*) similar, but larger and has all-rust belly, and rust-red under wing

The only kingfisher found across most of North America, the Belted Kingfisher is common, and frequently spotted near woodland water. It is a solitary bird, defending its fishing territory and only associating with others of its kind in the breeding season. Following mating, the female lays her eggs in a tunnel up to 7 feet long in the side of a steep river bank. The eggs are incubated for around 3-4 weeks and the young birds leave the burrow after about 7 weeks when they are fully fledged. When flying between perches, the Belted Kingfisher often gives a loud, harsh, rattling call. It alights on a branch over a lake or river until it spots a fish, then hovers over the water before diving for its catch. It also eats frogs, tadpoles and insects.

RUFOUS HUMMINGBIRD

Scientific name:	*Selasphorus rufus*
Length:	3¾ inches
Habitat / Range:	Woodlands and gardens, mainly in the north-western US and British Columbia
Identification:	Small and compact, with rather short wings. Male rufous above and on sides, with bright orange-red gorget and white breast. Female green above, with rufous on sides, white beneath with orange-red spotted throat patch. Outer tail feathers rufous at base, black in middle and white at tip
Similar species:	Male distinctive. Female is similar to female Broad-tailed (*Selasphorus platycercus*) but has shorter tail and reddish throat patch

Although it is mainly found along the north Pacific coast in summer, the Rufous Hummingbird is also sometimes seen over much of the east in fall, as it migrates south. Some birds stay along the Gulf coast in winter, but most fly on to southern Mexico. Its nest is a carefully woven cup of plant down, decorated with moss and lichen, usually fastened to a horizontal branch. In flight, the male may produce a whistling buzz with its wings. Both male and female defend their territory and nectar sources. They also eat tiny flying insects and running tree sap.

RUBY-THROATED HUMMINGBIRD

Scientific name:	*Archilochus colubris*
Length:	3¾ inches
Habitat/Range:	Gardens and woodland edges in much of eastern North America
Identification:	Small, with long, straight, thin bill. Bright green back, white underparts. Male has black face and chin and iridescent scarlet gorget
Similar species:	Male Broad-tailed Hummingbird is similar to male Ruby-throated, but has rose-red throat rather than ruby. Female very similar to other female humming birds

The Ruby-throated is the only hummingbird regularly seen in the east. They are anti-social birds, pairing only to mate. The female builds a tiny nest of spiders' webs and plant down, often near water, where she incubates 2 white eggs for 11–14 days. The male defends the breeding area and nectar resources with stylized displays. The female defends the nest in the breeding season, but also defends the nectar resources at other times. Despite its tiny size, the Ruby-throated Hummingbird migrates across the Gulf of Mexico to winter in Central America. Red tubular flowers are a particularly favorite source of food, but it also eats tiny flying insects and small spiders.

HAIRY WOODPECKER

Scientific name:	*Picoides villosus*
Length:	9½ inches
Habitat/Range:	Forests and suburbs through much of North America, but absent from the far north, and some southern areas
Identification:	White back, black forehead and crown, broad black eye stripe, white face and underparts, long, sturdy bill. Wings black with white spots. Male has red patch on nape
Similar species:	Downy Woodpecker almost identical, but is much smaller with a shorter bill

Fairly common across the whole continent, except in the southwest and the far north, the Hairy Woodpecker is seen in mature woodland with large trees. When breeding it excavates a hole high above the ground in a dead tree limb, and often uses the same cavity year after year. It lays 4-7 white eggs, which are incubated by the male at night and the female during the day, for around 2 weeks. The young birds leave the nest around 4-5 weeks after hatching. The Hairy Woodpecker drills into trees to find the wood-boring insects under the bark and also eats berries and seeds. Like many other woodpeckers, it also drums on trees and posts to proclaim its territory.

DOWNY WOODPECKER

Scientific name:	*Picoides pubescens*
Length:	6¾ inches
Habitat/Range:	Woodland, suburbs and parkland. Widespread, but absent from the far north and arid, southwestern regions
Identification:	Small, with very short bill. White back, black forehead and crown, broad black eye stripe, white face and underparts. Wings black with white spots. Male has red patch on nape
Similar species:	Hairy Woodpecker almost identical, but is larger and has a longer bill

The Downy Woodpecker is the smallest North American woodpecker and is common across the whole continent, except in drier regions in the southwest and the cold far north. It is often seen in suburbs, parks and orchards as well as woodland. When nesting, it excavates a hole up to 50 feet above the ground in a dead tree trunk or branch, in which it lays 4-7 white eggs. The Downy Woodpecker will often come to bird tables for suet, but also eats wood-boring insects, berries and seeds. In the Pacific northwest, these birds tend to have a gray-brown back and underparts, but are otherwise the same.

RED-HEADED WOODPECKER

Scientific name:	*Melanerpes erythrocephalus*
Length:	9¼ inches
Habitat/Range:	Open and dense woodland, in much of southern Canada and the eastern US
Identification:	Medium-size, broad-winged woodpecker. Bright red head, neck and throat, blue-black back, pure white underparts
Similar species:	Unmistakable

Although still common across its extensive range, the Red-headed Woodpecker population is declining in many areas, partly due to the loss of its breeding habitat and partly because of competition from starlings and other birds for nesting holes. Like other woodpeckers it favors dead wood in which to excavate its hole, but dead and dying trees are now routinely removed. In a suitable cavity, it lays 4-6 white eggs, which are incubated by both parent birds for around 14 days; the young leave the nest around 4 weeks after hatching, and there is often a second brood. The Red-headed Woodpecker pecks at bark to find insects and beetles, but also sometimes flies out to catch insects in midair and eats nuts and acorns.

LEAST FLYCATCHER

Scientific name:	*Empidonax minimus*
Length:	5¼ inches
Habitat/Range:	Deciduous woodland and parks in Canada and the northern US, moving south in winter
Identification:	Small, and compact, with short wings and a short triangular bill. Olive above, white throat and eye ring, gray wash across breast, pale-yellow belly. Lower bill pale, two buffy-white wing bars
Similar species:	All the *Empidonax* flycatchers are very alike and mainly told apart by habitat and song

Fairly common in the east but less so in the west, the Least Flycatcher is found in summer across the north in deciduous woods, orchards and parks, but in fall it migrates to the Southern Hemisphere for the winter. In the summer breeding season it builds a nest of stems and plant fibers up to 60 feet above the ground on a horizontal branch, in which it lays 3–5 white eggs. These are incubated for up to 2 weeks and the young birds are ready to leave the nest around 14 days after they have hatched. The song of the adult is a snappy *CHE-bek* and its call a dry *whit*. The Least Flycatcher eats flying insects and berries.

EASTERN KINGBIRD

Scientific name:	*Tyrannus tyrannus*
Length:	8½ inches
Habitat/Range:	Woodland clearings and forest edges across much of eastern and central North America, migrating south in fall
Identification:	Black head, slate-gray back, white underparts with pale gray wash on breast. Tail is black with white tip. Strip of red feathers on crown usually not visible
Similar species:	Coloring and habits distinctive

A conspicuous and common bird, the Eastern Kingbird is often seen perching on treetops, fences and utility poles in summer. In its breeding area, it builds a large and bulky nest of twigs, roots, straw and grass, lined with hair, up to 60 feet above the ground on the horizontal limb of a tree. The female lays 3–5 white eggs, spotted with brown, which are incubated for up to 2 weeks. The Eastern Kingbird is an aggressive bird that perches out in the open and defends its territory vigorously even against much larger birds. It darts out to catch passing winged insects, but also sometimes eats berries and seeds.

LOGGERHEAD SHRIKE

Scientific name:	*Lanius ludovicianus*
Length:	9 inches
Habitat/Range:	Open grasslands and farmland throughout North America
Identification:	Blue-gray above, with black mask, wings and tail, white throat, rump and outer tail feathers. Large white wing patches, dark, hooked bill
Similar species:	Northern Shrike (*Lanius excubitor*) is slightly larger, and its face mask does not meet above bill

Fairly common over much of its range, the Loggerhead Shrike is seen all year round across southern North America, with many birds moving further north in the summer, though its exact range varies from year to year. It builds a nest of twigs, well-lined with feathers, in a tree or thorny bush, in which it lays 3–8 greenish-white eggs, speckled with brown. These are incubated by the female bird for just over 2 weeks, and the young leave the nest about 3 weeks after they have hatched. The Loggerhead Shrike feeds mainly on large insects, but will hunt mice and other birds when other food is scarce. It stores excess food on a thorn or barbed wire.

BLUE JAY

Scientific name:	*Cyanocitta cristata*
Length:	11 inches
Habitat/Range:	Suburbs, parks and woodland, mainly east of the Rocky Mountains
Identification:	Crested, broad-winged, rather short-tailed woodland bird. Blue above, gray-white underneath with black necklace, black barring on wings and tail, white patches on wings, outer feathers of tail white
Similar species:	Coloring distinctive, but often mimics the calls of other birds

Common in suburbs, woodlands and parks, the Blue Jay is found across most of eastern North America and is occasionally seen in the northwest and west. Some birds migrate south in the fall, moving in large flocks. Like other jays, it has a harsh, strident voice and often mimics other birds, particularly the Red-shouldered Hawk. The Blue Jay builds a bulky nest of twigs, moss and leaves on a branch or in the crotch of a tree, in which it lays 3–5 olive, blue or buffy eggs spotted with brown. These are incubated by the female for about 17 days and the young birds leave to fend for themselves around 3 weeks after hatching. The Blue Jay eats nuts, seeds, fruit and insects.

STELLER'S JAY

Scientific name:	*Cyanocitta stelleri*
Length:	11½ inches
Habitat/Range:	Pine-oak woods, suburbs and coniferous forests, from Alaska to California
Identification:	Crested, broad-winged, rather short-tailed woodland bird. Head, throat, chest and upper back all black, with deep blue wings, rump, tail and belly
Similar species:	Steller's Jay is the only crested jay that is all dark

Steller's Jay is North America's largest jay and lives in dense forests It often travels in small groups and its blue coloration makes it conspicuous. It prefers conifers for nesting, building a neat and sturdy bowl of twigs lined with mud on a high branch, in which it lays 3–5 greeny-blue spotted eggs that are incubated by the female alone for about 16 days. Like other jays, Steller's Jay is an accomplished mimic. It is bold and aggressive and often visits bird feeders and picnic grounds, but otherwise likes to eat nuts, seeds, fruit and insects.

GRAY JAY

Scientific name:	*Perisoreus canadensis*
Length:	11½ inches
Habitat/Range:	Mountain forests across Canada, south into the northern US, and through the Rocky Mountains
Identification:	Dark gray above, white or pale gray beneath, white forehead and face
Similar species:	Looks rather like a very big chickadee, but much larger size is distinctive

Previously known as the Canada Jay, the Gray Jay is a familiar visitor to mountain camp sites and cabins, where it will help itself to as much food as possible, earning itself the nickname "camp-robber". The adult is a long-tailed bird with a short bill and distinctive fluffy plumage; however, there are three distinct color variations; birds in the far north on the taiga have a brownish crown and nape; those in the Rocky Mountains have a mostly white head, and northwest coast birds have a large dark crown. The Gray Jay stores scraps of frozen meat and other morsels in trees, to eat when its other staples of insects, fruit, mice and birds' eggs are not available. It breeds very early, often when there is still snow on the ground, building a bowl-shaped nest of twigs lined with feathers or moss.

CLARK'S NUTCRACKER ▲

Scientific name:	*Nucifraga columbiana*
Length:	1 foot
Habitat/Range:	Coniferous mountain forests, from British Columbia and Alberta, south through the western US
Identification:	Long-winged, short-tailed woodland bird with long, pointed bill. Mostly light gray, black wings with large white patch on trailing edge, black tail with white outer feathers, white face and belly
Similar species:	Gray Jay has much smaller bill and lacks white on wings and tail

A mountain bird, Clark's Nutcracker commonly frequents camp sites, picnic spots and cabins where it comes to seek handouts or to steal scraps. Although it normally lives far inland, it sometimes ranges further afield and may reach the Pacific coast when food is scarce. Clark's Nutcracker flies with slow, deep wingbeats, rather like a crow. It mainly eats pine nuts, which it stores in fall for the following winter and spring. It also eats juniper berries, and insects in summer.

AMERICAN CROW

Scientific name:	*Corvus brachyrhynchos*
Length:	1½ feet
Habitat/Range:	Varied; open country, woodland, coasts and cities. Found from British Columbia east to New Foundland, south to southern California, Florida and the Gulf Coast
Identification:	Large, short-tailed crow with powerful bill and broad wings. All black
Similar species:	The Fish Crow (*Corvus ossifragus*) is slightly smaller, and may be distinguished by its call

The largest of the crows, the American Crow is very common across most of America, also ranging further north and up into Canada during the summer months. Once a mainly woodland bird, it has adapted to changing circumstances over the years and now also lives on farmland and in urban areas. It generally breeds in rather loose colonies, which can consist of hundreds of birds, building a well-constructed nest of sticks and plant fibers in a tree. The American Crow is both resourceful and intelligent and has developed a communication system to alert others in the colony of approaching danger and to pass on the position of new food supplies. It is a predator that will eat almost anything – including the eggs and chicks of other birds.

COMMON RAVEN

Scientific name:	*Corvus corax*
Length:	2 feet
Habitat / Range:	Mountains, deserts, forests and tundra. Found from the far north, south into mountainous parts of the US
Identification:	Large, long-winged raven with long heavy bill and low, resonant voice. All black
Similar species:	Chihuahuan Raven (*Corvus cryptoleucus*), is slightly smaller, and has a shorter bill

The most widespread raven in North America, the Common Raven is numerous in the north and west and spreading in the east, moving into cities in some areas. Pairs of birds mate for life and are often seen soaring high in the sky. It builds a large, loose nest of sticks and branches, which is lined with soft animal fur or wool, and placed high in a tree or on a cliff face. Its call is a low, resonant *craaak*, deeper than that of the Chihuahuan Raven, but it also makes a variety of other noises including screams, whistles and a melodious *kloo-klok*. The Common Raven is a resourceful and intelligent bird, which learns new behavior in different situations. It eats carrion, rodents, insects and the eggs and chicks of other birds, and often feeds at garbage dumps.

BLACK-BILLED MAGPIE

Scientific name:	*Pica pica*
Length:	1½ feet
Habitat/Range:	Open woodlands, thickets, suburbs and in trees along streams. Occurs in the west from Alaska to California, and east into the Great Plains
Identification:	Large, with a long tail, stout black bill and broad wings. Black head, back and breast, iridescent green-blue on wings and tail, white shoulders and belly, white wing patches in flight
Similar species:	Very similar Yellow-billed Magpie *(Pica nuttalli)* is slightly smaller and has yellow bill, but is only seen in a tiny part of California

Often seen in pairs or small flocks walking on the ground in the open, the Black-billed Magpie is very common across most of western North America. It generally nests in pairs, but also sometimes in loose colonies, building a very large, bulky nest of sticks in a tree, which is covered with a thorny dome of twigs to protect the eggs and chicks. The female lays 7-9 greenish-buff, brown-splotched eggs, which are incubated for about 17 days; details of the nestling period are not known. The Black-billed Magpie eats insects and carrion, but is also known to steal the eggs and chicks of other birds.

BARN SWALLOW

Scientific name:	*Hirundo rustica*
Length:	$6\frac{3}{4}$ inches
Habitat/Range:	Rural buildings, culverts and bridges, across most of North America in summer
Identification:	Long, slender, pointed wings and long, deeply-forked tail. Blue-black above, pale cinnamon or buffy-white below, chestnut-red throat and forehead, white spots under tail
Similar species:	Shape and plumage are unmistakable

A graceful and elegant bird, the Barn Swallow is found across most of North America in summer, gathering in large flocks in fall to migrate south to winter in South America. It breeds in small colonies, building a cup-shaped, straw and feather-lined nest on a wall or the vertical surface of a bridge. It rarely nests away from man-made structures. It lays 3–6 white, red-brown-spotted eggs that are incubated for around 14–18 days. The Barn Swallow feeds on insects caught in flight, and hunts communally. In flight, it may fold its forked tail into one long point.

▼ # CLIFF SWALLOW

Scientific name:	*Hirundo pyrrhonota*
Length:	$5\frac{1}{2}$ inches
Habitat/Range:	Cliffs, rural buildings and bridges, across most of North America in summer
Identification:	Broad rounded wings, short square tail. Blue-black crown, wings, tail and back, pale rust rump, chestnut throat and cheeks, buff collar, white forehead and belly
Similar species:	Cave Swallow (*Petrochelidon fulva*) is very alike, but has cinnamon forehead and buff throat. Found in areas of Texas and Florida

A summer visitor, the Cliff Swallow is common in the west, but much less numerous in the east. It migrates in fall in large flocks to spend the winter in South America, returning in early spring. It breeds in very large colonies of hundreds of birds, building a gourd-shaped nest of mud, lined with grass and feathers on a natural cliff face, under the eaves of a building or on a bridge. It lays 4–6 creamy, lightly spotted eggs that are incubated for around 2 weeks by both parent birds, and the young chicks are ready to leave the nest about 3 weeks after hatching. The Cliff Swallow feeds on small insects caught in flight, but sometimes takes berries or other fruit when insects are scarce.

TREE SWALLOW

Scientific name:	*Tachycineta bicolor*
Length:	5¾ inches
Habitat / Range:	Woodland near water, across much of North America in summer
Identification:	Stocky, broad-winged swallow with shallow forked tail. Metallic blue-black above, white beneath. Juvenile gray-brown above, often with indistinct dusky breast band
Similar species:	Violet-green Swallow (*Tachycineta thalassina*), has white on cheek and sides of rump, variable iridescent color in good light

The Tree Swallow is common and widespread in much of North America in summer, and spends the winter in the southern states and down into Central America. It is seen in a variety of habitats, often in huge flocks as it prepares to migrate in fall, but is never found far from water. It builds a cup nest of grass lined with soft feathers in a tree hollow, abandoned woodpecker hole or nesting box, in which it lays 4–6 white eggs. The Tree Swallow often perches in long rows on wires and branches. It eats insects caught on the wing, but turns to berries in winter when other food is scarce.

BANK SWALLOW

Scientific name:	*Riparia riparia*
Length:	4¾ inches
Habitat/Range:	Riverbanks and gravel pits. Widespread in summer
Identification:	Small, slender, narrow-winged swallow with long, notched tail. Brown above, white beneath with brown band across upper breast
Similar species:	The Northern Rough-winged Swallow (*Stelgopteryx serripennis*), is larger, and has a brown wash on the throat instead of the breast band

The smallest swallow in North America, the Bank Swallow is common across most of North America in summer, migrating south in large flocks to spend the winter in South America. It breeds in very large colonies, sometimes containing hundreds of birds, digging a deep tunnel in a soft earth bank, with a chamber at the end which is lined with grass and feathers. Tunnels are often renovated and reused the following year, due to a shortage of sufficient suitable sites. It lays 4–6 white eggs that are incubated for around 2 weeks by both parent birds. The Bank Swallow flies with very fast, shallow wingbeats and eats insects caught in flight.

BLACK-CAPPED CHICKADEE

Scientific name:	*Parus atricapillus*
Length:	5¼ inches
Habitat/Range:	Open woodland and suburbs. Found from Alaska to Newfoundland, south to Arizona and North Carolina
Identification:	Bold, long-tailed woodland songbird, with large head and fluffy plumage. Gray above, creamy beneath with buff flanks, black throat patch and cap, white face
Similar species:	Mountain Chickadee (*Poecile gambeli*) has black stripe through eye

A small and constantly active bird, the Black-capped Chickadee is found right across central North America in open woodland, but also often visits suburban bird feeders, where it is particularly fond of sunflower seeds and suet. It nests in a tree hole, often in a rotten stump, making a loose cup of plant material and feathers to hold 4–8 eggs. These are incubated for 10–12 days and the young are ready to leave the nest just over 2 weeks after hatching. After the breeding season is over, the Black-capped Chickadee forms small flocks to roost and forage together. It eats insects, seeds and berries.

BUSHTIT

Scientific name:	*Psaltriparus minimus*
Length:	4½ inches
Habitat/Range:	Woods, parks and gardens. Occurs from sothwestern Canada, to California and Texas, south into Mexico
Identification:	Small, long-tailed songbird with short stubby bill. Gray above, lighter beneath.
Similar species:	Juvenile Verdin (*Auriparus flaviceps*) may be mistaken for Bushtit, but has shorter tail and is never seen in flocks

The Bushtit spends most of the year in flocks of up to 30 birds, flitting through the trees of deciduous woods and constantly twittering. The flocks only break up in the breeding season, when birds pair up to build a hanging, gourd-shaped nest of tightly-woven plant fiber. The female lays up to 14 white eggs. These are incubated for about 11–13 days by both birds, and the young leave the nest about 2 weeks after hatching but join the parents to form a family group. Pacific coast birds have a brown crown, and some in west Texas may have a black ear patch. These were once considered to be a separate species, the Black-eared Bushtit. The Bushtit forages in flocks, moving from one feeding spot to another in a unit. It eats insects, spiders and berries.

TUFTED TITMOUSE

Scientific name:	*Parus bicolor*
Length:	6½ inches
Habitat/Range:	Deciduous woodland, parks and gardens, mainly in eastern North America
Identification:	Stocky woodland songbird with broad tail and distinctive crest. Gray above, whitish beneath with pale orange flanks, gray crest and black forehead. Some birds have black crest and pale forehead
Similar species:	Coloring is distinctive

The Tufted Titmouse is fairly common across eastern North America and often visits feeders, particularly in winter. It is usually seen in pairs or in small flocks, but will also join other small birds in winter to form mixed flocks. In the breeding season it nests in a natural tree cavity, similar hole or a nesting box, building a loose cup of moss, bark and hair at the bottom to hold its eggs. In parts of Texas, birds have a black crest and a pale forehead and were formerly considered a separate species, the Black-crested Titmouse. The Tufted Titmouse is an active and sociable bird. It mainly eats insects, fruit and seeds and is particularly fond of sunflower seeds.

BROWN CREEPER

Scientific name:	*Certhia americana*
Length:	5¼ inches
Habitat/Range:	Coniferous and mixed forests, wooded swamps, from Southern Canada to New Mexico
Identification:	Small and slender with long, thin, stiff tail and thin down-curved bill. Mottled brown above, white eyebrow and underparts
Similar species:	Behavior makes it unmistakeable

Unlike the nuthatch, the Brown Creeper uses its tail as a brace so it can only climb trees upwards, circling the trunk in a spiral from the base until it reaches the top, then flying to the base of the next. It is quite common, but easy to overlook, and although it is usually a solitary bird, it sometimes joins flocks of other birds in winter. It builds a nest of bark, moss and twigs held together with spider webs, often concealed behind loose bark. The Brown Creeper eats spiders and insects, as well as insect eggs and larvae, which it digs out of the cracks and crevices of tree bark.

RED-BREASTED NUTHATCH ▲

Scientific name:	*Sitta canadensis*
Length:	4½ inches
Habitat/Range:	Coniferous and mixed forests, adjacent suburbs. Found in suitable habitats through much of North America
Identification:	Blue-gray above, black cap over white eyebrow, broad black eye stripe, rusty-red breast, belly, undertail coverts. Female and juvenile slate-gray cap, paler beneath
Similar species:	Coloring is distinctive

Nuthatches climb up, down and around tree trunks and branches, using their strong legs and feet. Since they do not use the tail as a brace, they can also move head downward. The Red-breasted Nuthatch is fairly common across North America, spreading through most of the south in winter. In the summer, it prefers the conifer forests and mixed woodland of the north, nesting in an excavated tree cavity up to 100 feet above the ground, or in a nesting box. It lines the nest cavity with feathers, moss, grass and bark and lays 5–8 white, red-brown-speckled eggs. The Red-breasted Nuthatch eats conifer seeds and insects. It stores excess food in larders and in lean years will migrate further south.

HOUSE WREN ▼

Scientific name:	*Troglodytes aedon*
Length:	4¾ inches
Habitat/Range:	Scrub, farmland, gardens and parks. Occurs north of Florida and Texas to Southern Canada
Identification:	Small and slender, with long, slightly curved bill and short tail. Gray-brown above, cross barring on back and tail, faint eyebrow, gray-brown beneath
Similar species:	Winter Wren (*Troglodytes troglodytes*) has more prominent barring on belly and is smaller

Familiar and common across America, the House Wren is found in a variety of habitats and often visits suburban gardens. Its loud, fast, bubbling song is very musical and is heard throughout the summer. It builds a simple nest of twigs and sticks, lined with feathers, in a natural or man-made hole, or in a nesting box. It competes with other birds for a suitable nest site, sometimes throwing out the nest, eggs or chicks of its rival. It lays 5-7 white eggs, finely speckled with brown, which are incubated by the female alone for around 2 weeks. The House Wren eats insects and spiders.

AMERICAN DIPPER ▲

Scientific name:	*Cinclus mexicanus*
Length:	7½ inches
Habitat/Range:	Fast-flowing mountain streams, from Alaska, south through the Rocky Mountains
Identification:	Large, stocky aquatic songbird with dark bill and quite long legs. Slate-gray overall, white eyelids seen when blinking
Similar species:	The American Dipper is the only songbird that swims

The American Dipper is only found along clear, fast-flowing, rocky streams in the west. It is solitary most of the year, and never seen in flocks or away from water. Its nest is bulky, made of grass and moss with an entrance at the side, and built among roots, in a rock crevice, under a bridge or on rocks above the water. It lays 3-6 white eggs, which are incubated by the female alone. The American Dipper flies low over the water, or jumps in to swim, dive or walk along the bottom. It eats aquatic insects and water snails.

GOLDEN-CROWNED KINGLET

Scientific name:	*Regulus satrapa*
Length:	4 inches
Habitat/Range:	Dense coniferous woods. Widespread in winter, breeding in mountainous parts of the US and Canada in summer
Identification:	Small, with short, slender bill and short, slightly notched tail. Olive-green above, whitish beneath, yellow crown bordered with black. White eyebrow, black eyeline, white wing bars
Similar species:	Head coloring distinctive

Although in general it much prefers conifers, the Golden-crowned Kinglet is also found in mixed woodland in winter, foraging in flocks with other small birds. It has been helped by the advent of conifer plantations; when the mature trees are harvested, the birds move on to a new plantation home. In its breeding area it builds a delicate nest with high walls, made of lichens and moss and thickly lined with moss and feathers. It lays 5–11 gray-white eggs, heavily spotted with brown and lilac, which are incubated for around 2 weeks. The Golden-crowned Kinglet is an acrobatic bird that often hangs upside down to feed, hopping among the branches and flicking its wings while foraging; it eats insects and their larvae.

RUBY-CROWNED KINGLET

Scientific name:	*Regulus calendula*
Length:	4¼ inches
Habitat/Range:	Woodlands and thickets. Common in the south in winter, north in summer
Identification:	Small songbird with short, slender bill and short, slightly notched tail. Olive-green above, buffy-whitish beneath, white wing bars, incomplete white eye ring. Male has red crown, visible only when raised
Similar species:	*Empidonax* flycatchers have longer tails. Huttons's Vireo is larger, has a thicker bill and lacks dark area behind wing bars

The Ruby-crowned Kinglet breeds in northern coniferous woodland in summer, and builds a delicate, woven nest with high walls, made of lichens and moss, and thickly lined with moss and feathers. The nest is suspended from the tip of a conifer branch up to 100 feet above the ground. It lays 5-11 creamy-white eggs, speckled with brown and gray, which are incubated for around 2 weeks. The Ruby-crowned Kinglet is not particularly sociable, and is often seen foraging alone. It eats caterpillars, spiders, insects and their larvae.

Blue-gray Gnatcatcher

Scientific name:	*Polioptila caerulea*
Length:	4¼ inches
Habitat/Range:	Leafy woodlands and thickets, over much of the US in summer
Identification:	Small, with long tail, long, pale bill and pointed wings. Blue-gray above, white beneath, long black tail with white outer feathers and narrow white eye ring. Male has black eyebrow in summer
Similar species:	In winter many species of gnatcatcher can look very similar, but the Black-tailed has a tail that is mostly black when seen from beneath

In the east, the Blue-gray Gnatcatcher lives high in leafy trees in summer, but in the west it tends to be found lower in oaks and junipers. It is quite common in both areas, but is perhaps easier to spot at lower levels. It builds a tiny, woven nest of grass, bark and plant fibers, camouflaged on the outside with pieces of lichen. It lays 4 or 5 pale blue eggs, sometimes spotted with brown, which are incubated for about 2 weeks by both adult birds. The young become independent around 9-12 days after hatching. The Blue-gray Gnatcatcher is a very lively bird that constantly flicks its tail upward as it forages for spiders and insects.

HERMIT THRUSH

Scientific name:	*Catharus guttatus*
Length:	6¾ inches
Habitat/Range:	Coniferous and mixed woodland throughout much of the US, north into Canada in summer
Identification:	Stocky, with short wings. Olive-brown above, reddish tail, whitish belly, white eye ring and pale olive-gray flanks. Breast is buff with dark spots,
Similar species:	All the *Catharus* thrushes are very similar, mainly told apart by range and song

In summer, the Hermit Thrush is found in coniferous and mixed woodland across the north; it spends the winter in the south and down into Mexico. It is widespread and common, but spends much of its time in dense undergrowth. In its breeding area it nests on or just above the ground, building a neat cup of grass, leaves and rootlets, lined with moss. The song of the Hermit Thrush is loud and slow, with similar phrases repeated, moving up and down the scale. Its call is a soft *chup*. The Hermit Thrush forages on the ground in dense cover for berries, insects, spiders and earthworms.

VARIED THRUSH

Scientific name:	*Ixoreus naevius*
Length:	9½ inches
Habitat/Range:	Dense, moist woods and conifer forests from southern Alaska to California
Identification:	Large, long-necked songbird with short tail. Slate-gray above, rust-orange eyebrow, throat and breast, broad slate-black breast band, whitish belly
Similar species:	Plumage distinctive

Within its limited North American range, the Varied Thrush is common, but it is a fairly shy and elusive bird. It nests in trees, building a large, sturdy cup of stems, twigs, leaves and mud, lined with moss, to hold its 3-5 pale blue, brown-spotted eggs. These are incubated by the female bird for about 2 weeks. The Varied Thrush mostly stays hidden in trees and undergrowth, although it does forage in open areas for earthworms. It also eats insects, spiders, nuts, seeds and fruit.

AMERICAN ROBIN

Scientific name:	*Turdus migratorius*
Length:	10 inches
Habitat/Range:	Woodland, swamps, urban parks and gardens throughout North America
Identification:	Large, sturdy songbird with long legs and tail. Gray-brown above, white throat, red-orange breast, blackish head and tail, yellow bill
Similar species:	Plumage distinctive

Common and widespread, the American Robin is one of the best-known American birds and is often seen in suburban gardens. In summer it spreads right up into Canada and the far north, but it is found all year round across most of America. It nests in shrubs, trees or on buildings, building a sturdy cup of roots, twigs and mud, lined with soft material, to hold its 3 or 4 blue eggs. These are incubated by the female bird, with the young leaving the nest around 2–3 weeks after hatching. The American Robin often forages on lawns with its head held cocked, looking for earthworms. It also eats insects and berries.

EASTERN BLUEBIRD ▲ MOUNTAIN BLUEBIRD

Scientific name:	*Sialia sialis*
Length:	7 inches
Habitat/Range:	Open woodland, farmland, parks and forest edges. Found in the east, from southern Canada to Texas
Identification:	Stocky, with a stout bill, short wings and tail. Deep blue above, chestnut throat, sides of neck, breast and flanks. Belly and undertail coverts white. Female is grayer
Similar species:	Western Bluebird *(Sialia mexicana)* has blue throat and blue-gray belly

Scientific name:	*Sialia currucoides*
Length:	7¼ inches
Habitat/Range:	High open country and mountain meadows throughout western North America
Identification:	Male sky-blue, lighter blue breast, white belly. Female gray with brown tint, blue wash on wings, rump and tail, white belly
Similar species:	Pale blue of male is distinctive. Indigo Bunting is darker blue with thicker bill. Female has longer wings and tail than other bluebirds

Found in small groups in open country, often perched on wires or fence posts, the Eastern Bluebird was once in decline due to competition with other birds for suitable nesting sites. Specially-designed nesting boxes have reversed this trend and it will use these, or a natural cavity or woodpecker hole, lining the bottom with a loose cup-shape made of grass and plant stems. It lays 2–7 pale blue-white eggs, which are incubated by the female for around 2 weeks. The young are independent about 3 weeks after hatching, and are brownish and heavily spotted, but with a trace of blue above. The Eastern Bluebird eats insects, spiders and berries and will also visit bird feeders.

The Mountain Bluebird prefers open areas at higher altitude in summer, as long as there are trees nearby for cover. In the winter it will come lower down, and also migrates further south. It nests in a natural cavity, woodpecker hole or will even use a nesting box, lining the bottom of its chosen site with grass, bark chips and feathers. It lays 4–6 pale blue-green eggs, which are incubated for around 2 weeks. The Mountain Bluebird often hovers low over the ground, or darts out from a branch to catch insects and spiders. In fall and winter it also eats berries.

BROWN THRASHER

Scientific name:	*Toxostoma rufum*
Length:	11½ inches
Habitat/Range:	Hedgerows, brush, woodlands and suburbs in the east, from Canada to Texas
Identification:	Large, short-billed songbird with long, pointed wings. Bright red-brown above, buffy beneath with thin, dark streaks, two white wing bars, white outer corners to tail, yellow eyes
Similar species:	Wood Thrush (*Hylocichla mustelina*) has spotted rather than striped breast, dark eyes, shorter tail. Long Billed Thrasher (*Toxostoma longirostre*) has longer bill, orange eyes and is grayer above.

Spreading across most of the east in summer, the Brown Thrasher lives in hedgerows, brush and thickets, often close to human dwellings. Although it is declining it is still quite common within its range, and some birds are seen all year round in the southeast. It is often noticed singing from treetops in the breeding season. It nests on the ground or in a dense brush pile or thicket, building a well-hidden, bulky cup of twigs, leaves and grass to hold its 2–4 bluish-white, brown-speckled eggs. The Brown Thrasher forages on the ground, scattering leaves by moving its bill from side to side as it searches for insects, spiders and berries.

GRAY CATBIRD

Scientific name:	*Dumetella carolinensis*
Length:	8½ inches
Habitat / Range:	Woodland thickets and dense gardens, mainly in the eastern US
Identification:	Slender, long-tailed songbird. Overall slate-gray, black cap, chestnut-red under tail
Similar species:	Coloring is distinctive

Very common in the east in summer, the Gray Catbird is rarely found west of the Rockies. Its call sounds like the mewing of a cat, hence its name, and it is often found in suburban gardens as well as in dense woodland thickets. It nests fairly low down in a tree or dense shrub, building a rough cup of twigs and stems, lined with rootlets, to hold its 3–5 bluish-green eggs. The Gray Catbird is an excellent mimic, copying all the birdsongs in the area and adding its own shrieks and whistles. It forages on the ground for insects, either in dense cover or out in the open, and also eats berries in late summer and fall.

NORTHERN MOCKINGBIRD

Scientific name:	*Mimus polyglottos*
Length:	10 inches
Habitat / Range:	Woodland, urban gardens, desert and farmland. Found from northern California, to Nebraska, and southeastern Canada, southward
Identification:	Slender, with a long tail, long legs and short bill. Gray above, white beneath, two white wing bars
Similar species:	Coloring and shape are distinctive

A bird that prefers warmer climates, the Northern Mockingbird is in fact found mainly across the south. It nests low down in a tree or shrub, building a cup of twigs lined with soft plant fibers. It is an excellent mimic, not only copying birdsongs but also the sound of cars, machinery and sirens. The Northern Mockingbird is very territorial and defends its ground aggressively. It likes open grassy areas for feeding, with nearby foliage to hide its nest, and perches for the male to sing and warn off intruders. It eats insects, spiders and berries, often flashing its wings while foraging on the ground, possibly to scare insects out of hiding.

BOHEMIAN WAXWING

Scientific name:	*Bombycilla garrulus*
Length:	8¼ inches
Habitat/Range:	Open coniferous and mixed woods, spruce forest and bogs. Breeds in British Columbia and Alberta, spreading further south and east in winter
Identification:	Round body, short tail and crested head. Cinnamon-gray above, gray beneath, with chestnut under tail. Yellow and white wing markings, red spot on wing and yellow tail-tip. Black face mask edged with white, black chin
Similar species:	Cedar Waxwing is browner, lacks chestnut under tail

A bird of the far northwest, the Bohemian Waxwing is very sociable and is almost always seen in flocks. Although it usually spends the summer in boreal forests and the edge of the taiga, wintering in the prairie provinces, it is sometimes seen in large numbers much further afield, possibly due to food shortages in its normal range. In its breeding area it builds a twiggy nest, lined with moss, high in a conifer to hold its 4–6 bluish eggs. The Bohemian Waxwing mainly eats insects and berries.

CEDAR WAXWING

Scientific name:	*Bombycilla cedrorum*
Length:	7¼ inches
Habitat/Range:	Found in trees with wild berries, mainly across southern Canada and the northern US
Identification:	Round body, short tail, crested head. Brown-gray above, yellow beneath, with yellow and white wing markings, red spot on wing, and yellow tail tip. Black face mask edged with white, black chin
Similar species:	Bohemian Waxwing is grayer, has chestnut under tail and gray belly

The Cedar Waxwing is a very sociable bird, and is almost always seen in quite large flocks, except when the birds pair up to breed. It is found across most of North America at various times of the year, but flocks will move around a great deal in winter in search of berries. In its breeding area it builds a loose nest of twigs, grass and lichens, on a horizontal branch, where it lays 3-6 blue-gray eggs. They are incubated for 12-14 days, and the young birds are ready to start fending for themselves about 2 - 3 days later. The Cedar Waxwing is particularly fond of berries, but it will also eat flying insects and flower petals.

YELLOW WARBLER ▲ BLACKBURNIAN WARBLER

Scientific name:	*Dendroica petechia*
Length:	5 inches
Habitat/Range:	Willows and alders in wet open woodland. Occurs throughout much of North America, but largely absent from the southeast
Identification:	Stout, with a short tail and thick bill. Yellow overall, wings and tail yellow-olive with yellow markings and spots. Male has chestnut stripes on breast and flanks, female and juvenile duller
Similar species:	Male Wilson's Warbler *(Wilsonia pusilla)* has black cap, females difficult to tell apart

Scientific name:	*Dendroica fusca*
Length:	5 inches
Habitat/Range:	Coniferous and mixed forests, spruce woods, mainly in eastern parts of North America
Identification:	Slim, with long tail and pointed wings. Breeding male has orange throat, black ear patch, white wing patch, and black, white-striped back. Female similar but has orange-yellow throat, and black wings with white bars
Similar species:	Unmistakable

A very common and widespread bird across most of North America, the Yellow Warbler inhabits open woods, often preferring those along streams, and winters in the tropics, although some only move as far as Mexico. It nests in the crotch of a small tree or shrub, building a deep cup of plant material lined with down. The Cowbird will often deposit its egg in a Yellow Warbler nest, usually leading the bird to build another floor over the alien egg and begin all over again – nests have even been found with several floors. The Yellow Warbler usually forages around the mid-level in the foliage of trees, where it will hunt for insects and spiders.

The brilliantly colored Blackburnian Warbler is fairly common in conifer woods in the northeast in summer, although it is rare in the west. It can also be spotted as it migrates through the eastern states to winter in South America. The Blackburnian Warbler stays high in the upper branches of trees, and mainly eats insects and berries. Several species of warbler often share the same territory, but because they tend to forage at different levels in the trees they do not compete with each other for the available food.

YELLOW-RUMPED WARBLER

Scientific name:	*Dendroica coronata*
Length:	5½ inches
Habitat/Range:	Coniferous, mixed woodland and parks. Found across Canada, the northern US, and along the Pacific in summer. Winters south into the tropics
Identification:	Long tail, stout black bill. Dark gray above with black streaks. White belly, eyebrow, throat and wing bars. Breeding male has yellow rump, flank and crown patches, and white tail spots
Similar species:	Yellow-rumped Warbler is a hybrid of two former species, and may be difficult to distinguish from other warblers as there are many color variations

The Myrtle Warbler (*Dendroica petechia*), in the east, and Audubon's Warbler (*Dendroica auduboni*) in the west, combined and interbred where their ranges overlapped and this hybrid is now considered a separate species, the Yellow-rumped Warbler. It is found across the north in summer and spends the winter in the south and Central America, but is seen in migration across most of the continent. It nests fairly high in a conifer and lays 4 or 5 white eggs, spotted with brown and gray. Audubon's Warbler has a yellow throat and a white wing patch, the Myrtle a white eyebrow, a white throat extending up the side of the neck, a black cheek and two white wing bars. The Yellow-rumped Warbler eats insects and spiders, berries and seeds.

BLACK-AND-WHITE WARBLER

Scientific name:	*Mniotilta varia*
Length:	5¼ inches
Habitat/Range:	Mixed woodland east of the Rocky Mountains
Identification:	Mainly striped black and white, with white crown stripe. Male has black throat and cheeks when breeding, white chin in winter. Female and juvenile, white throat and cheeks, buff flanks with gray streaks
Similar species:	Black-throated Gray Warbler (*Dendroica nigrescens*) has black crown

Like a nuthatch, the Black-and-white Warbler creeps around the trunks and large branches of trees, the only warbler that behaves in this way. It is common in summer in the mixed woodlands of the eastern states, but also occasionally strays into the west; a few birds spend the winter in Florida, but most head much further south. It builds its nest on the ground, sheltered among the roots of a tree or tucked under a log or rock, creating a thickly-woven cup of bark, moss, twigs and plant fiber, in which it lays 4 or 5 whitish-cream, brown-speckled eggs. The Black-and-white Warbler probes tree bark with its long bill, hunting for insects and spiders.

MAGNOLIA WARBLER

Scientific name:	*Dendroica magnolia*
Length:	5 inches
Habitat/Range:	Damp, open conifer forests in Canada and the northern US, migrating into the east
Identification:	Male gray above, with a black mask, breast streaks and back, white eyebrow and wing patch, yellow rump and underparts. Female duller, more greatly streaked
Similar species:	Juvenile Prairie Warbler (*Dendroica discolor*) similar to juvenile Magnolia, but lacks eye ring and breast band

This species was given its name after being discovered in a magnolia tree, but otherwise there is no special connection. It nests fairly low down in a conifer, building a loose, shallow cup of grass and rootlets on a horizontal branch, in which it lays 3–5 eggs. These are incubated for up to 2 weeks by the female bird, with the young leaving the nest some 9 days later. The adult is a long-tailed bird with a round head and a small bill. Fall adults and juveniles are gray-olive above with a white eye ring, and yellowish beneath with a faint gray breast band. The Magnolia Warbler eats insects and spiders.

AMERICAN REDSTART ▲ COMMON YELLOWTHROAT

Scientific name:	*Setophaga ruticilla*
Length:	5¼ inches
Habitat/Range:	Second-growth woods. Found mainly in northern and eastern parts of North America
Identification:	Long-tailed woodland bird with short broad bill and rounded wings. Male black, white belly, orange patches on sides, wings and outer tail feathers. Female gray above, white beneath, with yellow patches on sides, wings and outer tail feathers
Similar species:	Coloring distinctive

Scientific name:	*Geothlypis trichas*
Length:	5 inches
Habitat/Range:	Grassy fields and open marshes through much of North America, most common in the eastern US
Identification:	Stumpy, with short neck, small bill, round tail and wings. Male olive-green above, bright yellow below fading to dull white belly. Black mask, edged with white across crown. Female olive-brown above, buff beneath with yellow on throat
Similar species:	Juvenile Mourning Warbler (*Oporornis philadelphia*) like female Common Yellowthroat but has yellow belly

A very distinctive warbler, the American Redstart is common in North America across much of the north and southeast in summer, where it prefers open deciduous woods. It is rare in the southwest and spends the winter in Mexico and northern South America. It nests up to 70 feet above the ground in an upright crotch of a tree, building a firm cup of twigs lined with finer material, in which it lays 3-5 eggs. The American Redstart fans its tail and spreads its wings frequently to flash its bright patches, so it is fairly easy to spot. It feeds mainly on flying insects, frequently catching them in midair.

One of the most widespread warblers in North America, the Common Yellowthroat is found in summer across most of the continent and some birds also spend the winter across the south. It prefers grassland, marshes and other open habitats with low vegetation, rather than woods. It nests on or near the ground among weeds or grasses or in a low shrub. The Common Yellowthroat spends much of its time hidden in dense under-growth, but the male climbs a tall stalk to sing in the breeding season. It eats insects and spiders.

SUMMER TANAGER

Scientific name:	*Piranga rubra*
Length:	7¾ inches
Habitat:	Pine-oak woods and cottonwood groves in the southern US
Identification:	Male rosy-red, female olive-yellow above, orange-yellow beneath, greenish under tail
Similar species:	Female similar to female Scarlet Tanager, but tail is greenish beneath instead of gray

Found across the south in summer, the Summer Tanager lives in pine-oak forest in the southeast and streamside cottonwoods in the southwest and rarely spreads any further north. It makes its nest in a tree, building a rather frail and shallow cup of grass and leaves on a horizontal branch, in which it lays 3 or 4 blue-green eggs with brown blotches. The Summer Tanager forages high in the canopy and eats insects, larvae, spiders and berries - it also eats fruit.

SCARLET TANAGER

Scientific name:	*Piranga olivacea*
Length:	7 inches
Habitat/Range:	Leafy forests in the east, north of the Carolinas
Identification:	Male has black wings and tail, white wing linings, in breeding season is brilliant red overall, in winter greenish-yellow. Female is greenish-yellow with darker wings and tail, and white wing linings
Similar species:	Male distinctive. Female similar to female Summer Tanager, but tail is gray beneath instead of greenish

WESTERN TANAGER

Scientific name:	*Piranga ludoviciana*
Length:	7½ inches
Habitat/Range:	Coniferous mountain woodland in the western US
Identification:	Male has brilliant red head, bright yellow body, black wings and tail, upper wing bar yellow, lower wing bar white. Female is yellow-green above, yellow below, wing bars as male
Similar species:	Male distinctive. Female similar to female orioles, but has thicker bill

The Scarlet Tanager lives in the leafy deciduous forests of the northeast in summer, but is also seen across the southeastern states as it migrates to the tropics in fall for the winter, and when it returns in spring. It nests in a tree, building a shallow cup of grass and leaves at the tip of a horizontal branch, in which it lays 3–5 blue-green eggs finely spotted with brown. These are incubated by the female for around 2 weeks. The Scarlet Tanager usually forages high in the canopy, but may come down lower to hunt for food as it migrates. It eats insects, caterpillars, spiders and berries – it is very popular with gardeners because of its voracious appetite for garden pests.

In cool conifer forests and mountain pine woods across the west the Western Tanager is fairly common in summer, but it is also seen in many different habitats during its migration across the western states. It nests near the top of a tall conifer, building a shallow saucer of moss, stalks and bark, in which it lays 3-5 bluish-green eggs finely spotted with brown. The Western Tanager usually forages high in the canopy, but may come down lower to hunt for food as it travels in migration. It generally eats insects, which it will often catch on the wing, berries and other small fruit. Although it looks striking, like other tanagers it does not have a notable song.

FOX SPARROW

Scientific name:	*Passerella iliaca*
Length:	7 inches
Habitat/Range:	Coniferous and mixed woodland undergrowth and scrub, migrating between Canada and the southern US
Identification:	Large, stocky, round-headed sparrow with heavy bill. Coloring variable; usually gray, dark brown or streaked rufous above, with heavy triangular spots beneath. White belly, reddish rump and tail
Similar species:	Hermit Thrush has white eye ring, lacks heavy streaking below

The Fox Sparrow is one of the largest sparrows in North America and is fairly common in many areas, but it lives in dense thickets and so it may be difficult to spot. It nests on or just above the ground, building a neat, solid cup of plant fibers lined with feathers hidden in a thicket or low in a bush. It lays 4 or 5 pale green eggs speckled with brown, which are incubated for up to 2 weeks by the female bird. The Fox Sparrow scratches at the ground under bushes with both feet, hunting for seeds and insects.

SONG SPARROW

Scientific name:	*Melospiza melodia*
Length:	5½ – 7½ inches
Habitat/Range:	Dense riverside thickets, parks and gardens. Widespread throughout North America
Identification:	Stocky sparrow with round head, long tail and stout bill. Coloring variable, but generally streaked red-brown above, heavily striped beneath with distinct central breast spot, white belly, gray crown stripe and eyebrow
Similar species:	Savannah Sparrow lacks central breast spot and has shorter tail

The Song Sparrow is the most widespread sparrow in North America, but it hides in dense cover, although it also lives in suburban gardens and parks, where it can become quite tame. It nests on or just above the ground, in vegetation, and lays 3–6 greenish-white eggs heavily spotted with brown. These are incubated for around 2 weeks by the female bird, and the young are ready to begin fending for themselves around 10 days later – there are often several further broods in a season. The Song Sparrow usually lives in family groups or pairs and is rarely seen in flocks. It eats seeds, grain, berries and insects.

WHITE-THROATED SPARROW

Scientific name:	*Zonotrichia albicollis*
Length:	6¾ inches
Habitat/Range:	Woodland undergrowth, brush, parks and gardens. Migrates between Canada and the southern US
Identification:	Large, heavy sparrow with long tail. Chestnut-brown above, black and white striped crown, bright yellow spot behind dark bill, either white or tan eyebrow, gray cheek and breast, white throat, two narrow white wing bars
Similar species:	White-crowned Sparrow is grayer with pink or yellow bill

The White-throated Sparrow is commonly seen in flocks in woods, parks and gardens in the southeast in winter, but is rare in the west. It spends the summer in the cool forests of the north and northeast. In the breeding season it nests on the ground, weaving a cup of moss, grass, rootlets and bark strips, lined with fine grass and hidden in vegetation, in which it lays 3–5 eggs. The White-throated Sparrow is usually found on the ground, where it forages for seeds, berries and insects, often in flocks with juncos and other sparrows.

WHITE-CROWNED SPARROW

Scientific name:	*Zonotrichia leucophrys*
Length:	7 inches
Habitat/Range:	Woodland edges, grassland, thickets, mainly in the west
Identification:	Large, with long tail. Gray-brown streaked above, black and white striped crown, pink or yellow bill, gray cheek and breast, white throat and belly, two narrow white wing bars
Similar species:	White-throated Sparrow is browner with dark bill

Abundant in the west but uncommon in the east, the White-crowned Sparrow is seen in flocks at the edges of woodland and in hedges across the south in winter and spends the summer in the north and northwest. In the breeding season it nests both on or high above the ground, weaving a neat cup of grass hidden in vegetation or in a tree, in which it lays 3-5 eggs. The White-crowned Sparrow eats seeds, grain and insects and often visits feeders in winter.

CHIPPING SPARROW

Scientific name:	*Spizella passerina*
Length:	5½ inches
Habitat/Range:	Lawns, grassy fields and woodland edges. Found throughout most of North America
Identification:	Rust-red crown above white eyebrow and black eyeline, gray cheeks, collar and underparts, brown back with dark streaking, two white wing bars
Similar species:	Rufous-winged Sparrow *(Aimophila carpalis)* larger and more secretive

Widespread and common across most of North America in summer, the Chipping Sparrow is often seen in backyards and gathers in flocks in the south in winter. It nests up to 40 feet above the ground in a bush or tree, building a neat cup of plant fibers lined with animal hair, in which it lays 3–5 pale blue eggs, marked with brown, black and purple. These are incubated by the female for up to 2 weeks and the young leave the nest after around 9–12 days. The Chipping Sparrow often feeds in the open and eats insects and seeds.

SAVANNAH SPARROW

Scientific name:	*Passerculus sandwichensis*
Length:	5½ inches
Habitat/Range:	Marsh, fields and grassy beaches across much of North America
Identification:	Small crest, short notched tail and pointed wings. Coloring variable, but generally streaked brown above, heavily striped beneath. White belly, light central crown stripe and eyebrow
Similar species:	Vesper Sparrow *(Pooecetes gramineus)* has pale eye ring, lacks bold eyebrow and white central crown stripe

A common and widespread bird, the Savannah Sparrow can often be seen perching in the open on marshes, fields or grassy beaches. It nests on the ground, hidden in vegetation, and lays 4–6 whitish eggs spotted with brown and purple. These are incubated for 10–12 days by both birds, and the young are ready to begin fending for themselves around 2 weeks later. The Savannah Sparrow usually lives in loose flocks and eats seeds and insects.

AMERICAN TREE SPARROW

Scientific name:	*Spizella arborea*
Length:	6½ inches
Habitat/Range:	Tundra, open areas with groves of trees and brushy fields. Found in the north, and winters across central North America
Identification:	Large, with long tail, chestnut cap and eye stripe, gray head and nape, gray underparts with dark spot on center of breast and chestnut patch at side. Red-brown back with dark streaking, two white wing bars
Similar species:	Chipping Sparrow is smaller and lacks breast spot

A bird which prefers colder climates and can tolerate subzero temperatures, the American Tree Sparrow spends the summer in the tundra zone . It nests on or very near the ground, building a cup of plant fibers lined with feathers, in which it lays 4 or 5 pale blue eggs, speckled with brown. These are incubated by the female for just under 2 weeks and the young leave the nest to start fending for themselves after around 9–11 days. The American Tree Sparrow mainly eats seeds, but will also take insects and spiders.

YELLOW-EYED JUNCO ▲

Scientific name:	*Junco phaeonotus*
Length:	6¼ inches
Habitat/Range:	Coniferous and pine-oak mountain slopes in the southern US
Identification:	Slender ground-dwelling bird with long tail. Gray head, sides and flanks, rust-red on back and wings. Pale throat, two-tone bill, whitish belly, dark tail with white outer feathers
Similar species:	Dark-eyed Junco (*Junco hyemalis*) has dark eyes, and often less red on back

Only found in the far south of North America and extending down into Mexico, the Yellow-eyed Junco lives in coniferous and pine-oak forests. It nests on the ground, building a compact saucer of rootlets and fine grass lined with horsehair, situated under a fallen log or protected by vegetation. It lays 3 or 4 eggs. The Yellow-eyed Junco forages on the ground, moving around slowly and deliberately and walking rather than hopping. It eats seeds, insects and berries.

INDIGO BUNTING

Scientific name:	*Passerina cyanea*
Length:	5½ inches
Habitat/Range:	Woodland clearings, farmland, brushy pasture, mainly in the east
Identification:	Stocky ground-dwelling bird, with short tail and stout bill. Breeding male indigo blue overall. Female and fall male brown, with fine streaks on chest and blue tint to tail
Similar species:	Male Blue Grosbeak *(Guiraca caerulea)* is bigger with larger bill and wide cinnamon wing bars

Common in the east in woodland clearings and on farmland in summer, the Indigo Bunting is rarely seen in the west although part of its range overlaps with that of the Lazuli Bunting (*Passerina amoena*), and the two sometimes interbreed. It nests above the ground, building a neatly-woven cup of grass, leaves and bark strips in a tree or bush to hold 3-5 plain pale blue-white eggs. These are incubated by the female for about two weeks. The Indigo Bunting mainly forages on the ground in flocks, looking for insects and seeds, but it also takes berries in fall.

SNOW BUNTING

Scientific name:	*Plectrophenax nivalis*
Length:	6½ inches
Habitat/Range:	Tundra, rocky shores, sand dunes, beaches, barren fields. Migrates between the Arctic and central US
Identification:	Stocky, with short tail and pointed wings. Black central tail feathers and wing tips, variable black patch at shoulder. Winter male white with buff crown, ear patch, collar and back. Female white with rusty-tan crown, ear patch, collar and back
Similar species:	Plumage distinctive

The Snow Bunting is fairly common across central North America in winter, and spends the summer on Arctic tundra, but is also often seen in various open habitats during migration. It nests in a crevice or a depression in the ground among rocks, lining the hollow with moss and feathers to hold 4–6 blue-white eggs, very heavily spotted with brown and lilac. These are incubated by the female for about 2 weeks and the young are ready to fend for themselves around 11–18 days after hatching. The Snow Bunting is often seen in large flocks along with Horned Larks and longspurs. It eats insects, seeds and spiders.

PAINTED BUNTING

Scientific name:	*Passerina ciris*
Length:	5½ inches
Habitat/Range:	Low thickets, brushy streams and woodland edges, mainly in the southeastern US
Identification:	Stocky, with short tail and rounded bill. Male has indigo-blue head, bright green back, bright red under parts and rump, dusky wings and tail. Female lime green above, lemony-green below
Similar species:	Coloring distinctive

Despite its bright and distinctive coloring, the Painted Bunting can be difficult to spot since it hides in foliage even when singing. The male was once a popular caged bird, but now its capture is illegal. It nests not far above the ground, in a low tree, or thick bush. It lays 3 or 4 gray-white eggs, spotted with brown, which are incubated by the female for about two weeks. The Painted Bunting sings all year round, except when it molts in late summer. It forages on the ground, looking for insects, spiders and seeds.

NORTHERN CARDINAL

Scientific name:	*Cardinalis cardinalis*
Length:	$8\frac{3}{4}$ inches
Habitat/Range:	Forest, swamps, thickets and suburbs throughout much of the US, but absent from most of the west
Identification:	Crested, long-tailed woodland bird with large triangular bill. Male bright red, with black face and throat and red bill. Female olive-buff with reddish crest, wings and tail
Similar species:	The coloring of this species is distinctive

The Northern Cardinal is common both in the east and the southwest in a wide variety of habitats, even city parks and backyards as long as there is sufficient cover. The Cardinal not only returns to the same breeding area, but pairs mate for life. It nests up to 12 feet above the ground, building a loosely-woven cup of twigs and plant fibers in a shrub or thicket, in which it lays 3 or 4 pale green eggs with brown-lilac spots. These are incubated by the female for just under 2 weeks, while the male provides food and helps feed the nestlings after they have hatched. The Northern Cardinal feeds mainly on the ground, out in the open. It eats fruits, seeds and insects and regularly comes to bird feeders in winter, particularly for sunflower seeds.

BREWER'S BLACKBIRD

Scientific name:	*Euphagus cyanocephalus*
Length:	9 inches
Habitat/Range:	Open ground and urban areas in the western US and Canada, breeding eastwards to the Great Lakes
Identification:	Slender, with a long tail and short, straight bill. Breeding male black with iridescent purple head, green-violet glossy body, yellow eyes. Winter male less glossy. Female light gray-brown with brown eyes
Similar species:	The Rusty Blackbird *(Euphagus carolinus)* has a longer, thinner bill, and duller plumage

Brewer's Blackbird is very common in the west and is not only seen regularly in open country but also in suburban parks and sometimes even in city areas. It is a gregarious bird, and outside the breeding season often flocks with other blackbirds and the Brown-headed Cowbird. It nests in small, loose colonies, building a bulky bowl of twigs and grass plastered with mud or cow dung and lined with finer material, in which it lays 4–6 light gray eggs blotched with brown and gray. These are incubated for around 2 weeks by the female and the young leave the nest some 2 weeks after hatching. Brewer's Blackbird forages on the ground and eats seeds, grain and insects.

RED-WINGED BLACKBIRD ▲

Scientific name:	*Agelaius phoeniceus*
Length:	8¾ inches
Habitat/Range:	Freshwater marshes, open fields and farmland across most of North America
Identification:	Stocky, with fairly short tail and rounded wings. Male black with bright red and buff-yellow shoulder patch. Female and juvenile streaked brown with buff eyebrow
Similar species:	Male Tricolored Blackbird *(Agelaius tricolor)* has dark red and white wing patch

Widespread and abundant, the Red-winged Blackbird is found on all kinds of wet ground across most of North America. Except in the breeding season, it forms huge flocks, often with other blackbird species. It nests near the ground, weaving a sturdy cup of grass attached to marsh reeds or in a low bush, in which it lays 3-5 pale blue-green eggs, heavily marked with brown and black. These are incubated by the female for around 10-12 days and the young birds begin to fend for themselves just under 2 weeks after hatching. Although the Red-winged Blackbird may be considered a pest for eating grain in spring, it catches large quantities of crop-damaging insects during the nesting season. It also eats seeds and spiders.

BROWN-HEADED COWBIRD

Scientific name:	*Molothrus ater*
Length:	7½ inches
Habitat/Range:	Open woodland, farmland and suburbs throughout most of North America
Identification:	Male black with metallic green sheen and coffee-brown head. Female light gray-brown, juvenile gray-brown with scaled upperparts
Similar species:	Male distinctive, but female drab and confusing

The Brown-headed Cowbird is very common across most of North America and its population has increased with the clearing of forests so that it now threatens the existence of many smaller birds. It does not build its own nest, but lays its white eggs speckled with brown in the nest of a finch, warbler or vireo or other songbird of similar size, one egg per nest. These are incubated by the host bird, and after hatching the young cowbird crowds and starves out the other nestlings. The Brown-headed Cowbird often feeds near livestock, walking on the ground with its tail held upward, and outside the breeding season it will often flock with other blackbirds in fields and pastures. It eats grain, seeds, berries and insects.

BOBOLINK

Scientific name:	*Dolichonyx oryzivorus*
Length:	7 inches
Habitat/Range:	Damp meadows and hayfields in the northern US and southern Canada
Identification:	Breeding male mostly black with buff nape and white patches on shoulder and rump. Female and winter male buff with dark streaks on back, rump and sides, buff and black stripes on crown
Similar species:	Breeding male distinctive

In summer the Bobolink is fairly common in meadows and hayfields across the northern states and into Canada, but its population appears to be declining. In fall it migrates across the southeast, east of the Great Plains, to spend the winter in South America. It nests on the ground in hayfields and grass meadows, creating a flimsy cup of grass hidden in a dense tuft of vegetation, in which it lays 4–7 eggs. The Bobolink often mixes with other species of blackbird in fall to form large, mixed flocks. It feeds on insects, grain and seeds.

EASTERN MEADOWLARK

Scientific name:	*Sturnella magna*
Length:	9½ inches
Habitat/Range:	Fields, meadows
Identification:	Heavy-bodied open-country bird with short tail and long bill. Dark gray-brown above with darker streaks and bars, buff-white stripes on black crown, gray cheek, yellow underparts with black V-shaped breast band, white outer tail feathers
Similar species:	Western Meadowlark almost identical and the two interbreed

The Eastern and the Western meadowlarks are almost identical and although they can sometimes be distinguished by range and call, where their ranges overlap they learn each other's call and interbreed. The Eastern Meadowlark tends to prefer taller vegetation. It nests on the ground, building a grass cup with a dome-shaped roof of grass stems hidden in dense vegetation, in which it lays 3–7 white eggs, spotted with brown. These are incubated by the female for up to 2 weeks and the young birds are ready to leave the nest to fend for themselves a further 10–12 days after hatching. Its song is a clear, whistled *te-seeyou see-yeeer*, its call is a high buzzy *drezzt*. The Eastern Meadowlark eats insects, spiders, grain and seeds.

WESTERN MEADOWLARK

Scientific name:	*Sturnella neglecta*
Length:	9½ inches
Habitat/Range:	Roadsides, grassland, open ground
Identification:	Heavy-bodied open-country bird with short tail and long bill. Dark gray-brown above with darker streaks and bars, buff-white stripes on black crown, cheek partly gray, yellow underparts with black V-shaped breast band, white outer tail feathers
Similar species:	Eastern Meadowlark almost identical and the two interbreed

Almost identical to the Eastern, the Western Meadowlark can sometimes be distinguished by range and call, although where the ranges overlap they learn each other's call and interbreed. The Western Meadowlark tends to prefer low vegetation and is often seen on roadsides. It nests on the ground, building a cup with a dome-shaped roof of grass hidden in dense vegetation, in which it lays 3-7 white eggs, heavily spotted with brown. These are incubated by the female for up to 2 weeks and the young birds begin to fend for themselves a further 10–12 days after hatching. Its song is a bubbling, flute-like and complex series of phrases speeding up towards the end and its call is a low-pitched *chook*. The Western Meadowlark eats insects, spiders, grain and seeds.

COMMON GRACKLE

Scientific name:	*Quiscalus quiscula*
Length:	12½ inches
Habitat:	Open fields, woods, swamps, parks, suburban lawns
Identification:	Medium-size long-billed open-country bird with long tail and yellow-white eyes. Male black with bronze sheen, blue gloss to head and breast, purple gloss on tail. Female smaller and duller. Juvenile dusky-brown, with brown eyes
Similar species:	Great-tailed and Boat-tailed larger and more evenly colored

East of the Rockies, the Common Grackle is found in a wide variety of habitats – even walking on suburban lawns. It is gregarious, traveling in huge, noisy flocks, sometimes with other blackbirds, and breeding in colonies. It nests high above the ground in an evergreen tree, building a bulky and sturdy cup of twigs and grass, lined with finer stems, in which it lays 4-6 greenish eggs marked with brown. These are incubated by the female for around 2 weeks; the young birds leave the nest just under 3 weeks after they have hatched. The adult is a medium-size, long-billed bird with a long, keel-shaped tail and yellow-white eyes. The most common male, the "Bronzed Grackle", is black with a bronze sheen to the body, a blue gloss on the head and breast, and a purple gloss to the tail. The "Purple Grackle" male is black with a bronze sheen, a dark green glossy back, a purple gloss on the head and breast, and a blue gloss to the tail. The female is smaller than the male and is less glossy. The juvenile is dark brown, with brown eyes. The Common Grackle feeds on the ground and eats almost anything, including grain, insects, small fish, salamanders, seeds and eggs and young of small birds.

EVENING GROSBEAK

Scientific name:	*Coccothraustes vespertinus*
Length:	8 inches
Habitat:	Mixed woods, suburban backyards
Identification:	Medium-size, short-tailed woodland bird, with short pointed wings and massive bill. Male dark olive-brown head, neck and breast, yellow forehead and eyebrow, yellow body, black wings and tail with large white wing patch. Female and juvenile grayish-gold, black wings and tail marked with white
Similar species:	Goldfinches smaller, with much smaller bill

A wandering nomad, both range and numbers of the Evening Grosbeak vary a great deal from year to year. It is often seen in large, noisy flocks, which may visit feeders to eat sunflower seeds. It breeds in woodland, building a loose, flimsy bowl of small twigs and rootlets near the tip of a branch in dense foliage - several pairs may nest quite near one another. It lays 3 or 4 bluish-green eggs with fine markings, which are incubated for up to 2 weeks by the female bird; the young birds leave the nest around 2 weeks later. The Evening Grosbeak forages high in trees in flocks, for seeds, berries, buds or fruit – it also sometimes eats insects.

RED CROSSBILL

Scientific name:	*Loxia curvirostra*
Length:	$6\frac{1}{4}$ inches
Habitat:	Coniferous woods
Identification:	Stocky woodland bird with short tail and large bill with crossed tip. Male mottled brick-red with dark wings and tail. Female mottled olive-gray with darker wings, dull yellow rump and underparts. Juvenile orange-tinted with dusky streaks
Similar species:	White-winged Crossbill has two broad white wing bars

The unique bill of this species has developed to allow it to open pine cones and extract the seed. The Red Crossbill lives in coniferous forests but wanders around in flocks in search of pine cones and breeds in any season when food is plentiful - even in the depths of winter. It nests well above the ground in a conifer, building a neat, shallow cup of twigs, rootlets and moss lined with lichens and fur in which it lays 3–5 bluish eggs spotted with brown at the rounded end. The female bird incubates the eggs for around 2 weeks and the young leave the nest around 15–17 days after they have hatched. The Red Crossbill eats pine nuts and insects.

INVERTEBRATES

CLOUDLESS SULPHUR ▼

Scientific name:	*Phoebis sennae*
Identification:	Males yellow, sometimes reddish below, females yellow or white with a black spot on each forewing and spots around wing edges
Wingspan:	2–2½ inches
Habitat/Range:	Woodland, grasslands and beaches. Abundant throughout the southern US, migrating north to Canada in summer
Similar species:	Other sulphurs are generally smaller

GREAT SOUTHERN WHITE

Scientific name:	*Ascia monuste*
Identification:	Large, white butterfly with dusky wingtips, though females often somewhat more gray or even brown
Wingspan:	2–2½ inches
Habitat/Range:	Shorelines, coastal salt marshes and plains from Texas to Florida, migrating north to Kansas and Virginia in summer
Similar species:	The Florida White (*Appias drusilla*) lacks dark tips on forewings

Encountered year-round in warmer parts, particularly in the south of its range, the Cloudless Sulphur tends to migrate farther north in summer, sometimes in great numbers. These emigrants may produce up to two broods of young, but typically die in fall as temperatures drop. As with many sulphurs, this species is found around clover, alfalfa and leguminous vegetable crops, where its pitcher-shaped eggs are laid. The mature caterpillars may be quite large, perhaps almost two inches long, and are green or yellow with dark bands. They spend much of their time sheltering amongst vegetation within silken tents.

Generally an inhabitant of southern coastal regions, the Great Southern White may be found throughout the year in the warmer parts of its range. However, large numbers migrate northwards along the Atlantic and through the Mississippi Valley in summer, at which time many of the females exhibit a darker coloration. These movements are probably connected to the availability of food, and may be quite dramatic, involving vast aggregations of butterflies flying quite close to the ground. The caterpillars are yellow or green and may be striped, and are found on a wide range of plants.

COMMON/CLOUDED SULPHUR

Scientific name:	*Colias philodice*
Identification:	Pale yellow, both forewings and hindwings bordered with brown or black, less distinctly in females. Small dark spot on each forewing, small orange spot on each hindwing
Wingspan:	2 inches
Habitat/Range:	Open grasslands and clover meadows throughout much of North America. Absent from much of Florida and dense woodland and desert areas
Similar species:	The Alfalfa Butterfly or Orange Sulphur (*Colias eurytheme*) is orange or deep yellow, but otherwise similarly marked

The Common or Clouded Sulphur is a familiar and widespread butterfly, found in a range of open grassy habitats, and it is often seen in groups, gathered at the edges of puddles. The bright green larval caterpillars are usually associated with clover, alfalfa and vegetable crops and can be quite destructive where particularly numerous. It is thought that agriculture has widened the range of this species. The caterpillars generally spend the winter in the pupal stage, transforming into adult butterflies, but several broods of eggs may be laid throughout the year, with the adults emerging during much of the year.

CABBAGE WHITE

Scientific name:	*Pieris rapae*
Identification:	White, with black or dark-gray forward wingtips. One or two spots present on each forewing. Underside yellowish, often mottled with gray
Wingspan:	2 inches
Habitat/Range:	Varied habitats, from open grasslands to urban areas, throughout the US and southern Canada
Similar species:	Similar whites usually lack yellow underside, or have dark veins on underside of hindwings

Amongst the most common and widespread of North American butterflies, the Cabbage White was originally introduced from Europe, and is still sometimes referred to as the European Cabbage White. Its introduction was unintentional, but it has since flourished across a wide range of habitats. As their name might suggest, the larvae of this species are often found feeding on cabbages, but they are also associated with other vegetables, clover and similar plants. Being so numerous, they can prove destructive to crops, and are also often regarded as a pest by gardeners as they feed on the flowers of nasturtiums.

SWALLOWTAILS AND PARNASSIANS

The swallowtails of the family Papilonidae are some of the largest and most beautifully colored of all butterflies, and have distinctive, long "tails", which project backwards from their hindwings. Many are found in more tropical climates, but there are a number of species which inhabit open areas and woodland edges in North America. Of these, the **Black Swallowtail** (*Papilio polyxenes*) is the most widespread, occurring from southern Canada across the US. It attains a wingspan of around four inches, and is primarily black, with red, blue and yellow markings. It prefers open habitats and is a regular visitor to gardens, where the caterpillars may become a pest, feeding on carrots and other vegetables. The **Zebra Swallowtail** (*Eurytides marcellus*) grows to a comparable size, but is known as a "kite swallowtail" because of its particularly long "tails". It is confined to the eastern US and parts of Ontario, and is often found close to water in woodland or marshes, usually where pawpaw grows. Its name is derived from its black and white coloring, and it has red and blue spots close to the base of its "tails". Amongst the most common swallowtails are the **Eastern Tiger Swallowtail** (*Papilio glaucus*) and the **Western Tiger Swallowtail** (*Papilio*

rutulus). The Eastern Tiger Swallowtail occurs from the Gulf of Mexico, northwards east of the Rocky Mountains to Alaska, whilst the Western Tiger Swallowtail is found from British Columbia, south to Colorado, New Mexico and California. Both are often found close to water and are similarly colored with black and yellow markings, but the eastern species is usually slightly larger, with a wingspan up to about five inches, and it has red or orange spots on the hindwings. These species are known to hybridize however.

The parnassians are grouped with the swallowtail butterflies, but lack the distinctive "tails" of their close relatives. They are however generally large and similar in appearance, with broad hind and forewings. Whilst many swallowtails are tropical, or at least prefer more temperate habitats, the **Phoebus Parnassian** (*Parnassius phoebus*) is a common inhabitant of mountainous areas and tundra, although it is most likely to be seen in warm weather. The adults mate soon after emerging, and in many parnassians, the females develop a sphragis which prevents further implantation. The caterpillars feed on alpine plants, and make small silken cocoons on the ground.

Below: A newly emerged Black Swallowtail

Above: The Eastern Tiger Swallowtail

BROWN ELFIN

Scientific name:	*Callophrys augustinus*
Identification:	Brown to gray, hindwings often red-brown. Wing edges usually marked with black, or black and white
Wingspan:	1 inch
Habitat/Range:	Varied; open woodland, forest edges, marshes, foothills and mountainous areas from Canada, south to Virginia, New Mexico and California
Similar species:	The Pine Elfin (*Callophrys niphon*) is heavily marked below, with dark checks and scallops

The Brown Elfin is closely related to the coppers and hairstreaks, and belongs to a group commonly known as the gossamer-winged butterflies. This species tends to be quite dull in adulthood, but the caterpillars go through various color stages as they grow, gradually turning from a dark yellow-green, through to a vivid green, finally developing red and yellow stripes. They feed on a variety of flowering and fruit-bearing plants, consuming flowers, buds, seed-pods and fruits. The adult butterflies are typically abroad from spring to summer, usually for a shorter period in the east than in western parts of their range.

AMERICAN COPPER ▲

Scientific name:	*Lycaena phlaeas*
Identification:	Bright orange forewings with dark spots and edges. The hindwings are brown with orange edges above and an orange band below
Wingspan:	1 inch
Habitat/Range:	Lowland meadows and alpine areas in Canada and the northern US, south to parts of Florida and California
Similar species:	The Smartweed Copper (*Lycaena Gorgon*) is very similar below, but purple above

The American Copper is most common in northern and eastern parts of North America, occurring in low-lying open grasslands. There is also an alpine form, however, which is more common in the west, and which inhabits mountainous areas, often being found on rocky slopes above the tree line. The adults are usually abroad from spring to fall, and lowland forms may reproduce several times in that period. Alpine and arctic inhabitants however, tend to produce one brood of young in summer. The caterpillars develop on sorrel, dock and other weedy plants, spending the winter in the pupal chrysalis.

GRAY HAIRSTREAK

Scientific name:	*Strymon melinus*
Identification:	Gray-brown above, with two orange or red spots close to the rear edge of the hindwings. Paler below. Two "tails" extend from hindwings
Wingspan:	1–1½ inches
Habitat/Range:	Widespread through a variety of open habitats in Canada and the US
Similar species:	The Coral Hairstreak (*Satyrium titus*) lacks "tails" on its hindwings

The Gray Hairstreak is the most abundant and wide-ranging of all the hairstreak butterflies in North America, a fact no doubt due in part to the wide variety of plants upon which the caterpillars of this species are able to feed, including commercial crops such as cotton. This species is sometimes considered a pest for this reason, and it is also thought to pose a threat to other hairstreaks due to hybridization. Notably, it breeds with the Avalon Hairstreak, on the Californian islands.

RED ADMIRAL

Scientific name:	*Vanessa atalanta*
Identification:	Dark brown or black with white spots on wingtips and orange-red bars across forewings and hindwing edges
Wingspan:	1½–2½ inches
Habitat/Range:	Widespread in parks, gardens, meadows, forest edges and shorelines from Canada to Central America
Similar species:	Unmistakable

A common and easily identifiable species, the Red Admiral, like the Painted Lady, is a year-round inhabitant of warm, southwestern states that migrates northwards in spring and summer, dispersing throughout North America. In mild conditions, the adults may remain in northern parts, and juveniles sometimes overwinter in their pupal stage, but otherwise, adults will often return south. The adults feed on fruit and the nectar of various flowers, whilst the spiny caterpillars are most commonly found on nettles.

PAINTED LADY ▲

Scientific name:	*Vanessa cardui*
Identification:	Orange, with dark forewing edges and wingtips, with white spots. Rear edge of hindwing is marked with small blue and black spots. The underside is dusky pink, with an olive, black, and white pattern
Wingspan:	2–2½ inches
Habitat/Range:	Extremely varied; from meadows, mountains and gardens to desert areas, throughout North America
Similar species:	The American Painted Lady (*Vanessa virginiensis*) has two large eyespots on the underside of its wings

The Painted Lady is a member of a large group known as the brush-footed butterflies. These are so-called due to their short, hairy front legs which are used for tasting. It is a widespread species across much of the world, but is not highly tolerant of cold conditions. For this reason, it is absent from most of the US in winter, but migrates northwards in summer from warm, southern parts, including Mexico, extending its range well into Canada. The adults feed on the nectar of various flowering plants, whilst the caterpillars are commonly found on thistles.

COMMON BUCKEYE

Scientific name:	*Junonia coenia*
Identification:	Dark brown, with two orange bars and a large eyespot on each forewing. Two eyespots are present on each hindwing, one larger than the other. Paler underside
Wingspan:	2–2½ inches
Habitat/Range:	Meadows, desert scrub and beaches in the southern US, migrating north to Oregon, New England and southern Canada in summer
Similar species:	The Dark Buckeye (*Junonia nigrosuffusa*) is almost black above

Easily recognizable due to its large eyespots, which somewhat resemble those found on the tail feathers of peacocks, the Common Buckeye is a year-round resident of warmer, southern states in the US. It migrates seasonally throughout much of North America in summer, sometimes returning south in fall, particularly along the Atlantic coast. The caterpillars are usually dark green with orange or yellowish markings and are found on a variety of plants, but especially plantain. There remains on-going discussion concerning the classification of this species, which is sometimes given the scientific names *Precis lavinia* or *Precis coenia*.

VICEROY ▲

Scientific name:	*Limenitis archippus*
Identification:	Orange, with pronounced black veins, white-spotted wingtips and white dashes around wing edges
Wingspan:	2½–3 inches
Habitat/Range:	Meadows, marshland and woodland, from southern Canada throughout most of the US. Absent from much of the Pacific coast
Similar species:	The Monarch (*Danaus plexippus*) grows larger and has spots rather than dashes on wing margins

The Viceroy is a mimic, being almost identical to the Monarch butterfly, an adaptation which protects it from predation by many birds. Monarch caterpillars feed on milkweed, and the adults remain distasteful if eaten. Viceroy caterpillars, however, are usually found on willow, oak and fruit trees. Even in the juvenile stages, this species uses its appearance as a defense. The caterpillars are generally well camouflaged and have horned foreparts, whilst the pupal chrysalis closely resembles a bird dropping. Adults in flight are distinctive, flying slowly and gliding between wing beats.

Zebra Heliconian

Scientific name:	*Heliconius charitonius*
Identification:	Wide, narrow wings, black with thin, yellow bands
Wingspan:	3–3½ inches
Habitat/Range:	Sub-tropical forests and thickets, from Texas to Florida and South Carolina, sometimes occurring in southern California and parts of the Great Plains
Similar species:	Unmistakable

The Zebra Heliconian is boldly patterned with black and yellow warning colors, which indicate to potential predators that it is poisonous. The caterpillars of this species grow and feed upon the poisonous flowers of passion vines and, as with the larva of some other butterflies, retain the ingested toxins into adulthood, as a deterrent to birds and other predators. The caterpillars themselves are also unappetizing and somewhat striking, possessing rows of black spines along their sides. The adults feed on pollen during the day and may be observed flying slowly in southern woodland areas, or gathering in the evenings at communal roosts.

MONARCH

Scientific name:	*Danaus plexippus*
Identification:	Large, bright orange with black veins. Wing margins are marked with white spots. Larger orange and white spots are present on the front wingtips
Wingspan:	3½–4 inches
Habitat/Range:	Varied; weedy meadows, marshes, forests, mountains and urban areas, particularly found where milkweed is present. Occurs from southern Canada, south through the US to Mexico
Similar species:	The Viceroy is usually smaller, and has dark lines across its hindwings

The Monarch is a familiar butterfly, which is found throughout much of North America, and it is particularly well known for the mass migrations that it undertakes. It typically overwinters in California and further south in Mexico, usually sheltering in mountain forests, feeding on nectar on warm days. These roosts may be extensive, containing millions of butterflies. As spring arrives, the Monarchs head northwards, breeding and laying their eggs on milkweed plants. The caterpillars develop and pupate, and the newly emergent adults migrate south in the fall, returning to the roosting sites of their parents. As the Monarch caterpillars feed on milkweed, most bird species find them, and the adult butterflies, poisonous and have learned not to eat them.

QUEEN ▲

Scientific name:	*Danaus gilippus*
Identification:	Large, reddish-brown with black-edged wings, speckled with white spots. Black veins more clearly visible on underside of wings
Wingspan:	3–3½ inches
Habitat/Range:	Deserts, grasslands and coastal areas, particularly where milkweeds are present. Usually restricted to the southern US
Similar species:	The Monarch is larger, more orange than brown, and has more prominently defined veins

Like the Monarch, the Queen is sometimes commonly referred to as a "milkweed butterfly", as the caterpillars feed almost exclusively on poisonous milkweed plants. They absorb these toxins without coming to harm, but are then poisonous to most predators. The adult butterflies also remain toxic. Unlike Monarchs, however, the Queen does not undertake extensive migrations, though it is known to move northwards when conditions allow, and has been found as far north as Utah, Kansas and Nebraska.

GREAT SPANGLED FRITILLARY

Scientific name:	*Speyeria cybele*
Identification:	Large, orange butterfly with black markings, paler underside with silver spotting. Female typically darker
Wingspan:	3–3½ inches
Habitat/Range:	Meadows and open woodlands across southern Canada, south as far as Georgia, New Mexico and central California
Similar species:	Western individuals are sometimes classified as a separate species, the Leto Fritillary (*Speyeria cybele leto*)

A common fritillary in the eastern US, the Great Spangled Fritillary is much more scarce in the west, and some butterfly experts, or lepidopterists as they are known, regard these western examples as a different species, or perhaps subspecies. The adults emerge to fly and mate in June or July, with females laying their eggs in late summer or early fall, usually on violets. The spiny caterpillars spend the winter feeding at night before entering the pupal stage, to emerge as butterflies the following summer. Adult Great Spangled Fritillaries are often found feeding on thistles.

EASTERN TAILED-BLUE

Scientific name:	*Everes comyntas*
Identification:	Small, silvery-blue butterfly with dark wing margin edged with white. Thin "tails" are present on the hindwings, preceded by small orange and black spots. Female is more gray or brown
Wingspan:	1 inch
Habitat/Range:	Open meadows and gardens from southern Canada through the US, south to Mexico and beyond
Similar species:	The Western Tailed-blue (*Everes amyntula*) is usually slightly larger

In spite of its name, the Eastern Tailed-blue is actually found from southern Canada, across the US, from the Atlantic to the Pacific. It is however more common east of the Rocky Mountains, where it is amongst the most numerous of butterflies. The adults may be encountered from spring through to late summer or fall, during which time they may reproduce on successive occasions. Females that emerge earlier in the year tend to be more vividly colored than those appearing in late summer. The eggs and larvae develop on the flowers of clover or leguminous vegetable crops, and the caterpillars may overwinter within bean pods.

COMMON WOOD-NYMPH ▼

Scientific name:	*Cercyonis pegala*
Identification:	Light to dark brown, with prominent dark veins and large eyespots on forewings, often smaller, more numerous eyespots on hindwings, particularly below
Wingspan:	2–3 inches
Habitat/Range:	Woodland, meadows and marshes across most of North America, but absent from parts of the south and the Pacific northwest
Similar species:	The Great Basin Wood Nymph (*Cercyonis sthenele*), which occurs in the western US, is usually smaller

Although the Common Wood-nymph and other closely related species may visit flowers to obtain nectar, they often have a more varied taste, feeding on rotting fruit, the sap from trees or even animal droppings. The caterpillars, however, typically feed on grasses. The females produce one brood of larvae each year, which hibernate during the winter and pupate in spring or early summer. The adult butterflies are large, but often well camouflaged when at rest, and are probably best recognized by their slow, somewhat erratic flight.

LEAST SKIPPER/SKIPPERLING

Scientific name:	*Ancyloxypha numitor*
Identification:	Small, moth-like, orange, gold and black butterfly with hooked antennae
Wingspan:	$\frac{3}{4}$–1 inch
Habitat/Range:	Moist meadows, marshes and watercourses in southern Canada and the eastern US to the edge of the Rocky Mountains in the west
Similar species:	The Hobomok Skipper (*Poanes hobomok*) is similarly colored, but may attain a wingspan of almost two inches

The Least Skipper or Skipperling is abundant in much of the east, and is most commonly encountered in damp habitats close to water. Like other skippers it flies relatively weakly, "skipping" amongst long grasses as it seeks out nectar from flowers growing close to the ground. Its yellow eggs are laid amongst grasses and sedges, often at the edge of a pool or stream, and are also frequently found on rice crops. Several broods may be produced each year from spring through to late summer or fall, depending on location.

POLYPHEMUS MOTH ▲ CECROPIA MOTH

Scientific name:	*Antheraea polyphemus*
Identification:	Large, sandy-colored moth with an eyespot on each wing. Those on the hindwings are larger, and edged with black and blue. Large, feathery antennae
Wingspan:	4–6 inches
Habitat/Range:	Varied; forests, deserts and suburban areas throughout much of North America, east of the Rocky Mountains
Similar species:	Unmistakable

Scientific name:	*Hyalophora cecropia*
Identification:	Large, gray-brown wings with red and white crescents and bands. The body is also red and white
Wingspan:	$4\frac{1}{2}$–6 inches
Habitat/Range:	Open woodland and suburban areas. Found in southern Canada and east of the Rocky Mountains in the US
Similar species:	Unmistakable due to their large size and distinctive markings

Named after the one-eyed giant of Greek legend, the Polyphemus Moth is a large distinctive species, common throughout the east in a range of habitats. The adults do not feed, but the caterpillars may be found on a wide variety of plants and trees, and are also easily recognizable. They may grow to over three inches long, and are plump and bright green in color, with red and gray tubercles. The caterpillars of this, and several related species, are known as giant silkworms, and when mature they spin large silken cocoons in which they pupate.

Along with the Polyphemus Moth, the Cecropia Moth is amongst the largest of North American moths, and both species belong to the family *Saturnidae*. They fly on summer nights, and do not feed, surviving long enough only to reproduce. The female Cecropia Moth may produce over one hundred eggs, typically laying them on the undersides of leaves. The caterpillars are tiny upon hatching, but with successive molts may reach around four inches in length. They are usually found in trees, particularly fruit trees, where they overwinter in their cocoons, emerging in spring or summer as adult moths.

REGAL MOTH

Scientific name:	*Citheronia regalis*
Identification:	Large orange body, gray forewings with orange veins and yellow spots. The hindwings are mostly orange with some yellow markings
Wingspan:	5 inches
Habitat/Range:	Deciduous forests and suburban areas in the eastern US from Missouri to Massachusetts, south to Texas and central Florida
Similar species:	Unmistakable

The Regal Moth is a saturnid species, and is one of the largest and most spectacular North American moths. Like most moths, it is nocturnal and not often seen, but it may be attracted to house or street lights in suburban areas. The larva of this species is known as the Hickory Horned Devil due to its fierce appearance, and it typically inhabits hickory and walnut trees. It is most likely to be seen on the ground when it descends from the branches in order to find a suitable spot to make its cocoon. These caterpillars burrow into soft soil where they hibernate in the pupal stage for the winter months.

LUNA MOTH

Scientific name:	*Actias luna*
Identification:	Large white body, pale green wings with yellow eyespots. The forewings have a brown or purple leading edge, and long "tails" are present on the hindwings
Wingspan:	3–4½ inches
Habitat/Range:	Broadleaf woodlands in southern Canada and the eastern US
Similar species:	Unmistakable

A particularly beautiful and distinctive species, the Luna Moth is easily recognised by the long "tails" which trail from its hindwings. It is a nocturnal forest inhabitant, and like other saturnid moths is quite shortlived and so is seldom seen. Populations of this species are also thought to suffer badly from the use of pesticides, but the Luna Moth is not currently classified as endangered. Like the Regal Moth, its caterpillars are most commonly associated with hickory and walnut trees, and they usually come down from trees to pupate amongst leaf-litter on the ground.

GYPSY/TUSSOCK MOTH   ▼   ORNATE TIGER MOTH

Scientific name:	*Lymantria dispar*
Identification:	Male is speckled brown or gray, whilst females are white with brown markings
Wingspan:	1–2¾ inches (female larger than male)
Habitat/Range:	Forest habitats from southern Canada into the northeastern US, but introduced more widely
Similar species:	The Spotted Tussock Moth (*Lophocampa maculata*) has yellow and brown forewings

Scientific name:	*Apantesis ornata*
Identification:	Black forewings and body crossed with ivory stripes. Hindwings pinkish-orange with black spots
Wingspan:	1–1½ inches
Habitat/Range:	Meadows, woodland edges and suburbs along the Pacific coast and surrounding areas
Similar species:	The Painted Tiger Moth (*Arachnis picta*), found in southwestern states, is somewhat paler

The Gypsy Moth, sometimes referred to as a Tussock Moth, was inadvertently introduced to North America in the nineteenth century and has since proved to be a major pest. Although the females are flightless and produce only one brood of larvae each year, they may each lay several hundred eggs, depositing them amongst leaf-litter or on the bark of trees such as apple, cherry, pine, oak and willow. When the caterpillars hatch in spring they begin feeding on leaves, and may be so numerous as to strip an area of woodland bare of foliage by the time they are ready to pupate.

The tiger moths are a large group, with species occurring throughout North America. Many are quite similar in appearance, and those of the genus *Apantesis* are often quite boldly colored and patterned, with "stained-glass" markings on the forewings. Whilst these moths are often regarded as amongst the most beautiful, their appearance is actually a defense against birds and other predators, warning that they contain chemicals which make them unpleasant to eat. The caterpillars of the Ornate Tiger Moth and related species, are commonly known as woolly bears, and are usually brown or black and particularly hairy. They feed on a variety of grasses and other plants.

White-lined Sphinx

Scientific name:	*Hyles lineata*
Identification:	Forewings brown with a tan band and white veins. Hindwings pink with dark bands. Body is brown with white stripes and paired black and white spots
Wingspan:	2½–3½ inches
Habitat/Range:	Varied open habitats, from deserts to meadows and gardens. Occurs throughout the US to southern Canada
Similar species:	The white veins on the forewings distinguish this species from other sphinx moths

Hummingbird Clearwing ▲

Scientific name:	*Hemaris thysbe*
Identification:	Large, furry, olive-green and plum or rust-red body, with a yellow tail horn. Wings mainly transparent with red-brown border
Wingspan:	1½–2½ inches
Habitat/Range:	Forest edges, meadows and gardens. Found from Alaska, through much of Canada, south to Oregon in the west, and throughout the eastern US to the Gulf
Similar species:	The Bumblebee Moth (*Hemaris diffinus*) also has clear wings, but resembles a bee in its coloration

The White-lined Sphinx is closely related to the Hummingbird Clearwing, and exhibits similar tendencies, hovering at flowers in order to feed upon nectar. However, whilst this species may be seen during the afternoon, it is more commonly abroad at dusk or during the night, and it is often attracted to lighted windows. It is an abundant and widespread moth, resident for much of the year in warmer, southern states, but found across the US and parts of Canada in summer. In arid regions it is often seen after rain. The female typically produces two broods of larvae each year, and the caterpillars may be found on a wide range of plants, including flowers and vegetable crops. They pupate below ground, burrowing into loose soil.

Whereas some adult moths do not feed, the sphinx or hawk moths tend to have a long proboscis which they use to drink nectar from flowers. The Hummingbird Clearwing is such a species, and it is most often encountered by day, hovering much like a hummingbird whilst feeding at flowers. The latter part of its common name is derived from the large transparent patches on its wings. These are initially covered in dark scales like those present on the wing margins, but they fall off during early flights. The adults are found throughout summer and typically lay their eggs beneath the leaves of honeysuckle or related plants. The caterpillars pupate on the ground, often amongst leaf-litter.

COMMON WHITETAIL

Scientific name:	*Libellula Lydia*
Identification:	Broad, slightly flattened abdomen, white in males, brown with yellow spots in females. Dark bands across wings
Length:	1½–2 inches
Wingspan:	2½–3 inches
Habitat/Range:	Found close to ponds, rivers and streams from southern Canada, throughout the US
Similar species:	The Western Widow (*Libellula forensis*) is a very similar species, but is bluish rather than white

The Common Whitetail is not particularly large, but it has a much broader abdomen than many species, and the brilliant-white male is particularly distinctive. The male Whitetail is territorial and flies strongly, darting rapidly to pluck small insects from the air, or to chase away other males. Following mating, the female flies over a pond or stream, repeatedly breaking the surface of the water with the end of her abdomen to deposit up to fifty eggs. The larvae hatch within a week and usually dwell amongst the detritus on the bottom, preying on small aquatic insects.

HALLOWEEN PENNANT

Scientific name:	*Celithemis eponina*
Identification:	Slender, yellow-brown head and body, yellow wings with brown markings
Length:	1½ inches
Wingspan:	2¾–3 inches
Habitat/Range:	Marshes and pond edges throughout much of the eastern US and Canada
Similar species:	The Biddie (*Cordulegaster dorsalis*) may be similarly marked on the abdomen, but has clear wings and is found in the west

The Halloween Pennant is a typical dragonfly, with two pairs of wings of approximately equal size which are held outwards from the body when the insect is at rest. It is typically encountered close to densely vegetated ponds, which it inhabits as a larva or nymph, but it has a relatively weak, fluttering flight and may be carried elsewhere by the wind. In summer, the aquatic nymphs crawl out of the water onto vegetation, where they shed their skin and transform into winged adults. Like other dragonflies, this species preys on small flying insects which it usually captures in mid-air.

RED SKIMMER

Scientific name:	*Libellula saturate*
Identification:	Reddish-brown, including body, legs and veins of wings
Length:	1–2½ inches
Wingspan:	3½–3¾ inches
Habitat/Range:	Small pools, streams and springs. Occurs from southern California to Kansas, north to Idaho, Wyoming and Montana
Similar species:	The Neon Skimmer (*Libellula croceipennis*) is brighter, often more pink than red, with a slightly wider body

Sometimes called the Flame Skimmer, this fiery colored dragonfly is most abundant in the southwestern US, around warm, sometimes stagnant ponds and pools. In northern parts of its range, however, it is often associated with hot springs, particularly in Idaho. Like the Common Whitetail, males establish territories during the breeding season in summer, and upon finding a mate, will often carry the female about in flight. After mating, the female is released, but the male may accompany her as she deposits her eggs in water. The larvae are quite large and stocky, and may feed on tadpoles and fish fry as well as insects.

COMMON GREEN DARTER/ DARNER ▼

Scientific name:	*Anax junius*
Identification:	Large, with a bright green head and thorax, blue or purplish abdomen and clear wings
Length:	3 inches
Wingspan:	4½ inches
Habitat/Range:	Marshes, vegetated ponds, lakes and slow-flowing streams. Found throughout North America
Similar species:	The Heroic Darner (*Epiaeschna heros*) may exhibit similar colors, but is larger with a wingspan up to 5 inches

The Common Green Darter, or Green Darner, as it is also known, is one of the largest commonly seen dragonflies in North America, and although it is more common in the east, it is widespread, ranging from coast to coast. The adults are powerful fliers, and are often seen hunting for mosquitoes or other flying insects at the edges of ponds and lakes. Males are also territorial and will chase other males of their species during the breeding season. Following mating, females deposit their eggs singly into the stems of aquatic plants. The nymphs live an aquatic existence for around a year, feeding on insects, small fish and tadpoles, before emerging to transform in spring or summer.

EBONY JEWELWING

Scientific name:	*Calopteryx maculata*
Identification:	Male has metallic green body and black wings, female is brown with a white spot on each forewing
Length:	1½–1¾ inches
Wingspan:	2–3 inches
Habitat/Range:	Forest streams, mainly in the east, from southern Canada to Florida and Texas
Similar species:	The wings of the male River Jewelwing (*Calopteryx aequabilis*) are black only at the tips

The Ebony Jewelwing is a damselfly, a group which can be distinguished from dragonflies by their relative slenderness and habit of resting with their wings folded above the abdomen. Damselflies also tend to fly less directly, with a more fluttering flight pattern. Otherwise, the two groups are much alike. The Ebony Jewelwing is usually found in shady areas along slow-moving streams where it moves amongst vegetation in search of its insect prey. As in dragonflies, the larval nymphs, or naiads, as they are also known, are wingless, aquatic creatures which feed on small insects.

CIVIL BLUET

Scientific name:	*Enallagma civile*
Identification:	Bright blue with black markings on abdomen and transparent wings
Length:	1–1¼ inches
Wingspan:	1¼–1½ inches
Habitat/Range:	Close to still or slow-moving water, often with abundant vegetation. Found throughout much of North America
Similar species:	The Northern Bluet (*Enallagma cyathigerum*) is more robust

The Civil Bluet, also known as the Familiar Bluet, is one of the most common and widespread of North American damselflies, and one of a large group of small, mainly blue species. The females however generally exhibit duller coloration, being gray to brown. The Civil Bluet is usually encountered along sandy, vegetated shores where it hunts for small flying insects. The adults normally fly from May to October, and breeding pairs may be seen on the wing in tandem throughout the summer months. The female deposits her eggs inside soft-stemmed aquatic plants, and they hatch into predatory aquatic larvae.

WHIRLIGIG BEETLE ▼

Scientific name:	*Gyrinus limbatus*
Identification:	Small, black, oval-shaped aquatic beetle
Length:	⅛–¼ inch
Habitat/Range:	Ponds, lakes and streams in eastern North America
Similar species:	Different species of Whirligig Beetle are virtually impossible to distinguish in the field, being identified by varying characteristics of the male sexual organs

Whirligig Beetles are generally encountered in groups, in quiet waters close to the shore, where they move about at the water's surface. Their name is derived from their defensive behavior, as they cluster together tightly, moving rapidly in circles when disturbed. As a further defensive measure, they also produce toxic secretions, which may deter such predators as fish, amphibians, birds and mammals. Whirligig Beetles feed on small aquatic insects and their larvae, as well as terrestrial insects which fall into the water. They are capable of flight, and overwinter on land amongst leaf-litter, returning to water in spring in order to breed.

COMMON BACKSWIMMER

Scientific name:	*Notonecta undulata*
Identification:	Elongated body with a keeled back, usually greenish-yellow and red. Very long, oar-like hindlegs
Length:	¼–½ inch
Habitat/Range:	Weedy lakes, ponds and quiet streams. Widespread in North America
Similar species:	Water boatmen are virtually identical, but swim on their front, however the term is sometimes applied to backswimmers

The Common Backswimmer spends much of its time swimming upside-down at the water's surface, breathing through a tube at the end of its abdomen. However, when disturbed, it may rapidly dive from view. It is mainly a predatory species, catching insects and even tadpoles, but it may consume some aquatic vegetation whilst scavenging at the surface. Backswimmers are also known to bite people from time to time, and should be handled carefully if caught. This species may produce one or two broods of young each year, attaching its eggs to submerged vegetation. The nymphs hatch around three weeks later and, like the adults, they prey on small aquatic insects.

AMERICAN/ELEPHANT STAG BEETLE

Scientific name:	*Lucanus elephas*
Identification:	Large, reddish-brown to black beetle with enlarged mandibles, those of the male being antler-like and perhaps as much as an inch long
Length:	1½–2 inches
Habitat/Range:	Woodland, grassland and suburban areas in the eastern US
Similar species:	The Eastern Hercules Beetle (*Dynastes tityus*) is usually yellowish with dark spots, and has three horn-like projections on the head, the central one being longest

The American Stag Beetle is large and fearsome-looking, but is in fact harmless, and feeds on the sap of leaves and trees. Its "antlers" are used to overturn rival males. The large, white, larval grubs develop in damp forests, usually living in rotting logs or stumps where they grow for a year or more, before typically emerging as winged adults in summer. In wooded areas, the adult American Stag Beetle is also likely to be found around decaying trees, but in suburbs it may be attracted to windows and other sources of artificial light.

JAPANESE BEETLE

Scientific name:	*Popillia japonica*
Identification:	Oval, metallic-green head and body, red-brown elytra, white hair on abdomen and hooked feet
Length:	½ inch
Habitat/Range:	Woods, meadows and gardens throughout North America, but mainly found in the northeastern US
Similar species:	The Hairy Bear Beetle (*Paracotalpa Granicollis*) is a similarly colored, but smaller, very hairy species found in the Pacific Northwest

Another scarab beetle, the Japanese Beetle was accidentally introduced to North America from Asia around 1916, and has since proved to be a major pest. It feeds on over two hundred different plants including trees, vines and many kinds of flowers, consuming leaves, fruits and the flowers themselves. The larvae are also destructive, eating the roots of vegetables, grasses and other plants. They normally pupate below ground in the spring and emerge as adults in the summer. Attempts to control the Japanese Beetle have involved the use of parasitic flies and wasps.

Ten-lined June Beetle

Scientific name:	*Polyphylla decimlineata*
Identification:	Brown with white stripes on wing cases, or elytra. Antennae are clubbed and flattened at the end
Length:	1–1¼ inches
Habitat/Range:	Found in forest habitats throughout the US, but absent from parts of the Midwest
Similar species:	This species can be easily distinguished from related June bugs by its distinctively marked carapace

Essentially a woodland dweller, the Ten-lined June Beetle begins life on the forest floor as a large white grub with a red head. This larva burrows into the ground, where it feeds on roots and other vegetation before entering a pupal stage and emerging as an adult in the summer. The adults fly on warm evenings, feeding on fruit, pine needles and leaves, and are often attracted to house lights. Like the American Stag Beetle, the Ten-lined June Beetle is a scarab beetle, a group characterized by their large size and long, clubbed antennae that often end in fan-like plates.

Common Black Ground Beetle

Scientific name:	*Pterostichus melanarius*
Identification:	Mainly black, slightly elongated with grooved wing cases
Length:	½–¾ inch
Habitat/Range:	Woodland, meadows and gardens throughout Southern Canada and extending southward down both the Atlantic and Pacific coasts
Similar species:	There are many virtually identical black ground beetles

This species is one of many which shares the common name "Common Black Ground Beetle", and it is a typical example, although some may grow much larger. It generally lives amongst leaf-litter or under logs and stones in moist habitats, and may ascend trees or bushes in search of food, but it does not fly. Ground beetles are carnivorous and prey upon smaller beetles, grubs, caterpillars, slugs and other small, soft-bodied invertebrates. They can be useful in controlling pests, but this particular species has been introduced from Europe and its potential impact on native wildlife is not yet fully understood. It does however provide a food source for many birds, rodents, amphibians and reptiles.

TWO-SPOTTED LADY (BIRD/BUG) BEETLE ▲ SIX-SPOTTED GREEN TIGER BEETLE

Scientific name:	*Adalia bipunctata*
Identification:	Small red beetle with a black and white head and thorax, and a black spot on each wing case
Length:	$\frac{1}{8}$–$\frac{1}{4}$ inch
Habitat/Range:	Woodland, meadows and gardens throughout North America
Similar species:	The California Lady Beetle (*Coccinella californica*) lacks spots. Other species are often identified by the number of spots present, such as the Nine-spotted Ladybird Beetle (*Coccinella novemnotata*)

Scientific name:	*Cicindela sexguttata*
Identification:	Iridescent green with white spots on edge of wing cases. Antennae and limbs are long
Length:	$\frac{1}{2}$–$\frac{3}{4}$ inch
Habitat/Range:	Open woodland through much of the eastern US
Similar species:	There are many species of tiger beetle which occur in iridescent colors. Most are found in the western US

Variously referred to as a Lady, Ladybird or Ladybug Beetle, this species is a small, familiar and easily identifiable beetle, beneficial to gardeners due to is consumption of aphids and other small insects which often damage plants. The larvae also feed on aphids, and are elongated, mainly black, with white and yellow spots. They hatch from eggs laid on plant stems or the underside of leaves, and also pupate in such locations. Breeding may take place throughout the year, but in northern parts of its range the Two-spotted Ladybird Beetle can often be found hibernating in houses or other sheltered places, sometimes in large numbers.

The Six-spotted Tiger Beetle is somewhat misnamed, for it usually has around four spots, and in some cases it may have none. The adults are fast moving in both the air and on the ground, and they are voracious predators, hunting small invertebrates such as other beetles, spiders, worms and slugs. The larvae are also carnivorous, and bury themselves in the ground where they wait for passing prey with their jaws exposed. They pupate in these burrows, emerging as flying adults in summertime. Due to their speed, these beetles are difficult to catch, but if they are caught they should be handled with care as they are capable of delivering a painful bite.

BOLL WEEVIL

Scientific name:	*Anthonomus grandis*
Identification:	Gray or brown with light, yellowish hairs, and a long, slender snout from which the antennae extend
Length:	⅛–¼ inch
Habitat/Range:	Found in cotton fields in the southern US
Similar species:	The Rose Weevil (*Rhynchites bicolour*) is about the same size, but is red in color and found mainly on rose bushes

A notorious pest, the Boll Weevil is well known for infesting and decimating cotton crops, but it also attacks related species such as the hollyhock. It originated in Central America, spreading rapidly into and across the southern US where cotton flourished in the nineteenth century. Both adults and larvae feed on cotton, and the female deposits her eggs within the bolls or seedpods of the plant. They are laid singly, but each female may produce up to three hundred eggs, several times a year. The larvae hatch within the seedpods and begin to eat their way from the inside out. The adults feed on the bolls, buds and flowers.

BLOODSUCKING CONENOSE

Scientific name:	*Triatoma sanguisuga*
Identification:	Dark, flattened body with a long, cone-shaped head and a prominent tapering "beak". Each side is marked with six orange spots
Length:	¾–1 inch
Habitat/Range:	Rodent nests and houses, mainly in the south eastern US
Similar species:	The Masked Hunter (*Reduvius personatus*) is narrower, with a wider, more curved proboscis

The Bloodsucking Conenose is an assassin bug, a group of insects named for their nocturnal, predatory behavior. Many assassin bugs prey on other insects, but *Triatoma* species feed on the blood of vertebrates. They are often found in rodent nests, but they also suck blood from humans, living in mattresses and other bedding, and feeding at night. Their bites can be painful, lead to allergic reactions or transmit disease, and they should be handled with care. This species may breed at various times of the year, but take up to three years to reach sexual maturity, passing through various molts as the nymphs transform into adults.

Below: Triatoma protracta

Bee Assassin

Scientific name:	*Apiomerus crassipes*
Identification:	Black and red or orange, flattened, with a long narrow head
Length:	$\frac{1}{4}$–$\frac{3}{4}$ inch
Habitat/Range:	On flowering plants in open woodland, meadows and gardens, most common in the western US
Similar species:	Bloodsucking Conenose tends to be found in Pack Rat nests or human dwellings

As its name suggests, The Bee Assassin feeds on bees, but it also consumes various other flower-visiting insects. The young, red nymphs are primarily ambush hunters, but adults will also follow their quarry from plant to plant. They pounce on their prey, holding it secure with their powerful front legs, and pierce its back with their beak-like mouthparts. As they do so, they inject a chemical which serves both to immobilize and to begin digesting their chosen victim. They then suck out its soft insides. The adults are most commonly encountered in summer, and are often highly visible due to their bright coloration, which also serves to deter predators.

SCARLET-AND-GREEN LEAF HOPPER ▼

Scientific name:	*Graphocephala coccinea*
Identification:	Slender and tapering, with brilliantly striped, turquoise and red thorax and wings. Head and limbs pale yellow
Length:	¼ inch
Habitat/Range:	Meadows and gardens in eastern parts of North America
Similar species:	The coloration of this species is distinct from that of other leaf hoppers

The Scarlet-and-Green Leaf Hopper is a herbivorous bug which feeds on the sap from the leaves and buds of ornamental shrubs such as rhododendrons, azaleas, and other vegetation. The damage they cause may not initially be noticeable, but they prevent the host plant from developing properly and may encourage fungal diseases. Females also lay their eggs within plant stems or buds. The young hatch in spring and the green or yellow nymphs are usually found on the undersides of leaves, transforming into adults by late summer. The adults are capable of flight, but as their name suggests they are more likely to be seen hopping from leaf to leaf.

COMMON EASTERN FIREFLY

Scientific name:	*Photinus pyralis*
Identification:	Head is partially concealed by a rounded plate on the thorax called the pronotum. This is orange in color with a large dark spot. The wing cases are black and edged with yellow
Length:	¾–½ inch
Habitat/Range:	Forests, meadows and gardens throughout the eastern US
Similar species:	The Scintillating Firefly (*Photinus scintillans*) is smaller

Commonly referred to as Lightning Bugs, most fireflies are well known for their ability to produce light, though in some species only the females do so, and others lack light organs altogether. Those that do emit light achieve this feat by combining chemicals within their bodies, and the resultant light is "cold", generating very little heat, which might otherwise damage the insect. This process is known as bioluminescence, and is used by fireflies as a means of communication, particularly during courtship. The males will often flash signals whilst on the wing, with the flightless females responding from amongst vegetation. Eggs are laid in soil and the larvae develop on the ground in damp leaf-litter or under bark. Like the adults, they prey on insects and soft-bodied invertebrates such as slugs and snails.

ANTS AND TERMITES

Ants are closely related to bees and wasps and, like many of these species, live in highly organized communal nests of hundreds, or even thousands of individuals, with different "castes" fulfilling distinct roles within the colony. In most cases the majority of ants are wingless workers, usually sterile females, that collect food, look after and protect the nest, eggs, larvae, and pupae. These ants are often capable of delivering painful bites. Periodically, fertile males and females are produced, that leave the nest to breed and establish new colonies. In many species, these reproductive individuals are winged and mate during swarming flights. Following mating, the males typically die and the females shed their wings, returning to the ground to start new colonies as queens. Ants are generally easy to recognize, and are usually red, brown or black, around $\frac{1}{16}-\frac{1}{4}$ inch long, with a distinctive bead-like pedicel or joint between the thorax and abdomen. However, as many ants are so similar, it can often be difficult to distinguish between individual species, even when considering their habitat and geographical range, or observing their behavior. Some ants even assimilate other species into their colonies, generally introducing them as pupae, which they intend to eat, but accepting those that reach maturity as their own. The **Little Black Ant**

(*Monomorium minimum*) is amongst the most common and widespread of ant species. It ranges throughout most of North America, except for the Pacific Northwest, and it is also one of the most likely to be found in and around homes, collecting morsels of sugary produce and other human foods. The **Harvester Ant** (*Pogonomyrmex rugosus*), by contrast, mainly gathers seeds, which are then stored in the nest. It will also consume dead insects however. This species is found in the southwestern US, and makes its nests in sandy soils. It may be recognized by its large, black head and red abdomen. The (**Black**) **Carpenter Ant** (*Camponotus pennsylvanicus*) is uniformly black, but may be distinguished from the Little Black Ant, and indeed many other species, by its comparatively large size. This ant is heavily built, and may grow to about $\frac{1}{2}$ an inch long. It occurs from southern Canada throughout much of the eastern US and, as its name might suggest, it is typically found living in wood, sometimes in buildings where it can cause extensive damage. It does not feed on timber, but tunnels through it to form its nests. This species often feeds on fruits, nectar and insects, but interestingly, obtains much of its nourishment from "milking" aphids of their honeydew.

Below: The Carpenter Ant

EASTERN SUBTERRANEAN TERMITE

Scientific name:	*Reticulitermes flavipes*
Identification:	Ant-like, but lacking the characteristic "wasp-waist". Workers are white or cream in color, whilst soldiers are slightly larger with an enlarged dark head and strong jaws. Reproductives are black with wings and visible eyes.
Length:	¼ inch
Habitat/Range:	Soil and wood in damp forests, also in buildings. Occurs from southeastern Canada, throughout the eastern US
Similar species:	The Western Subterranean Termite (*Reticulitermes hesperus*) is found along parts of the Pacific coast

In their natural woodland habitat Eastern Subterranean Termites build a network of tunnels, both above and beneath the soil, forming tubes above ground made of earth. They live in huge colonies, sometimes numbering over one million members, and they share a similar social organization to many ants, bees and wasps. They have three castes; workers, soldiers and reproductive individuals, the latter taking the form of kings, queens or alates. Alates are winged individuals that are capable of starting new colonies, whereas kings and queens are flightless, remaining with a colony for life. Most of the individuals in a nest will be workers that tend and feed nymphs, construct and repair the nest, and search for food. The soldiers meanwhile, guard foraging workers and defend the nest against intruders such as ants. Termites eat wood, and are aided in its digestion by a tiny organism that lives inside them. They are beneficial to their habitat in speeding up the decomposition of wood, allowing nutrients to re-enter the soil more quickly, but they also extend their colonies into wooden buildings, and are regarded as being amongst the most destructive insects in North America.

GREEN STINK BUG

Scientific name:	*Acrosternum hilare*
Identification:	Shield-shaped, with a central ridge along the back. Bright green, but often with thin yellow bands along its edges
Length:	$\frac{1}{2}$–$\frac{3}{4}$ inch
Habitat/Range:	Cultivated fields, woodland, meadows and gardens throughout North America
Similar species:	The Red-shouldered Stink Bug (*Thyanta accerra*) has a red stripe across its thorax

Although some stink bugs are predatory, the Green Stink Bug is herbivorous, and can be a major pest to both farmers and gardeners alike. It feeds on leaves, flowers, fruits and seedpods, extracting sap, which can cause plants to deform. Favored host plants include fruit trees, tomato plants, leguminous vegetables and crops such as cotton and corn. It lays its eggs in rows on the underside of leaves, and they hatch in spring. Stink bugs are aptly named as they produce musky secretions when disturbed or handled.

Above: Harlequin Cabbage Bug nymphs

SMALL MILKWEED BUG

Scientific name:	*Lygaeus kalmii*
Identification:	Oval, but elongated. Black and red, with bands forming a red X-shape on the forewings
Length:	$\frac{1}{2}$ inch
Habitat/Range:	Meadows and fields where milkweed is present, throughout North America
Similar species:	The Large Milkweed Bug (*Oncopeltus fasciatus*) may reach almost an inch in length

The Small Milkweed bug feeds on the white sap of the milkweed plant, and as one of a small number of insects which can tolerate its toxins it is a useful ally in controlling the plant. These bugs are commonly found in small groups, usually on the underside of leaves, or on the seedpods, which they pierce with their beak-like mouthparts. Due to their ingestion of milkweed sap, most birds and other predators find them unpleasant to eat, and their bold colors are designed as a warning of this fact. Milkweed bugs are abundant in warm conditions, but during the winter they often take shelter, hibernating in leaf-litter, under logs and stones, or sometimes in houses.

HARLEQUIN CABBAGE BUG

Scientific name:	*Murgantia histrionica*
Identification:	Shield-shaped, with black and red or orange markings
Length:	$\frac{1}{4}$–$\frac{1}{2}$ inch
Habitat/Range:	Cultivated fields, meadows and gardens. Found in the southern US, north to New England and southern Canada in the east
Similar species:	Similar to other stink bugs, but distinctively colored. Milkweed Bugs are more elongated

This stinkbug, also known as the Calico, or Fire Bug, can devastate commercial crop fields in a relatively short period, with just a few individuals able to destroy a plant in a matter of days. The adults and their larvae feed upon the sap of cabbage and related plants, as well as root crops, leguminous vegetables and surrounding vegetation. In warm areas this species may reproduce throughout the year, and in the north of its range, where only one generation is likely, the adults hibernate in winter, to begin feeding again in spring. The larvae also grow quickly, maturing in one to two months.

DIFFERENTIAL GRASSHOPPER

▲ # PERIODICAL CICADA

Scientific name:	*Melanoplus differentialis*
Identification:	Yellow-brown, with black markings and spines on the hindlegs. Antennae short
Length:	1½– 1¾ inches
Habitat/Range:	Woodland and meadows throughout the US and southern Canada
Similar species:	The Meadow Grasshopper (*Chorthippus curtipennis*) has longer antennae and is often found in more marshy habitats

Scientific name:	*Magicicada septendecim*
Identification:	Stocky, black body, large red eyes, and large transparent wings with prominent orange veins
Length:	1¼ inches
Habitat/Range:	Woodlands and meadows in the eastern US
Similar species:	The Dogday Harvestfly (*Tibicen canicularis*) is a large black and green cicada

The Differential Grasshopper is probably the most abundant and widespread of the North American grasshoppers, and is well known as an agricultural pest, often devastating crops where it occurs in large numbers. It also feeds on grasses and fruits, leaping from plant to plant with its long, powerful back legs. Like other grasshoppers, the Differential Grasshopper is also capable of flight, but unlike some species it does not migrate. It is most numerous in summer, when it can be heard "singing" in open grasslands, producing a loud buzzing or chirping sound by rubbing its hind legs against its wings. The female lays around eighty eggs in small clusters, depositing them in soil.

Although sometimes referred to as locusts, these rather unusual insects are in fact more closely related to leafhoppers. They are divided into two main groups, the Thirteen-year and Seventeen-year Cicadas, each consisting of three species which take either thirteen or seventeen years to reach maturity. However, certain broods have been known to switch life cycles. This species, *Magicicada septendecim*, usually remains as a nymph for seventeen years, living underground, before climbing a tree to shed its skin and emerge as an adult, often with large numbers of insects transforming simultaneously. The males produce a loud, distinctive, buzzing song.

CAROLINA LOCUST

Scientific name:	*Dissosteira Carolina*
Identification:	Gray-brown to tan, with black hindwings which have wide yellow margins. Antennae short
Length:	1½–2 inches
Habitat/Range:	Dry, grassy fields and roadsides throughout Canada and the US
Similar species:	The Long-winged Locust (*Dissosteira longipennis*), is usually yellowish, and has much narrower borders on the hindwings

The Carolina Locust is widespread, but most often found in sandy or dusty habitats where its coloration provides the best camouflage. It feeds on a range of vegetation, including grasses, and sometimes also consumes leguminous vegetables, but it is somewhat less destructive than many closely related species. The Carolina Locust emits sound only during flight, rather than when at rest as many grasshoppers do, producing a whirring drone followed by fluttering, as it hovers from one place to another. It deposits its eggs in soft earth, laying masses which may contain up to seventy eggs.

FORK-TAILED BUSH KATYDID

Scientific name:	*Scudderia furcata*
Identification:	Green overall, with long legs and antennae, and long, narrow wings which extend well beyond the abdomen
Length:	2 inches
Habitat/Range:	Woodland and forested areas throughout North America
Similar species:	The True Katydid (*Pterophylla camellifolia*) has large, rounded, leaf-like wings

Closely related to grasshoppers, locusts and crickets, the Fork-tailed Bush Katydid can be distinguished by its extremely long back legs, extensive, thread-like antennae and long wings. The male also has a pair of forked claspers at the end of the abdomen. However, this species is well camouflaged amongst the trees and shrubs in which it lives, and is perhaps more likely to be heard than it is seen, particularly during the breeding season. The males produce a loud and somewhat rasping call, which females may reply to with a series of chirps. Following mating, eggs are laid on the underside of leaves or branches.

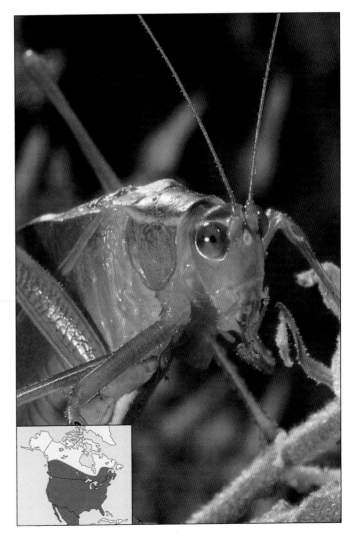

PRAYING MANTIS

Scientific name:	*Mantis religiosa*
Identification:	Elongated, green, or light brown body, with wings reaching beyond the abdomen. Forelegs enlarged with a white, black-ringed spot beneath. Head triangular with large eyes
Length:	2–2½ inches
Habitat/Range:	Meadows and gardens in southeastern Canada and the eastern US
Similar species:	The Carolina Mantis (*Stagmomantis carolina*) lacks spots below forelegs

Fearsome-looking, but harmless to humans, the Praying Mantis takes its name from the way in which it holds its two front legs together, as if in prayer. These are specially adapted for grasping and holding onto prey. This species eats various smaller insects such as butterflies, moths and their caterpillars, and may be a useful ally to the gardener in controlling herbivorous pests. However, many mantids are also cannibalistic, with the female typically consuming the male following mating. Eggs are laid on the branches of shrubs in fall and overwinter, with the nymphs emerging in spring. This species is non-native, and sometimes referred to as the European Praying Mantis, having been accidentally introduced from Europe in the nineteenth century.

NORTHERN MOLE CRICKET

Scientific name:	*Gryllotalpa hexadactyla*
Identification:	Brown and hairy, with an enlarged head and large, spade-like forelegs
Length:	$\frac{3}{4}$–$1\frac{1}{2}$ inches
Habitat/Range:	Meadows and prairies, often close to water. Found from Nebraska to Ontario, south to Texas and Florida
Similar species:	The large Jerusalem Cricket (*Stenopelmatus fuscus*) is wingless, and typically found in the west

A large, distinctive species, the Northern Mole Cricket is however, seldom seen. As its name suggests, it is a mainly subterranean, burrowing insect, although it can fly and is sometimes attracted to house lights. It forms tunnels in soft, moist soil using its powerful forelegs, and the females excavate an egg chamber when breeding in early summer. This is typically positioned close to plant roots, upon which both the adults and nymphs feed. The female remains with her brood until some time after hatching, which usually occurs in June or July. Although its feeding habits may at times damage crops, trees and other vegetation, the Northern Mole Cricket is not considered to be a serious pest.

FIELD CRICKET ▼

Scientific name:	*Gryllus pennsylvanicus*
Identification:	Black or brown, with long antennae. Tail-like cerci extend from the tip of the abdomen
Length:	$\frac{1}{2}$–1 inch
Habitat/Range:	Undergrowth in meadows and also in houses. Found throughout North America
Similar species:	The Snowy Tree Cricket (*Oecanthus fultoni*) is pale green and more elongated

The most common and widespread cricket in North America, the Field Cricket, as its name suggests, is usually found in grassy habitats, either dwelling on the ground or in trees and bushes. However, as temperatures drop in fall, this species often seeks warmth in human homes. At this time it is often most numerous, active and vocal, as it reaches maturity and breeds. The females lay their eggs in soil or decomposing wood, and the eggs hatch in spring. Following several molts, the juveniles emerge as adults around three months later. Their song is a series of high pitched chirps, or a sustained trilling when breeding. The Field Cricket is omnivorous, feeding on plant material, small insects and carrion.

AMERICAN COCKROACH

Scientific name:	*Periplaneta americana*
Identification:	Light brown or reddish, with a yellow thorax. Flattened body, and long antennae
Length:	2 inches
Habitat/Range:	Moist vegetation, wall cavities, sewers and basements. Occurs mainly in the southern US, but introduced in the far north
Similar species:	The more widespread Oriental Cockroach (*Blatta orientalis*) is smaller, darker and more rounded

Although cockroaches are known to infest houses and other buildings, the American Cockroach is quite slow to reach maturity, taking about a year, and so tends not to be present in such large numbers as some species of cockroach. Adult females may, however, produce over one hundred offspring throughout their lifetime, which is usually a further year. They lay around twelve eggs at a time, contained within an egg-case, which is carried on the females' abdomen for one or two days, before being deposited in a dark, secluded location. The American Cockroach feeds at night, consuming human foodstuffs and decaying plant or animal matter. The adults are capable of flight and may be attracted to artificial lights.

EUROPEAN EARWIG

Scientific name:	*Forficula auricularia*
Identification:	Brown or black, with an elongated abdomen which terminates in a pair of yellowish forcep-like spines or cerci
Length:	$\frac{1}{2}$–$\frac{3}{4}$ inch
Habitat/Range:	Cultivated fields, meadows, gardens and buildings. Found across much of Canada, the eastern US and parts of the west
Similar species:	The native Spine-tailed Earwig (*Doru aculeatum*) has dark cerci and is found mainly in marshy habitats

Inadvertently introduced to North America around 1900, the European Earwig has become something of a pest in some areas. It may damage crops, fruits and flowers, and at times be found in large colonies in houses, but it is generally solitary. Despite being potentially destructive, in addition to vegetation, this species also feeds on small insects and their larvae, and so can be beneficial. The European Earwig can fly, but very rarely does so; it is more commonly seen in leaf-litter, woodpiles, on shrubs, or in damp places indoors. Breeding takes place in fall, with the females laying around seventy or eighty eggs in loose soil. They then hibernate with the eggs until spring.

Green Lacewing ▲ Ant Lion

Scientific name:	*Chrysopa Carnea*
Identification:	Pale green, with a delicate body, long antennae, golden eyes and large, transparent, pale green wings. Becomes more brown in fall
Length:	¾ inch
Habitat/Range:	Deciduous woodland, meadows and gardens throughout North America
Similar species:	Another lacewing species, *Chrysopa downesi*, remains dark green throughout the year, and is found in coniferous forests

Scientific name:	*Brachynemurus Ferox*
Identification:	Elongated body, long transparent wings of almost equal length, and long, clubbed antennae
Length:	1½–1¾ inches
Habitat/Range:	Found close to sandy soils in the southern US
Similar species:	Damselflies are similar, but have shorter antennae which are not clubbed at the ends

Closely related to ant lions, the adult Green Lacewing is a flying insect which feeds on nectar, pollen and the honeydew produced by aphids, whilst its larvae are highly predatory, feeding on aphids, mites, small caterpillars and other small insects and their larvae. As such, they are highly beneficial to gardeners, and are even bred for release in commercial growing environments such as vineyards and greenhouses. The female lays her eggs in spring and summer, attaching them to the underside of leaves. The larvae hatch after a few days and pupate only two or three weeks later within a silken cocoon. The emergent adults then typically disperse in order to seek food.

The Ant Lion is so called due to the predatory nature of its larva, a large-headed, oval-shaped insect with huge jaws. It digs a circular or conical pit in sandy soil and buries itself at the bottom with only its mouthparts exposed, feeding on small insects such as ants and aphids which fall in. The feeding habits of the adults are not well understood, but it is thought that they may feed on pollen or nectar, if indeed they feed at all. The larvae are commonly referred to as "doodlebugs" due to the trails that they leave in the sand whilst digging their pits, and the traces of their activity are often more conspicuous than the insects themselves. Active only at dusk, the adult Ant Lion is also rarely seen, but it closely resembles a damselfly, with a similarly weak flight, and a habit of resting with its wings held open.

FLIES

Flies belong to a large and fairly diverse group of insects which contains some of the most notorious species, many of which are found close to farmland and human habitations. The **House Fly** (*Musca domestica*), is a common and widespread insect, well known for its potential to transmit disease-causing bacteria and parasitic worms. It feeds on sugary foods and various other, often decaying, organic matter and is frequently found around garbage or sewage where it acquires the pathogens which are then passed on to humans. The House Fly is known to spread such illnesses as typhoid, cholera and tuberculosis. It may grow up to $\frac{1}{2}$ an inch long and has a gray and black striped thorax, and a dark, hairy abdomen and legs. Its mouthparts are designed only for sucking up liquids and it liquefies solid food by regurgitating saliva on to it. The life cycle of this species may be extremely short, with eggs hatching within a day, and the larval and pupal stages being complete in as little as a week. Although the adults might then survive for less than a month, many generations may be produced within a single season. The **Blow Fly** (*Phaenicia Sericata*), more commonly known as the Green Bottle Fly due to its metallic green abdomen, also has

a very short life cycle and multiplies rapidly, with each female capable of producing thousands of eggs in a period of only two to eight weeks. The larvae mature in wounds, carrion or garbage within a matter of days, before pupating in the soil and emerging as adults a few days later. The Blow Fly, like the House Fly, is known to transmit diseases to humans, but it is perhaps more troublesome to poultry, sheep, cattle and other livestock, often laying its eggs in open wounds, which can lead to inflammation and infection. The larval maggots generally only consume decaying matter, but they may occasionally also attack healthy tissue. Unlike those flies with mouthparts capable only of ingesting liquids, the female **Deer Fly** (*Chrysops flavidus*) is a biting insect, although the male of this species feeds mainly on pollen and nectar. The female inflicts a bite on a warm-blooded animal, and then proceeds to drink blood from her victim. They are known to transmit disease, but are perceived to pose less of a threat to humans than House Flies, for example. Deer Flies belong to the family *Tabanidae*, more commonly known as the Horse Flies, and are typically found around livestock, particularly close to water. Eggs are most commonly deposited on aquatic

Below: **The House Fly**

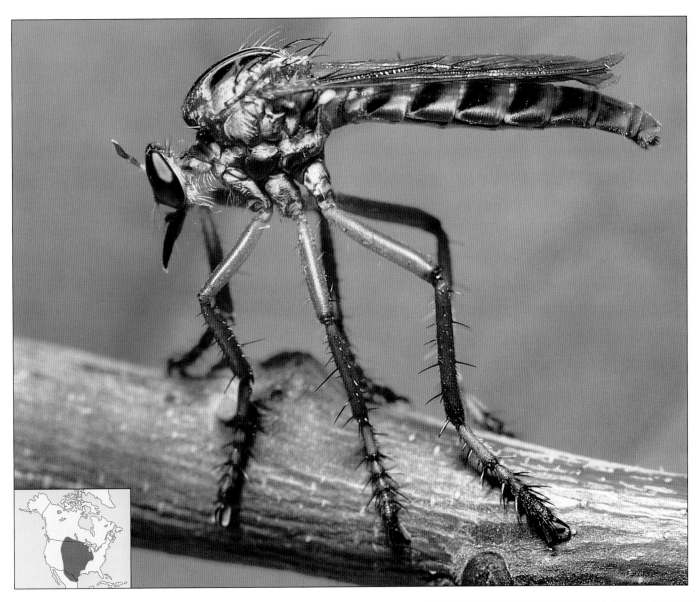

Above: The Robber Fly
Right: Green Bottle Fly

vegetation, just above water, and the larvae are semi-aquatic, living in mud and marshy areas, seeking drier soil when ready to pupate. The adults grow to around $\frac{1}{4}$ inch, and are black with yellow markings on the thorax and abdomen. Mainly found amongst tall grass in the Great Plains area the **Robber Fly** (*Diogmites angustipennis*) is a large, reddish-brown fly with black markings, spiny, orange legs and large, bulging eyes. It is a predatory insect which catches its food on the wing, securing its prey with its spiny legs. It then settles on vegetation where it sucks out the innards of its victim with beak-like mouthparts. It catches and eats insects such as flies, bugs, bees, wasps, butterflies and moths, often tackling quite large specimens. Its larvae are also carnivorous, preying on small insects and their larvae in soil or decaying vegetation. The adult female Robber Fly lays her eggs on the ground in fall, and the juveniles burrow into the soil where they pupate in spring. The adults usually emerge in late summer.

EASTERN YELLOW JACKET

Scientific name:	*Vespula maculifrons*
Identification:	Stout-bodied, with a mainly black thorax, yellow and black banded abdomen, and dark wings
Length:	½–¾ inch
Habitat/Range:	Woodland, meadows, parks and gardens. Occurs throughout the eastern US, west to eastern parts of Texas and North Dakota
Similar species:	The Common Yellow Jacket (*Vespula vulgaris*), is found across Canada and the northeastern US

GIANT ICHNEUMON

Scientific name:	*Megarhyssa macrurus*
Identification:	Brown or black body with yellow markings. Legs are long and mainly yellow, wings are smoky with dark veins. Female has long ovipositor
Length:	1–2 inches, but ovipositor of female may be a further 3 inches
Habitat/Range:	Woodlands and gardens. Giant Ichneumons occur throughout North America, wherever there are trees
Similar species:	The species *Megarhyssa greenei*, usually has a much smaller ovipositor

Yellow Jackets are probably the most widespread and well known of the wasp species found in North America, and are notorious for their painful stings. However, they tend only to be particularly aggressive when threatened, or if defending their nests. The Eastern Yellow Jacket tends to nest in the ground or amongst decaying wood, building a paper-like structure from chewed material, but this wasp will also nest in buildings; in wall cavities, or under the eaves of houses. The queens usually overwinter in leaf litter following mating, establishing new colonies of sterile female workers in spring. New queens and fertile males tend not to appear until summer. The workers tend the larvae, bringing pre-chewed food to the nest, and although they drink nectar from flowers, they also consume fruit, smaller insects and carrion, as well as sugary human foodstuffs.

The Giant Ichneumon is a large, slender wasp, which parasitizes the larvae of the related Pigeon Horntail (*Tremex columba*) by laying its eggs on them, or in their tunnels. Adult Pigeon Horntails lay their eggs beneath the bark of hardwood trees, and the larvae bore into the tree whilst they develop. In fall, the female Giant Ichneumon may be observed flying from tree to tree, stopping to rest her antennae against the bark to feel for vibrations produced by horntail larvae. When a larva is discovered, the Ichneumon then inserts her ovipositor into the tree and lays an egg. When this hatches, the Ichneumon larva feeds upon the juvenile Horntail, before pupating and emerging as an adult in spring. Although fearsome-looking, the Giant Ichneumon is harmless to humans.

HONEY BEE

Scientific name:	*Apis mellifera*
Identification:	Dark thorax with light hairs, slender orange abdomen with dark bands
Length:	½ inch
Habitat/Range:	Woodland, meadows, cultivated fields and gardens. Occurs throughout most of North America, but absent from far north
Similar species:	The American Bumblebee is larger and usually hairier

Originally imported from Europe, the Honey Bee is now widespread, and is one of the most important insects in North America. It is responsible for pollinating a huge range of plants, including many fruits and vegetables which man relies upon for food, as well as producing honey. Honey Bees live in large colonies within hives, but may be found nesting in hollow trees where they have reverted to living in the wild. The majority of bees in a colony are workers; sterile females which spend their time maintaining the hive, collecting pollen and looking after the eggs which are produced by the queen. In spring or summer, the queen will start a new hive with a swarm of workers, leaving behind a new queen and fertile males, or drones. This bee may sting if provoked.

AMERICAN BUMBLE BEE

Scientific name:	*Bombus pennsylvanicus*
Identification:	A large, heavy-bodied, hairy bee. Black and yellow, with dark-veined wings
Length:	½–1 inch
Habitat/Range:	Woodland, meadows, marshes and gardens, throughout North America
Similar species:	The Honey Bee is smaller and less hairy

The Bumblebee is closely related to the Honey Bee, and like its smaller relative is an important pollinator of many flowering plants. Unlike the domesticated Honey Bee, however, this species is a native, wild insect which tends to live underground or in some other natural hollow. Bumblebees also differ slightly in their reproductive habits, with the queens spending the winter alone after mating, rather than with a colony of workers. She prepares a nest in early spring, laying eggs from which the larvae of new workers will soon emerge and pupate. New queens and males are produced in the summer and go on to establish new colonies, with the males dying after mating takes place.

SPIDERS

Of the many spiders encountered in North America, grass spiders and wolf spiders are amongst some of the most common and widespread species, and along with the **American House Spider** (*Achaearanea tepidariorum*), are frequently encountered around homes and gardens. **Grass spiders** belong to the family *Agelenidae*, which is more commonly referred to as the Funnel Web Weaver family. These spiders spin large, horizontal webs, either along the ground, amongst grass, or in other low vegetation, which typically taper toward a funnel at one corner, where the spider will reside for much of the time. This funnel is usually positioned in a sheltered spot; amongst leaf litter, in a crevice, or sometimes in an abandoned rodent burrow. The webs of these spiders are not sticky, but the vibrations made as insects land on them alert the spider, which will rush from its funnel to seize its prey. They typically feed upon small beetles, grasshoppers, butterflies and moths. The **Carolina Wolf Spider** (*Hogna carolinensis*) does not construct a web, but is a ground-dwelling species, which inhabits burrows in all kinds of habitats. It is rarely seen by day, being a nocturnal hunter, but males may be abroad in daylight hours as they wander in search of a mate, and females will sometimes sun themselves and their eggs at the entrance of their burrow. Following mating, the female produces an egg sac which she attaches to her spinnerets, carrying it with her for about a month. Upon hatching, the spiderlings may then be transported on their mother's back for a further month, clinging to hairs. Adults grow to around an inch long.

The *Argiope* species are some of the most striking of the spiders commonly seen in North America. Sometimes known as the **Black-and-yellow Garden Spider** or **Golden Orb Weaver**, the **Black-and-yellow Argiope** (*Argiope aurantia*), is found from southern Canada throughout the US. It is often quite large, and with its bold coloration, it is generally easy to spot. The female makes a large web, spanning between tall grass-stems or other vegetation, and is usually visible during the day, hanging in the center of the web, waiting for flying insects to become entangled. The male meanwhile, often resides in a smaller one at its edge. After mating, the female produces one or more egg cases, which may contain over one thousand eggs, and she guards them until winter approaches and she dies. The eggs hatch in fall, but the young will remain in their cocoon until spring. Whilst at rest, this spider frequently holds its legs together in pairs, producing a distinctive x-shape. The **Silver Argiope** (*Argiope argentata*) is a closely related species, but is far less widespread in North America. It is essentially a tropical species, and is generally only found as far north as the southern US, where the adults may survive until fall. As with other *Argiope* spiders, the male often lives at the edge of the female's web until mating takes place, following which, the female may consume the male. Before dying, a female that has mated successfully will produce an egg case and attach it to vegetation close to the web. The young hatch soon afterwards and disperse. They are able to produce silky threads almost immediately and begin building small webs amongst grass and other vegetation during the spring and summer, tending to build larger webs, higher in the vegetation as they grow.

Below: **The Silver Argiope (left) and the Black and Yellow Argiope**

DESERT TARANTULA/ ARIZONA HAIRY MYGALOMORPH

Scientific name:	*Aphonopelma chalcodes*
Identification:	A very large, heavy-bodied spider. Usually gray-brown to black in color, and very hairy
Length:	2–3 inches
Habitat/Range:	Desert areas in southern California, Arizona and New Mexico
Similar species:	Trapdoor spiders are similar in appearance, but smaller and less hairy

Also known as the Bird-eating Spider, the Desert Tarantula is a formidable predator which feeds mainly on large insects, but it is capable of overpowering and consuming small vertebrates such as birds, rodents and lizards. It is not generally aggressive to humans however, and though it may bite or shed irritating hairs if threatened, its venom is relatively mild and comparable to that of a bee sting. This species is a nocturnal predator but it does not venture far from its burrow until the breeding season. At this time the male wanders in search of a mate, cautiously tapping on the silky threads at the mouth of female burrows. Following mating the male retreats to avoid predation. The female lays her eggs in the burrow and may remain with them until the young hatch and disperse.

SOUTHERN BLACK WIDOW SPIDER

Scientific name:	*Latrodectus mactans*
Identification:	Black and shiny, female has round abdomen with red hourglass marking beneath and some red spots on back, male has an elongated abdomen, with red and white stripes
Length:	$\frac{1}{8}$–$\frac{1}{4}$ inch (Female larger than male)
Habitat/Range:	Woodpiles, crevices, vegetation and basements. Found from southern New England to Florida, west to parts of Texas, Oklahoma and Kansas
Similar species:	The Western Black Widow (*Latrodectus hesperus*) is most common from southwestern deserts, north along the pacific to southern Canada

The Black Widow Spider is perhaps the most notorious of all arachnid species, and maybe not without reason, as it is venomous. Its bite is potentially fatal to humans and it is sometimes found indoors, where it may seek shelter amongst clothing or in shoes. However, unless guarding egg cases, this spider will not usually become aggressive, preferring to hide, or drop to the ground and play dead if disturbed. The female makes an irregular, often somewhat frayed web, with a silken tunnel in which she spends most of her time, whilst, as with most spiders, the males wander in search of a mate. The Black Widow is well known for the behavior that provides its common name, that is, that following mating, the female typically consumes the male. In some cases though, the male may be spared, and go on to mate with another female.

PALE WINDSCORPION

Scientific name:	*Eremobates pallipes*
Identification:	Yellow-brown, spider-like, with an enlarged head and large pincer-like mouthparts
Length:	½–1 inch
Habitat/Range:	Found mainly in desert and scrub areas in the southwestern US
Similar species:	Unmistakable

Although this arachnid species is referred to as a scorpion, and looks much like a spider, it is in fact neither, belonging to the order *Solpugida*. It does not posses venom glands or spinnerets, but uses a large pair of leg-like organs called pedipalps to seize and pass prey to its crushing jaws. The mouthparts are a distinctive feature of windscorpions, operating vertically and in pairs. It is a voracious and highly active, nocturnal predator, and its name comes from its speed – as it is said to "run like the wind". This species feeds upon small insects and spiders, sucking the innards from their bodies. When breeding, the female excavates a burrow in the ground, where she lays between 50 and 200 eggs. She then usually remains with the eggs until they hatch, at which time the young will emerge from the burrow with their mother. They will remain together for some time, with the female capturing prey to feed her family.

GIANT (DESERT) HAIRY SCORPION ▲

Scientific name:	*Hadrurus arizonensis*
Identification:	A large, yellow-brown scorpion with a dark back and paler legs. Dark hairs on pincers, legs and abdomen
Length:	5½–6 inches
Habitat/Range:	Desert valleys in southern California, Utah, Nevada, and western Arizona
Similar species:	This species may be distinguished from other scorpions by its size

Like spiders, scorpions are arachnids, but most species are characterized by having large pincers, and long tails that often terminate in a venomous barb. The Giant Hairy (Desert) Scorpion is the largest scorpion found in North America, and is a venomous species. It is particularly fearsome in appearance due to its large size, but although it has been known to become aggressive and to sting humans, an attack by this scorpion seldom proves to be fatal. This species is active at night, using its stinger to defend itself from potential predators and to subdue its prey. Though it mainly hunts for large insects, it will also kill and eat small snakes and lizards, dismembering them.

CENTRUROIDES SCORPION

Scientific name:	*Centruroides exilicauda*
Identification:	Dark brown to yellowish, often with a greenish central stripe
Length:	1–3 inches
Habitat/Range:	Found under rocks, logs and bark in arid southwestern regions
Similar species:	The closely related Florida Bark Scorpion (*Centruroides gracilis*) is found in the south eastern US

Often referred to as a bark scorpion, this species is the most venomous scorpion in North America, and its sting can prove fatal to humans, particularly children or the infirm, and it may cause severe allergic reactions in otherwise healthy people. As its alternative name suggests, it is often found beneath bark, and it is one of the few scorpions that climbs. It may however also be found under stones and amongst logs or other debris, often close to termite nests. Like most scorpions it is nocturnal, and it hunts for its insect prey at night. The female of this species produces live young following a gestation period of several months. The juveniles are then carried on the mother's back until their first molt.

FRESHWATER
FISH

ATLANTIC SALMON

Scientific name:	*Salmo salar*
Identification:	Dark back, silvery sides with X-shaped markings. During spawning males develop more reddish sides and a prominently hooked lower jaw
Length:	Up to 4½ feet
Weight:	Up to 70 lb+ (usually considerably less)
Habitat/Range:	Coastal waters from the Arctic Circle to Maine, also in rivers and lakes in the New England area and in Lake Ontario
Similar species:	Other salmon inhabit the Pacific Ocean

The Atlantic Salmon is an anadromous species, undertaking migrations between the sea and freshwater in order to spawn. They begin their lives in freshwater, and may remain in river systems for a number of years whilst developing, prior to beginning their downstream migration towards the sea. Here they remain for between one and three years, before heading back to the rivers of their birth to reproduce. Salmon tend not to feed when re-entering freshwater, but at sea they typically feed on small fish and crustaceans. Unlike many salmonids, this species is weakened by the experience, but does not necessarily die following spawning. The Atlantic Salmon is a majestic-looking fish, and is well revered for its arduous existence, good sport and fine meat. It is, however, endangered in various waterways around Maine where only small numbers now breed naturally in the wild. There are also a number of landlocked populations in surrounding states.

Above: **The Red Sock-eye Salmon during spawning**

PACIFIC SALMON

There are several species of salmon found in the Pacific, distributed from the Arctic Ocean to southern California. Like the Atlantic Salmon, they are anadromous, and migrate upstream from the sea into river systems to spawn, though there are also landlocked populations, with some fish having been introduced or stocked in lakes outside of their natural range. The largest species is the **Chinook Salmon** (*Oncorhynchus tshawytscha*), or **King Salmon**, which may reach almost five feet in length. Like most salmon it is dark blue-green on the back with silvery sides, and this species has a spotted back and tail. Males become tinged with red or pink in the breeding season, and develop a pronounced, hooked lower jaw. It is highly valued for both sport and food, but as with almost all salmon it is now considered to be endangered in much of its range. Whereas most related fish return to freshwater only to spawn, this species may be found in rivers and streams throughout the year. The **Coho**

Salmon (*Oncorhynchus kisutch*) is also prized as a game fish, but is today largely absent from areas where it was once prolific. It looks much like the Chinook Salmon, but only the upper part of its tail is spotted, and it is a smaller fish, growing to around three feet long. It spawns in small streams in fall, often quite far inland, after which both males and females die. Perhaps the most striking salmon, certainly during spawning, the male **Sockeye Salmon** (*Oncorhynchus nerka*) becomes almost completely bright red, except for its head. At sea it is speckled or blotched, but lacks the prominent dark spots of related species. It is the most commercially valuable salmon, but is protected in the Pacific northwest in parts of Washington, Oregon and Idaho. In contrast, the least sought after salmon species, the **Pink Salmon** (*Oncorhynchus gorbuscha*), is abundant throughout much of the Pacific Ocean. It has also been introduced into the Great Lakes and Canadian maritime provinces.

RAINBOW TROUT

Scientific name:	*Oncorhynchus mykiss*
Identification:	Blue-green back, pale belly and silvery flanks marked with small dark spots. A violet stripe runs along each side, which becomes more intense during spawning
Length:	Up to $3\frac{1}{2}$ feet
Weight:	Up to 40 lb
Habitat/Range:	A native inhabitant of lakes and streams along the Pacific, this species has been widely introduced elsewhere
Similar species:	The Brook Trout is a similarly brightly colored species, but is usually smaller, growing to about 2 feet long

Some Rainbow Trout may spend their entire lives in freshwater, whereas others are anadromous, leaving their home streams after a few years to enter the sea, returning to spawn in winter when sexually mature. These sea-run trout are referred to as Steelheads and are normally silver with black spots, lacking the reddish stripe common to freshwater individuals. Freshwater Rainbow Trout normally spawn in spring, and are often quite brightly colored throughout the year. As with most members of the salmon family, these are popular game fish, but they have also declined in number due to disruption of habitat and pollution. Many Steelhead populations are classified as endangered or threatened.

OTHER TROUT

There are numerous species of trout found in North America, and although some migrate between streams and the oceans, many are more frequently found in freshwater. As its name might suggest, the **Brook Trout** (*Salvelinus fontinalis*) is an inhabitant of small streams, often in mountainous areas. Its natural range extends throughout eastern Canada and the Great Lakes, south into the Appalachian Mountains, but it has been introduced in the Rocky Mountains, and is also sometimes found close inshore off the Atlantic coast. It is amongst the most colorful of freshwater fish, with a red or yellow hue on the back and sides and markings which consist of light stripes, and red spots outlined with blue halos. It grows to about two feet long, and is a popular fish with anglers. A much scarcer fish, the **Apache Trout** (*Oncorhynchus apache*), is also an inhabitant of clear mountain streams and pools, but it is only found in Arizona. It is a small species, about eighteen inches long,

and is a golden yellow color, with a dark spot behind each eye and numerous spots on its head, body and fins. It is classed as endangered, having hybridized and been forced to compete with non-native species. The **Brown Trout** (*Salmo trutta*) is not native to North America but has become widespread, having been introduced in the nineteenth century. It is somewhat larger than the two other species mentioned here, at around three feet long, but is not as widely caught for consumption as the Brook Trout. It is usually olive in color with a silvery underside, and tends to be scattered with orange spots, often surrounded with a light halo. Young brown trout feed mainly on insects and small crustaceans, but as they grow they often begin to eat small fish such as minnows, with the largest specimens preying on quite large fish and even becoming cannibalistic. In some areas this species has upset the natural balance, to the detriment of indigenous fish.

Above: Brook Trout
Opposite: Brown Trout

PADDLEFISH

▼

LAKE STURGEON

Scientific name:	*Polyodon spathula*
Identification:	Long, mottled blue or gray, with a pale underside. Mouth is large, snout is long and paddle-shaped and opercular flaps, or gill covers, taper, extending well back towards pelvic fins
Length:	Up to 7 feet
Weight:	Up to 200lb
Habitat/Range:	Lakes and slack portions of large rivers often in murky water. Found throughout the Mississippi river basin
Similar species:	No similar species

Scientific name:	*Acipenser fulvescens*
Identification:	A long, powerful fish with a gray or olive back and lighter sides which are lined with bony plates
Length:	Up to 8 feet
Weight:	Up to 300lb
Habitat / Range:	Large, clear lakes and rivers with sand or gravel bottoms. Found from Alberta in western Canada to Hudson Bay, south to parts of Louisiana and Georgia
Similar species:	The Shovelnose Sturgeon (*Scaphirhynchus Platorynchus*) is found in parts of this species' range, but grows to only around 3 feet

The Paddlefish is one of only two species belonging to the family *Polyodontidae*, and the only one found in North America, the other occurring in China. It is a highly distinctive and curious-looking fish, somewhat resembling a (long-nosed) Basking Shark as it swims with its huge mouth agape, feeding on plankton. Like sharks and freshwater catfish, the Paddlefish also lacks scales, instead having smooth skin. It also has a cartilaginous skeleton. Once found in the Great Lakes, this fish is now reduced in number and range, partly due to overfishing. An edible species, it is typically caught during its breeding season in spring and summer, and its eggs are also eaten as caviar.

A close relative of the more common Shovelnose Sturgeon, the Lake Sturgeon belongs to the family *Acipenseridae*, and is considered along with Paddlefish and Gars as a primitive, or ancestral fish, a predecessor of more advanced species. Its sides bear rows of bony plates which are sharply spined in juveniles, and the mouth, which is set below the snout, is preceded by four sensory barbels, used to detect food such as small fish or crustaceans on the lake or river bed. It is amongst the largest of North American freshwater fish, and can be incredibly long-living. It is also one of the most fertile, with females producing millions of eggs at a time. However, as it prefers clean, clear water, pollution has had a detrimental effect on populations in recent years.

Above: Alligator Gar (*Lepisosteus platostamus*)

LONGNOSE GAR

Scientific name:	*Lepisosteus osseus*
Identification:	Long and streamlined with a very long snout containing large, needle-like teeth. Back is a dark olive-green fading to a pale or white belly. Dark spots are usually present toward the rear
Length:	Up to 6 feet
Weight:	Up to 50lb
Habitat/Range:	Large still-waters or slow-flowing rivers, usually with abundant aquatic vegetation. Sometimes found in brackish water. Occurs throughout much of the eastern and central US
Similar species:	The Alligator Gar (*Lepisosteus platostamus*) is much larger, up to ten feet long and weighing 200lb. Also, no other Gar has such an elongated snout

The Longnose Gar is a highly predatory species, well equipped for catching fish and other small animals with its long, toothy snout. Prey is normally taken at or near the surface by ambush, and may include small birds, mammals, reptiles and amphibians. This species is also extremely tough and resilient, protected from potential predators by thick, hard scales, and able to tolerate stagnant or brackish water. In such conditions, the Longnose Gar is able to breathe air at the surface, having a modified swim bladder which operates much like a lung. Although this species is fished for sport, and sometimes eaten, some anglers consider it a pest as it preys on game fish.

NORTHERN PIKE ◄

Scientific name:	*Esox lucius*
Identification:	Long and streamlined, large head and protruding lower jaw. Usually olive green with yellow spots. Underside is pale, fins pale green, white or orange. Dorsal fin set well back, close to tail
Weight:	Up to 46lb
Habitat/Range:	Lakes and large slow-moving rivers. The Northern Pike is found from Alaska throughout most of Canada, south through the central US to Missouri, and northeast to New York
Similar species:	The Pickerels are smaller, whilst the Muskellunge is often much larger, with blotches or bars rather than spots

Four of the five species of pike found throughout the world occur in North America, and the Northern Pike is the most widespread of all freshwater fish, being found in North America, Europe and Asia. It has a long, powerful head and body, and large tooth-lined jaws. Rather than pursuing prey, the Northern Pike prefers to conserve energy by ambushing its quarry, lying hidden amongst aquatic vegetation, and propelling itself toward its target with a sudden burst of speed. Pike have large, high-set eyes and hunt mainly by sight, preferring quite clear waters. Once widely eaten, this large and aggressive species is now more highly valued as a sport fish.

MUSKELLUNGE

Scientific name:	*Esox masquinongy*
Identification:	A very large pike, with a broad head and deeply forked tail. Back is green or brown, sides gray-green to silver, with dark markings, and underside pale
Length:	Up to 6 feet
Weight:	Up to 65lb
Habitat/Range:	Densely vegetated lakes, reservoirs and slow-moving rivers from Manitoba to the Great Lakes and northeastern US, south to Missouri, Kentucky and Virginia
Similar species:	The Northern Pike is smaller with small yellow spots rather than large, dark markings

The Muskellunge, or "Muskie", is the largest member of the pike family, *Esocidae*, and the most highly prized by anglers, presenting something of a challenge to even an experienced fisherman. It is a powerful and voracious carnivore, feeding mainly at night, on fish, amphibians, waterfowl and small aquatic mammals. Usually ambushing its prey from the cover of vegetation, this species is an instinctive, aggressive predator, which will strike at any passing fish or animal that comes within its field of vision. Larger individuals may, however, become predominantly scavengers, feeding on dead or dying fish, whilst younger Muskellunge tend to prey on small schooling fish.

Above: The Redfin Pickerel (*Esox americanus*)

PICKERELS

The Pickerels are small members of the pike family but share the same body shape and predatory nature of their larger relatives. Only the **Grass**, or **Redfin Pickerel** (*Esox americanus*), which is the smallest of the group, at about fifteen inches, is not frequently fished for sport. It is usually green, with lighter sides that are marked with dark, vertical bars or stripes, and it is sometimes also known as the Barred Pickerel. It inhabits ponds and streams throughout the eastern US, but is absent from the Appalachian Mountain range. The slightly larger **Chain Pickerel** (*Esox niger*), attains a maximum length of about two and a half feet, weighing perhaps nine pounds. It is quite similar in appearance to the Grass Pickerel, both having a dark line below the eyes, but this species has a more deeply forked tail, and its markings are chain-like. It is also an inhabitant of eastern states, but is not found as far from the coast. Both species feed on small fish, amphibians and invertebrates.

CATFISH

The term "catfish" is derived from the presence of "whiskers" or, more accurately, barbels around these fishes' mouths. The barbels are sensory organs, sensitive to both touch and taste, and they are used in detecting food on the bottom. All North American catfish have four pairs of barbels. Other distinctive features include the fact that most catfish lack scales, instead having smooth skins, and they also have sharp spines in their pectoral and dorsal fins. In some species, such as the Tadpole Madtom (*Noturus gyrinus*), these spines are capable of delivering venom. Catfish are typically elongated, but often quite heavy-bodied. Amongst the largest of the native freshwater catfish is the **Flathead Catfish** (*Pylodictis olivaris*), which may grow to five feet long and weigh in excess of one hundred pounds. It has a characteristically long body, a wide, flat head and a broad mouth. Being particularly large, this species is often sought by sport fishermen. It is found throughout much of the eastern US, and has also been introduced further west. Like most catfish it inhabits large bodies of water which offer plenty of cover, in the form of vegetation or submerged debris. Another large species with a similar range is the **Channel Catfish** (*Ictalurus punctatus*) which may attain a length of three feet and weigh over fifty pounds. It too is often caught for sport, but it also sustains a large commercial industry and is widely farmed for food. Amongst the most common and widespread catfish species are the bullheads. The **Yellow Bullhead** (*Ameiurus natalis*) and **Brown Bullhead** (*Ameiurus nebulosus*) grow to about eighteen inches and weigh up to four and six pounds respectively. They inhabit deep pools with abundant vegetation, and are also caught for both food and sport. Both originate in the eastern US and parts of Canada, but have been widely stocked outside of this range. Like other catfish, they are often most active at night, slowly moving along the bottom in search of mollusks, crustaceans and small fish.

Below: Ictalurus nebulosus

YELLOW PERCH

Scientific name:	*Perca flavescens*
Identification:	Brassy-colored, with dark vertical bands across the back and sides. The anal, pelvic and pectoral fins are often red or orange. Two dorsal fins, the first of which is spiny
Length:	Up to 15 inches
Weight:	Up to 4lb
Habitat/Range:	Usually quite shallow, weedy areas of rivers, lakes and ponds. Found from Saskatchewan east to Nova Scotia, south to the Carolinas and northern parts of the Mississippi drainage
Similar species:	The Walleye is larger and more elongate, whilst smaller related species such as darters rarely exceed a few inches

The Yellow Perch is an aggressive predatory species, but due to its size is considered less of a sport fish than some of its larger relatives. It is however widely caught and eaten by man, and provides a source of food for larger fish. Found in a range of habitats, they are quite opportunistic in their feeding habits, often using their camouflage to hide amongst vegetation before ambushing prey, but they will also chase small schooling fish. Young perch also school in large groups and are often found in the shallows feeding on fry and insects, particularly at sunrise and sunset. Older Yellow Perch tend to form smaller groups, and feed mainly on small fish, even cannibalizing the young of their own species. The spawning method of these fish is unusual in that eggs are laid in long gelatinous strings.

WALLEYE

Scientific name:	*Stizostedion vitreum*
Identification:	Olive-green or brown back, with dark saddle-shaped markings and two dorsal fins. Belly is pale and the tip of the lower tail fin is white
Length:	Up to 3 feet 5 inches
Weight:	Up to 25lb
Habitat/Range:	Generally large bodies of water with sand or gravel bottoms, throughout much of Canada and the US
Similar species:	The Sauger (*Stizostedion canadense*) is a closely related and very similar fish, but is more slender and has spotted dorsal fins

The largest member of the Perch family in North America, the Walleye is a fairly large predatory species, and is popularly caught for both sport and food. It is typically found in cool, slightly cloudy water over a hard bottom, where aquatic insects and the small fish which feed on them tend to congregate. The Walleye will eat both invertebrates and smaller fish, with the Yellow Perch being its favored prey in many lakes. It feeds mainly at dusk and dawn, relying on its acute vision, which is provided by large, glassy eyes. The range of this species was once somewhat smaller, but it does well in a range of temperatures and water conditions, and has been successfully introduced across North America.

RAINBOW DARTER ▲

Scientific name:	*Etheostoma caeruleum*
Identification:	Yellow-green or olive back, blue-green belly. Around 8 darker vertical bands are present on sides. Fins are red with blue borders, that of the leading dorsal fin being widest
Length:	Up to 3 inches
Weight:	Up to $\frac{1}{8}$oz
Habitat/Range:	Clear streams and creeks, from the Great Lakes area, south through the Mississippi River system
Similar species:	There are several similar darters, but all have slight variations in color and pattern

A member of the perch family *Percidae*, the Rainbow Darter shares a similar body shape and dorsal fin arrangement with the Yellow Perch and Walleye, but it is much smaller and is strikingly colored, hence the name "Rainbow". The term "Darter" is derived from the rapid movements exhibited by these fish as they search for food close to the bottom. The Rainbow Darter feeds on tiny insects and crustaceans, inhabiting areas of relatively fast moving water where a good supply of food is swept along in the current. This species also prefers clean, clear water, and being highly sensitive to pollution, can prove a good indicator as to the cleanliness of a stream or river.

COMMON CARP ▲ HITCH

Scientific name:	*Cyprinus carpio*
Identification:	Deep-bodied with large, olive or brass-colored scales, long dorsal fin and two pairs of barbels on the upper jaw
Length:	Up to 2½ feet
Weight:	Up to 60lb
Habitat/Range:	Varied freshwater habitats in southern Canada and throughout the US
Similar species:	The Quillback is of similar appearance, but smaller, with silvery sides and greatly extended leading rays on the dorsal fin. The Smallmouth Buffalo is often larger. Both species lack barbels

Scientific name:	*Lavinia exilicauda*
Identification:	Dark brown or yellowish back, silvery sides, small head and upturned mouth and a deeply forked tail fin. The tail section prior to the caudal fin is distinctively slender
Length:	Up to 13 inches
Habitat/Range:	Found in the Sacramento, San Joaquin and Russian River systems of California, also in Clear Lake
Similar species:	This species may be distinguished from similar fish by the narrow caudal peduncle

The Common Carp is a non-native species, originally from Asia, which was introduced to North America from Europe in the nineteenth century. It has since become well-established, and is now widespread across the US. It is rarely eaten, and though quite powerful, it is not as popularly fished for sport as some native species. It occurs in a variety of habitats, but favors still water with plentiful vegetation, and can withstand quite stagnant conditions. It feeds on both plants and invertebrates, rooting around at the bottom or feeding on weeds and insects at the surface. The closely related Grass Carp (*Ctenopharyngodon idella*), which can grow to one hundred pounds, was introduced more recently in an attempt to control aquatic vegetation, but the growth rate and huge appetites of both of these species have proved detrimental to habitats in some areas.

The Hitch is native only to California, inhabiting river systems such as the Sacramento, San Joaquin, the Russian River and their surrounding tributaries. There is also a population in Clear Lake, often identified as a subspecies due to its geographical isolation. In spite of the relatively small range of this species, which is shared with an abundance of predatory birds and fish, the Hitch has proved quite adaptable, and although populations have been depleted, it continues to thrive in many areas. Additionally, this species tends to spawn in temporary channels, but its eggs hatch within about a week and juveniles become free-swimming within a further seven days. They then move into larger bodies of water, seeking refuge and food amongst bankside vegetation. Adults move into deeper water, feeding almost exclusively on planktonic crustaceans.

COMMON SHINER

Scientific name:	*Luxilus/Notropis cornutus*
Identification:	Quite deep-bodied, olive back, lighter sides, becoming silvery, tinted with blue, red or purple in breeding males. Fins transparent to rosy red
Length:	Up to 12 inches (usually considerably smaller)
Habitat/Range:	Clear, moderately fast-flowing water from Saskatchewan to Nova Scotia, south to Colorado and Virginia
Similar species:	Other shiners can generally be distinguished by specific markings or color differences

▼ # NORTHERN HOG SUCKER

Scientific name:	*Hypentelium nigricans*
Identification:	Tapered, with a disproportionately large head which is concave between the eyes. Olive or rusty-colored back, mottled with brown and marked with dark saddles. Sides green, belly white
Length:	Up to 2 feet
Habitat/Range:	Pools and riffles of quite fast-flowing streams. Occurs from Ontario, south to parts of Louisiana and Georgia
Similar species:	Alabama Hogsucker (*Hypentelium etowanum*) lacks concave section on head

Abundant throughout most of its range, the Common Shiner is however, highly sensitive to changes in water conditions, and is only able to tolerate relatively clean, clear water, free of pollution and silt. It is usually quite small, around three or four inches in length, and feeds on both plant material, insects and other invertebrates, although larger specimens may eat smaller fish. In turn, the Common Shiner is preyed upon by numerous larger species, and is often used as bait by anglers. It usually spawns in early summer, at which time males develop tubercles on the head and a red or purplish coloration along their sides and fins. Eggs are often deposited in a shallow gravel nest dug by the male, generally where there is a moderate current.

The Northern Hog Sucker is a fairly large, almost cylindrical species, which inhabits quite shallow, clear streams and rivers, favoring areas with a fairly fast flow and a gravel or rock bottom. It is well adapted to such conditions, being streamlined, but with a large, heavy head and large pectoral fins. Like other suckers it feeds on the bottom, but tends to be found close to riffles, searching out food brought down by the current and deposited amongst stones and rocks. They feed mainly on invertebrates such as insects, snails and crustaceans. Spawning occurs in late spring or early summer, and more than one male may fertilize the eggs of a single female.

LARGEMOUTH BASS

Scientific name:	*Micropterus salmoides*
Identification:	Large, olive-green, heavy-bodied fish with large mouth and divided dorsal fin
Length:	Up to 3 feet
Weight:	Up to 22lb
Habitat/Range:	Quiet, vegetated bodies of water in Ontario and the eastern US, but widely introduced elsewhere
Similar species:	The Smallmouth Bass (*Micropterus dolomieu*) grows to about 2 feet long

The Largemouth Bass belongs to the family *Centrarchidae*, or the Sunfishes, and is the largest bass occurring in freshwater. It is also amongst the most popular of all fish caught for sport in North America. Although it was originally native only to the eastern US and the Great Lakes region, it has been widely introduced and now thrives across much of the continent. In some parts however, this has proved detrimental to populations of the small fish upon which it feeds. It is found in a variety of habitats, but prefers quiet waters with abundant vegetation which provides shelter for juveniles. Spawning takes place in spring, with males making nests on the bottom which they then guard until some days after hatching.

GREEN SUNFISH

Scientific name:	*Lepomis cyanellus*
Identification:	Olive-green or yellowish, dark bars on sides may or may not be present. Mouth reaches to below center of eye. Dark spot on ear flap
Length:	Up to 12 inches
Weight:	Up to 2lb
Habitat/Range:	Usually found in still water. Its native range extends from the Great Lakes south to New Mexico and Alabama, but it is now found elsewhere
Similar species:	Other sunfish are usually more brightly and distinctively colored

The Green Sunfish is one of the most common sunfish in the US, having been widely introduced outside of its natural range, and it thrives in a variety of conditions. It is most commonly found in ponds or lakes, but also inhabits streams and rivers, particularly in quiet stretches or pools. Spawning takes place in spring and summer, and as with related species, the male Green Sunfish use their fins to form a nest in gravel or sand. They will then guard the nest until the fry are free-swimming. Juveniles feed mainly on tiny planktonic crustaceans, but the large-mouthed adults consume aquatic insects, small crayfish and small fish.

PUMPKINSEED ▼

Scientific name:	*Lepomis gibbosus*
Identification:	Yellow-green mottled with orange and blue. Black spot on ear flap is bordered with white. Mouth extends back to eye
Length:	Up to 16 inches
Weight:	Up to 1lb 14 oz
Habitat/Range:	Ponds, lakes and the quiet, shallow pools of rivers around the Great Lakes, south along the Atlantic coast to Georgia. Introduced elsewhere
Similar species:	Longear Sunfish (*Lepomis megalotis*) has elongated ear flap

A deep-bodied, colorful sunfish, the preferred habitat of the Pumpkinseed consists of still or slow-moving water with abundant vegetation. It feeds on a variety of invertebrates, foraging for small mollusks, crustaceans and insects, and although they have quite small mouths, adult Pumpkinseeds may also consume smaller fish. The young however, typically feed on plankton. During the breeding season the male of this species makes a depression on the lake or river bed into which one or more females will deposit eggs. These nests are often made in shallows quite close to the bank, and where space allows, many of these fish may nest together. The males guard the eggs until they hatch.

BURBOT

Scientific name:	*Lota lota*
Identification:	Elongated, olive in color, with mottled sides and fins. A long barbel is present on the chin
Length:	Up to 3 feet
Weight:	Up to 18lb
Habitat/Range:	Cold, deepwater lakes and rivers throughout Canada, south into the northern US
Similar species:	The Atlantic Tomcod (*Microgadus tomcod*) may enter freshwater, but it grows to only 15 inches

The Burbot is an unusual species, being the only member of the cod family, *Gadidae*, which occurs solely in freshwater, and although it is quite widespread, it is not particularly common. It is primarily an inhabitant of large cold, northern waters, though it will sometimes be found in smaller streams, but perhaps surprisingly, it actually spawns in the winter, usually when there is still ice at the surface. The eggs take about eight weeks to hatch, and the young Burbot feed mainly on insects and their larvae, with adults consuming fish and crayfish. This species is seldom caught by anglers, being a reclusive fish which prefers to hide amongst rocks or underwater structures.

▼ THREE-SPINE STICKLEBACK

Scientific name:	*Gasterosteus aculeatus*
Identification:	Gray-brown with lighter sides which bear bony plates. Head and undersides red during spawning. Three dorsal spines, the most posterior of which is smallest
Length:	Up to 4 inches
Habitat/Range:	Coastal, brackish and freshwater around north Atlantic, Hudson Bay and the Pacific coastline
Similar species:	The Blackspotted Stickleback (*Gasterosteus wheatlandi*) has black spots. Other Sticklebacks have more dorsal spines.

Although small, the Three-spine Stickleback is quite remarkable for a number of reasons, and perhaps best known for its unusual mating behavior. Often found along coastal shores, during the breeding season this fish enters brackish water or ascends freshwater streams where the male of this species constructs a nest from twigs, leaves and other aquatic vegetation. He then attempts to attract a female to lay her eggs there with an elaborate courtship "dance". The male guards the nest for some weeks whilst its young develop. This fish is also notable for its spines and lack of scales, instead possessing bony plates along its sides.

Western Mosquitofish

Scientific name:	*Gambusia affinis*
Identification:	Full-bodied, particularly the larger females. Olive or gray with yellowish belly. Anal fin has nine rays, and is extended in males to form gonipodium
Length:	Up to 2½ inches
Habitat/Range:	Fresh or brackish ponds, lakes and streams from central Mississippi, south and west through Texas to New Mexico, but introduced elsewhere
Similar species:	Eastern Mosquitofish (*Gambusia holbrooki*) has a larger number of rays on fins

The Mosquitofish belongs to the family *Poeciliidae*, and unlike most fishes which rely on the external fertilization of their eggs, these are a live-bearing species that reproduce by means of internal fertilization. The smaller males possess an adapted anal fin, part of which has developed into a sexual organ used to deposit sperm within the female. This organ is known as the gonipodium. Females may then carry sperm for several months during which time a number of eggs can be fertilized. The Mosquitofish is so named due to its consumption of mosquito larvae, a trait which has seen it introduced outside of its native range in a largely unsuccessful attempt to control numbers of these insects.

AMERICAN EEL

▲ # SOUTHERN CAVEFISH

Scientific name:	*Anguilla rostrata*
Identification:	Serpentine in appearence with a dark back, yellow-brown sides and a lighter belly. The long dorsal and anal fins converge at the tail
Length:	Up to 5 feet
Habitat/Range:	Brackish or freshwater along the Atlantic coast, inland through much of the eastern US. Spawns at sea
Similar species:	Lampreys have similar snake-like bodies, but lack jaws

Scientific name:	*Typhlichthys subterraneus*
Identification:	Broad head which lacks eyes. Body appears naked, lacking pigment and pelvic fins.
Length:	Up to 3½ inches
Habitat/Range:	Subterranean pools in caves close to the Mississippi River system
Similar species:	Alabama Cavefish (*Speoplatyrhinus poulsoni*) has a much longer, flattened snout

American Eels begin life in the Sargasso Sea as larval *leptocephali*, before migrating inland and developing into elvers, sometimes over a period of many years. It is thought that only the females then enter freshwater, whilst males reside in coastal waters. The females remain in freshwater for some years until they reach sexual maturity, when most return to the sea to spawn. Some eels however, may remain in freshwater for life, particularly if they become landlocked, although they are capable of moving overland to find water. The American Eel is mainly nocturnal, hiding in hollows or amongst debris during the day, and scavenging for food at night.

The Southern Cavefish is found only in the subterranean waters of caves in the eastern US, and due to environmental isolation it has developed various characteristics specific to its habitat. It lacks pigment and is highly sensitive to ultraviolet light, being unable to survive for any length of time if exposed to sunlight. It is also eyeless, and instead has a well developed lateral line and sensory papillae. The metabolic rate of this species is also low, allowing the fish to subsist on a low food intake. It tends to be most abundant where there is a flow of water which brings organic matter into the cave, attracting invertebrates upon which it feeds.

SOUTHERN BROOK LAMPREY

Scientific name:	*Ichthyomyzon gagei*
Identification:	Slender and eel-like, green or brown with a lighter underside. The circular mouth lacks jaws, but is surrounded with bicuspid rasping teeth
Length:	Up to 7 inches
Habitat/Range:	Clear, gravel-bottomed streams from Texas and Missouri, east to Georgia and parts of Florida
Similar species:	The Northern Brook Lamprey (*Ichthyomyzon fossor*) has singularly cusped teeth

Lampreys are primitive cartilaginous fish, many of which are parasitic species that attach themselves to other fish, feeding on them with their disc-like mouths. The Southern Brook Lamprey however, is non-parasitic. During its larval stage it is a filter feeder, usually remaining buried at the bottom of the stream where it consumes vegetable matter and tiny planktonic organisms, but upon reaching sexual maturity it does not feed. As with spawning eels, the development of reproductive organs coincides with the shrinking of the digestive system. This normally occurs after about three years, at which time the lamprey will emerge to spawn in spring, surviving only until it has reproduced.

MARINE FISH

(GREAT) WHITE SHARK

Scientific name:	*Carcharodon carcharias*
Identification:	A very large, torpedo-shaped shark. Black to slate-gray or brown above, predominantly white below. Bluntly pointed snout
Length:	Up to 21 feet
Weight:	Up to 2500lb+
Habitat/Range:	Open sea and inshore waters, along both the Atlantic and Pacific coasts
Similar species:	The Tiger Shark may reach a similar size, but has a more rounded snout and dark markings on its back and sides

The White Shark, commonly known as the Great White, is the largest and potentially most dangerous predatory fish in North American waters. It is not particularly common however, and attacks on humans are therefore quite rare. It feeds mainly on large fish, including other sharks, and marine mammals such as small whales, dolphins and seals, often attacking its quarry from below. It will also eat turtles, large crustaceans and carrion. It has a good sense of smell, and also uses sensory organs in its snout in order to detect electrical signals given off by its prey. The White Shark has a formidable array of large, serrated, triangular teeth that it uses to tear into its food. These are arranged in rows, and constantly replaced as they are broken or lost. A viviparous fish, the female gives birth to well developed pups, probably in litters of up to around five.

BLUE SHARK ▲

Scientific name:	*Prionace glauca*
Identification:	Long and slender, with narrow, elongated pectoral fins. Back and sides are intensely blue, underside white
Length:	Up to 12½ feet
Weight:	Up to 400lb+
Habitat/Range:	Shallow coastal waters along both the Atlantic and Pacific
Similar species:	Color, long pectoral fins and slender body shape make this species unmistakable

Like the Tiger Shark, this species is a member of the family known as the Requiem Sharks, a large group of mainly pelagic species. The Blue Shark, however, is commonly found quite close to the shore, often feeding at the surface on small schooling fish. It also consumes birds, marine invertebrates and carrion. Although it may grow quite large, and attacks on humans are not unknown, the Blue Shark is not considered to be particularly dangerous. It is probably the most prolific breeder of the large sharks, producing live young in large litters, sometimes numbering more than one hundred at a time.

TIGER SHARK

Scientific name:	*Galeocerdo cuvieri*
Identification:	Large shark with a heavy body and slender tail. Back is gray or brown, sides and belly lighter. Juveniles are spotted, whilst adults develop dark bars. Markings fade with age however
Length:	Up to 18 feet
Weight:	Up to 1700lb+
Habitat/Range:	Often close to the surface in inshore waters, but also found further offshore. Occurs from Maine to the Gulf in the Atlantic, and south from southern California in the Pacific
Similar species:	The only shark of comparable adult size is the (Great) White Shark, which has a more pointed snout

The Tiger Shark is generally found in tropical and sub-tropical seas, but may also be found in warm, temperate waters, probably migrating seasonally in pursuit of food. It is usually solitary and nomadic, and although it may sometimes appear sluggish, it can travel large distances each day, at speeds of over twenty miles an hour. When feeding, the Tiger Shark is also highly active and capable of rapid bursts of speed. This species is amongst the most dangerous of sharks, and although it seems to be omnivorous, this is probably due to its voracity, rather than because of dietary preference. It hunts for fish, crustaceans and cephalopods, turtles, birds and aquatic mammals, but is also known to consume a great deal of inorganic and indigestible matter, which it may then regurgitate later. As with most large sharks, the Tiger Shark produces live young.

349

SCALLOPED HAMMERHEAD SHARK

Scientific name:	*Sphyrna lewini*
Identification:	Gray-brown back with a pale yellow or white underside. Distinctive hammer-shaped head with scalloped leading edge that includes a central indentation
Length:	Up to 13½ feet
Weight:	Up to 335lb
Habitat/Range:	Offshore at depth, but also in coastal shallows and estuarine habitats
Similar species:	Indentations on front edge of head distinguish this species from other hammerheads such as the Great Hammerhead (*Sphyrna mokarran*)

Hammerhead sharks take their name from their highly unusual head-shape, and although this feature is thought to relate largely to sensory activity, it remains as yet, not fully understood. This species may occur singly, in pairs or in schools, and groups of several hundred have been observed. The Scalloped Hammerhead feeds on a variety of smaller fish, squid, octopus and crustaceans, often appearing in very shallow coastal waters. Most attacks on humans are thought to arise from defensive, rather than predatory behavior, but the Scalloped Hammerhead should be regarded as potentially dangerous. They bear live young, in litters of up to thirty pups, following a gestation period of around nine months.

NURSE SHARK

Scientific name:	*Ginglymostoma cirratum*
Identification:	Yellowish to gray-brown, with a broad, flat head, and two barbels. The dorsal and pectoral fins are large and rounded, and the caudal fin is very long
Length:	Up to 14 feet
Weight:	Up to 600lb
Habitat/Range:	Shallow, warm coastal waters, particularly around Florida in the Atlantic, also in the Gulf of California
Similar species:	Presence of barbels makes this species easily identifiable

Although the Nurse Shark may grow to a large size, and is often encountered in water only a few feet deep, it is a sluggish creature, spending much of its time at rest on the ocean floor. Most sharks obtain their oxygen from the water that flows through their gills whilst they are swimming, but the Nurse Shark will actively pump water through its gills whilst lying otherwise motionless. It is not aggressive by nature, but may bite if roughly handled or otherwise provoked. There have however, been some reports of unprovoked attacks on swimmers. It feeds on shellfish, crustaceans, sea urchins, and small fishes. Mating typically takes place in spring or summer, and although internal fertilization occurs, the nurse shark is an ovoviviparous species. Embryonic development occurs in an egg case within the female, with no placental nourishment from the mother.

▼

WHALE SHARK

Scientific name:	*Rhincodon typus*
Identification:	Huge streamlined body and broad, flattened head with a very wide terminal mouth. Upper body is dark, patterned with light spots
Length:	Up to 45 feet (though larger specimens have been reported)
Weight:	Up to 26000lb (13 tons)+
Habitat/Range:	Found in the Atlantic ocean from New York to the Gulf of Mexico, and around southern California in the Pacific
Similar species:	Unmistakable

The Whale Shark is the largest of the sharks, and is in fact the largest of all known fish species, including those from fossil records. It is however harmless, and generally encountered swimming at the surface, where, much like some species of whale, it feeds on tiny planktonic crustaceans, other invertebrates and small fish by sucking in large quantities of water. It is found in warm waters around the world, and is pelagic, mainly occurring in the open ocean, but it will also often come close inshore, sometimes entering bays and lagoons, probably in order to feed. At one time it was thought that the Whale Shark reproduced externally; however, it is now known to be ovoviviparous, with the young developing in egg cases within the female, who then gives birth to live young.

ATLANTIC MANTA

Scientific name:	*Manta birostris*
Identification:	Disk-shaped, flattened body with wing-like pectoral fins, a long slender tail, and a terminal mouth flanked by two cephalic fins
Width:	Up to 22 feet
Weight:	Up to 3000lb
Habitat/Range:	Offshore at depth, but also in coastal shallows, along the Atlantic from the Carolinas, south to the Gulf of Mexico. Also occurs around southern California
Similar species:	Unmistakable

The Atlantic Manta is a huge, graceful ray which swims through the water by beating its large pectoral fins like wings. Despite its imposing size, however, it is a harmless filter-feeder, consuming plankton and small fish, and it is not dangerous to people. Its food is guided into the mouth with the aid of cephalic fins, two projections which extend from the pectorals on either side of the head. This species occurs in the open ocean, but it is also found close to the shore, particularly around reefs or islands, where food is more plentiful. It is frequently encountered near to the surface, and may breach, leaping completely clear of the water. As with some sharks and other large fish, the Atlantic Manta is often accompanied by Remoras such as the Sharksucker, which attach themselves to the underside of the manta close to the gill openings, where they scavenge scraps of food.

SOUTHERN STINGRAY ▼

Scientific name:	*Dasyatis americana*
Identification:	Brown or gray, flattened, almost diamond-shaped, with wing-like pectoral fins and a long slender tail which bears a spine
Width:	Up to 5 feet
Weight:	Up to 210lb
Habitat/Range:	Inshore waters with sandy bottoms, from New Jersey to the Gulf of Mexico
Similar species:	The Atlantic Stingray is considerably smaller, growing to about two feet wide

Like most skates and rays, the Southern Stingray is a bottom-dweller, and it spends a great deal of time buried under sand, with only the eyes, tail and spiracles visible. The spiracles are vestigial gill openings on the Stingray's upper side which enable it to breathe whilst lying on the seabed. Stingrays are so-called as they possess a venomous barb or spine on their tails, and although they are not aggressive fish, they are likely to deliver a painful sting if trodden on. They feed as they move along the bottom, consuming various invertebrates and small fish. This species produces live young in litters of around four pups.

SMALLTOOTH SAWFISH ▲ BIG SKATE

Scientific name:	*Pristis pectinata*
Identification:	Flattened, but elongate, with large pelvic, dorsal and upper caudal fins. Saw-like snout
Length:	Up to 18 feet
Habitat/Range:	Coastal shallows, estuaries and freshwater, along much of the Atlantic coast to the Gulf of Mexico
Similar species:	The Largetooth Sawfish (*Pristis pristis*) has larger, but fewer teeth on its snout, with a maximum of 20 pairs

Scientific name:	*Raja binoculata*
Identification:	Brown or gray, flattened, with large, angular pectoral "wings" and a pointed snout
Width:	Up to 8 feet
Habitat/Range:	Mud, sand or gravel bottoms along the Pacific coast, from the Bering Sea, south to Baja California
Similar species:	The California Skate (*Raja inornata*) has more deeply notched pelvic fins. The Little Skate (*Leucoraja erinacea*) is a small, closely related species found in Atlantic waters

Like sharks, skates and rays, the Smalltooth Sawfish has a cartilaginous skeleton and lacks a true backbone, and although its body-shape resembles that of a shark, this species is more closely related to the rays. It is quite flat, with enlarged pelvic fins, but its most distinctive feature is undoubtedly the elongated, saw-like snout, which bears up to thirty-two pairs of teeth. It uses its snout to wound or kill small schooling fish, and also to disturb the seabed in search of invertebrates such as crustaceans. The Smalltooth Sawfish prefers the soft-bottomed areas of estuaries and coastlines, but is also known to ascend large tidal rivers. Females give birth to up to twenty live young.

A large, docile flatfish, the Big Skate is the largest skate species found in North American waters. Like other rays and skates it is most commonly encountered lying motionless on the ocean floor, often partially buried under sand, but it may occasionally be seen actively foraging for food over the soft bottom. It feeds on fish, crustaceans and other marine invertebrates. This species is oviparous, producing large egg sacs which are laid on mud or sand. These sacs may be almost twelve inches long and contain several embryos. The young skate emerge after about nine months.

Green Moray

Scientific name:	*Gymnothorax funebris*
Identification:	Serpentine, but heavy-bodied. Uniformly dark to light green, or brownish
Length:	Up to 6 feet
Weight:	Up to 60lb
Habitat/Range:	Rocky shorelines, reefs and harbors, often over sand and mud. Found around southern Florida and the Keys, sometimes further north
Similar species:	The Spotted Moray (*Gymnothorax moringa*) is another common species within this range, but is smaller, with dark markings

The Green Moray is a muscular predator, but it is usually quite sedentary for much of the time. During the day, this species tends to rest in cavities amongst rocks or other debris, often with only its head exposed. It may feed opportunistically at such times, but it becomes more active at night, emerging to hunt for its prey. It feeds on fish, crustaceans, squid and octopus, searching around crevices in the reefs and rocks where it makes its home. Like other morays, this species has large teeth, may be aggressive if disturbed, and is potentially dangerous to humans. Eating the Green Moray may also result in ciguatera poisoning, as it consumes herbivorous fish which accumulate toxins in their bodies through feeding on tiny algae.

SEA LAMPREY ▼ ATLANTIC HAGFISH

Scientific name:	*Petromyzon marinus*
Identification:	Long, slender and eel-like. Adults have a circular mouth filled with rows of horny teeth. Fins are absent, except for a rounded tail fin and a dorsal fin divided into two parts
Length:	Up to 3 feet
Habitat/Range:	Along the Atlantic coast, in estuaries and rivers. Also a landlocked population in the Great Lakes
Similar species:	The Atlantic Hagfish lacks eyes and has barbels around its mouth

Scientific name:	*Myxine limosa*
Identification:	Worm-like, lacking pectoral and dorsal fins, but with a rounded tail fin, much like that of an eel. Star-shaped mouth is surrounded by barbels. Body is often exceptionally slimy
Length:	Up to 2½ feet
Habitat/Range:	Muddy bottoms at depths of around 100 to 150 feet. Occurs in the Atlantic, from Canadian waters, south to North Carolina
Similar species:	The Sea Lamprey lacks barbels, has visible eyes and a dorsal fin

The Sea Lamprey is a primitive, jawless fish, which parasitizes other species. It begins life in freshwater however, where the young are not initially parasitic. The larvae burrow into muddy streambeds and filter-feed on organic matter, lacking the teeth of adults. They may remain in streams or rivers for some years until reaching adulthood, whereupon they swim downstream and enter the sea. It is at this stage that the adult lamprey attaches itself to a fish with its circular mouth and rasping teeth, and begins to feed on the blood of the unfortunate host. After perhaps two or three years at sea, the sexually mature adults return to rivers to spawn and die.

The Atlantic Hagfish is a primitive, worm-like species which feeds on both dead and dying fish, burrowing into them with rasping teeth, much like those of a lamprey, before consuming the internal organs. However, it does not go through a larval stage, and the mouthparts are well developed in juveniles. Sometimes referred to as a slime eel, this species produces a thick coat of mucus as a defence against predators, which it casts off by sliding a coiled knot along the length of its body. Due to its feeding habits, The Atlantic Hagfish is unpopular with commercial fishermen.

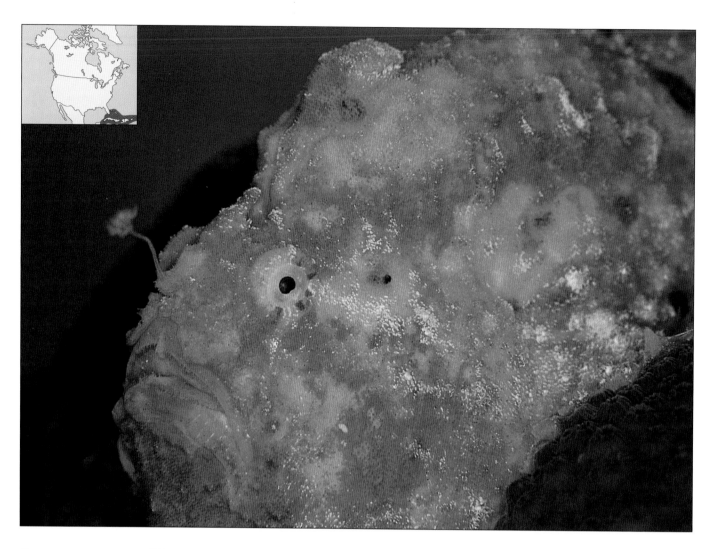

LONGLURE FROGFISH ▲ GOOSEFISH

Scientific name:	*Antennarius multiocellatus*
Identification:	Small and globular with a warty appearance and large upturned mouth. First dorsal spine is modified into a lure
Length:	Up to 6 inches
Habitat/Range:	Warm, shallow waters from Florida to South America
Similar species:	The Dwarf Frogfish (*Antennarius paucira diatus*) grows to only 2½ inches long

The Longlure Frogfish is mainly found around reefs where sponges are abundant, and its unusual appearance enables it to mimic its surroundings. It moves around the bottom, supporting itself on its pectoral and pelvic fins, and hides amongst sponges, moving its lure to attract prey. It feeds primarily on fish, and is capable of tackling quite large specimens, but it will also eat crabs and other crustaceans. A further unusual feature of this species is the means by which spawning takes place. The female releases her eggs at the surface encapsulated in a mucous "egg raft", which may allow them to be more widely dispersed.

Scientific name:	*Lophius americanus*
Identification:	Large brown fish with dark fins, a wide, flat head and large mouth. The first dorsal spine is adapted into a long lure
Length:	Up to 4 feet
Weight:	Up to 50lb
Habitat/Range:	Bottom dwelling, often at depth, closer inshore in northern range. Occurs from Florida to Newfoundland
Similar species:	The Blackfin Goosefish (*Lophius gastrophysus*) has pectoral fins with black inner edges

The Goosefish, which is often sold commercially as Monkfish, is also known as the Anglerfish, on account of its long lure. It lies in wait for a passing meal on the ocean floor, attracting fish and other prey with its rod-like lure. Having a large mouth and body, the Goosefish is capable of swallowing fish equal to its own weight. It is also known to eat turtles and large invertebrates. Spawning takes place from spring through to fall, depending on latitude, and like the Longlure Frogfish, the eggs of this species are released in long, ribbon-like sheets of mucus, often referred to as a veil.

OYSTER TOADFISH

Scientific name:	*Opsanus tau*
Identification:	Stout, with a broad, flat head and large mouth surrounded by fleshy appendages. Body is olive brown and the large pelvic fins are marked with light bars
Length:	Up to 15 inches
Habitat Range:	Shallow water around reefs, jetties, wrecks and vegetation. Found along the Atlantic coast from New England to Florida
Similar species:	The Leopard Toadfish (*Opsanus pardus*) is yellowish with dark blotches

Oyster Toadfish are bottom-dwelling, predatory fish that are most commonly found in sheltered areas, often around man-made structures. They spend their time lying on the bottom, hiding amongst vegetation or debris, and wait for passing food, which they then seize in their large, powerful jaws. The diet of this species includes fish, worms and mollusks, but crustaceans are probably its main prey. The Oyster Toadfish breeds in spring and summer, at which time males attract females with long resonant calls, produced by vibrations of internal muscles. Eggs are laid amongst rocks or beneath similar hard surfaces and guarded by the male.

ATLANTIC COD ▲ HADDOCK

Scientific name:	*Gadus morhua*
Identification:	Tapered, with a narrow caudal peduncle. Gray or green to reddish brown, speckled with spots. Three dorsal and two anal fins. Long barbel beneath chin
Length:	Up to 4 feet (Usually smaller)
Weight:	Up to 60lb
Habitat/Range:	Relatively shallow water, often over rocky bottom areas. Found from Greenland, south to North Carolina
Similar species:	The Greenland Cod (*Gadus ogac*) lacks spots

The Atlantic Cod is probably one of the best known fish in the Western world due to its importance as a commercial food fish, and it is also caught for sport. When young it may be found nearer to the surface, but adults are essentially bottom-dwelling, tending to be found over hard surfaces, particularly where there are steep rocky ledges giving way to deeper water. The Atlantic Cod feeds on a variety of smaller fish, mollusks and other invertebrates such as starfish, but it is omnivorous and will also consume vegetation. A particularly fertile species, a single spawning female may produce between two and ten million eggs; however the majority of juveniles will die before reaching maturity.

Scientific name:	*Melanogrammus aeglefinus*
Identification:	Cod-like, but has a large, pointed, leading dorsal fin and a much smaller chin barbel. Large dark blotch above pectoral fin
Length:	Up to 3½ feet (Usually smaller)
Weight:	Up to 35lb
Habitat/Range:	Typically in deep waters, from Newfoundland to North Carolina
Similar species:	Atlantic Cod lacks pointed dorsal, and is spotted, with a long chin barbel

Like the closely related Atlantic Cod, the Haddock is an important food fish, but overfishing has severely depleted populations in many areas. It tends to be found in deeper waters than cod, but is also a bottom-dwelling species, favoring rocky, sand or gravel bottomed areas. It is an omnivorous species, but feeds mainly on quite small marine animals, including mollusks, crustaceans, echinoderms, and small fish. Sexual maturity is reached at about four or five years, and spawning usually takes place in spring. The female may expel over a million eggs at a time, which are freely dispersed in the ocean.

HOGCHOKER

Scientific name:	*Trinectus maculatus*
Identification:	Small, right-eyed flatfish with a blunt head and small mouth.
Length:	Up to 8 inches
Habitat/Range:	Shallow, coastal waters and estuaries, from Maine to Mexico. Also in freshwater
Similar species:	This species is distinctive as it lacks pectoral fins on either side

A small flatfish of little commercial value, the Hogchoker is thought to have acquired its name in colonial times, as pigs which attempted to eat discarded fish found the rough scales of this species unpalatable. It is however, sometimes consumed by anglers. As with other flatfish the Hogchoker begins life in an upright position, transforming as it grows. It gradually becomes flattened, and moves to the bottom where the disproportionate growth of the left side of the head results in a migration of its eye onto the uppermost side. It is generally confined to coastal waters, and is common in bays and estuaries where spawning takes place in late spring and summer. It feeds mainly on small invertebrates such as annelid worms and crustaceans.

STARRY FLOUNDER ▼

Scientific name:	*Platichthys stellatus*
Identification:	Right or left-eyed, brown to black with a white underside. Dark bars alternate with white or orange bars on dorsal, anal, and caudal fins
Length:	Up to 3 feet
Weight:	Up to 20 lb
Habitat/Range:	Coastal shallows, estuaries and freshwater, also found offshore at greater depths. Found along the Pacific coast, from Alaska to California
Similar species:	This species has distinctive barred fins

This flatfish may be right or left-eyed, and it is thought that in American waters, fifty percent of all starry flounder are right-eyed and fifty percent are left-eyed. It lives on the bottom in both shallow and deep water environments, but is dependent upon estuarine habitats when spawning, and the juveniles particularly, are known to enter freshwater. The Starry Flounder feeds primarily on zooplankton, crustaceans, and other small invertebrates, but also eats small fishes. In turn it is preyed upon by other fish, marine mammals and birds, but as a defense it is able to change its coloration in order to blend in with its surroundings. It is an abundant flatfish in much of the Pacific and is fished both commercially and for sport.

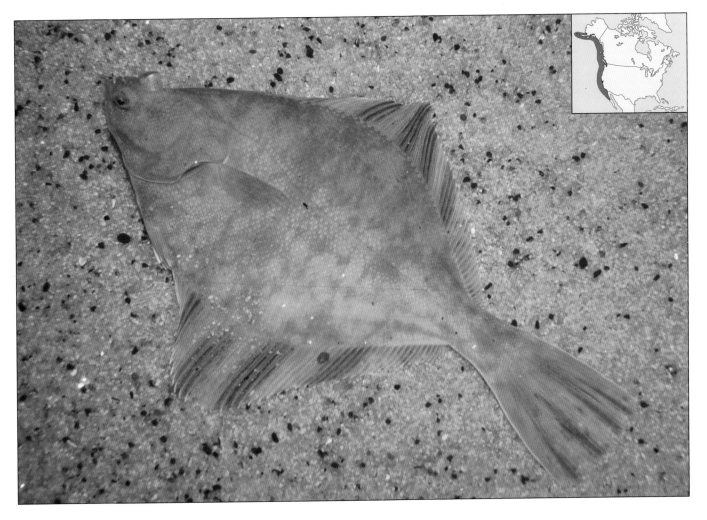

Above: King Mackerel (*Scomberomorus cavalla*)

BONEFISH

Scientific name:	*Albula vulpes*
Identification:	Elongated, blue or green back, silvery sides, sometimes striped. Deeply forked tail
Length:	Up to 3 feet
Weight:	Up to 19 lb
Habitat/Range:	Shallow waters over sand on both coasts, most abundant around Florida and California
Similar species:	A closely related fish once believed to be the same species has been identified, but remains unnamed

The Bonefish is predominately a coastal species, and is frequently found in estuaries and adjacent deeper waters. It uses its conical snout to root amongst vegetation in sandy flats in search of prey, which it crushes with its powerful teeth. Bonefish feed primarily on crustaceans, mollusks, worms, and fishes including toadfish. They are often found in schools but large adults tend to be solitary and spend more time at greater depths. They spawn throughout the year in deep water, and the juveniles go through an eel-like *leptocephalus* larval stage. This species is fast moving and is popular amongst sport fishermen.

ATLANTIC MACKEREL

Scientific name:	*Scomber scombrus*
Identification:	Elongated, dark blue back, fading to silver below. Dark bands on sides
Length:	Up to 22 inches
Weight:	Up to 6 lb
Habitat/Range:	Open seas and coastal waters, from Newfoundland to North Carolina
Similar species:	The Atlantic Chub Mackerel (*Scomber colias*) is spotted or blotched below its lateral line

The Atlantic Mackerel is an important commercial fish which is abundant in cold and temperate waters, particularly over the continental shelf. It overwinters in fairly deep waters, but moves inshore in spring to spawn as water temperatures rise. It is mainly diurnal and found in large schools, often feeding near to the surface, either catching individual prey such as small fish, or filter-feeding on zooplankton. Feeding activity is often greatly increased following spawning. In addition to being caught in large numbers by man, the Atlantic Mackerel is also an important food source for a number of fish, marine mammals and birds.

BLUEFIN TUNA

Scientific name:	*Thunnus thynnus*
Identification:	Deep blue above and silvery white below. The first dorsal fin is yellow or blue, the second is red or brown. The anal fin and finlets are yellow, edged with black
Length:	Up to 14 feet (Usually smaller)
Weight:	Up to 1000lb+
Habitat/Range:	Pelagic, found from Newfoundland, south to the Gulf of Mexico
Similar species:	No other tuna achieves such size

The Bluefin Tuna is highly valued as both a food and game fish, and is especially sought for sport in North America. It is very fast-swimming, and is mainly found in the open ocean, but it is able to tolerate a range of temperatures, and migrates between deep and coastal waters. Spawning typically occurs in warm waters relatively close to the shore, and the Bluefin is known to spawn in the Gulf of Mexico from April to June. The young exhibit strong schooling behavior, whilst the large adults become much more solitary. The Bluefin Tuna feeds mainly on smaller schooling fishes, particularly mackerel, but is also known to consume smaller organisms and to eat invertebrates and bottom-dwelling fish in coastal regions.

SWORDFISH

Scientific name:	*Xiphias gladius*
Identification:	Torpedo shaped, blackish or brown above, pale below, with a long, toothless bill. Leading dorsal fin is high, second is small and set well back. Adults lack scales
Length:	Up to 15 feet (Usually smaller)
Weight:	Up to 1000lb+
Habitat/Range:	Generally in open water, from the surface to depths of over 2000 feet. Found along both US coastlines
Similar species:	The swordfish is the only member of the family *Xiphiidae*, and can be distinguished from other billfishes by its relatively long, toothless bill and lack of scales

The Swordfish is a fast-swimming, mainly open-ocean species, and it is known to undertake seasonal migrations between temperate and more tropical waters. It is also found at a range of depths, and is well adapted to temperature variations, possessing a large bundle of tissues in the head which insulates the brain. This species feeds both at the surface and at depth, eating a range of smaller fish, and invertebrates such as squid. It swallows smaller prey whole, but may use its sword-like bill to wound larger fish prior to consuming them. Generally solitary, males and females form pairs during the breeding season. In the warm waters of the Gulf of Mexico and Florida coast, spawning often occurs year-round however, in cooler regions it takes place in spring and summer.

GREAT BARRACUDA ▲ BLUE MARLIN

Scientific name:	*Sphyraena barracuda*
Identification:	Slender and streamlined, with a dark back and silvery sides which may be barred or blotched. The head is flattened between the eyes and the large mouth contains many sharp teeth
Length:	Up to 6 feet
Weight:	Up to 100lb+
Habitat/Range:	Common in coastal waters and around reefs, sometimes also found in brackish water. Occurs from Massachusetts to the Gulf of Mexico
Similar species:	The Pacific Barracuda (*Sphyraena argentea*) is a similar species found in Californian waters

Scientific name:	*Makaira nigricans*
Identification:	Dark blue back, fading to a silvery white belly, with blue spots on the sides forming vertical bars. Pectoral fins fold against the body. Leading dorsal fin is high, and the upper jaw forms a long bill
Length:	Up to $14\frac{1}{2}$ feet
Weight:	Up to 1000lb+
Habitat/Range:	Surface waters in open seas. Found along the Atlantic coast, south from New England. Also off southern California
Similar species:	The Black Marlin (*Makaira indica*) which occurs in the Pacific, has rigid pectoral fins

Superficially resembling the freshwater pike, the Great Barracuda is an efficient predatory species. It is often encountered in inshore waters, but feeds at a range of depths, hunting largely by sight. It preys upon various fish, and with its large gape and many sharp teeth, it is able to tackle even large species such as tuna. Attacks on humans are quite rare, but this is an inquisitive, aggressive fish, and in addition to a number of reported attacks, there have been some documented fatalities. Usually solitary, the Great Barracuda is sometimes found in small groups, and may congregate in larger aggregations at sea during spawning. This species is thought to breed seasonally, spawning off the Florida Keys in spring.

An important food and sport fish, the Blue Marlin is a large powerful species, capable of great speeds. However, it is protected in some coastal waters by a catch and release policy. It is found primarily at the surface where it feeds on fishes such as mackerel, tuna, and dolphinfish, but it is also known to feed at greater depths on squid and deep-sea fish. Being so large and fast-swimming, the Blue Marlin has relatively few natural predators itself, but it is preyed upon by sharks, including the White Shark. Breeding occurs in warm waters between early summer and fall, with millions of eggs being produced at a single spawning.

QUEEN ANGELFISH

Scientific name:	*Holacanthus ciliaris*
Identification:	Deep-bodied and highly compressed with a blunt, rounded head and a continuous dorsal fin. Bright blue and yellow in color with a dark, blue-ringed spot on its forehead
Length:	Up to 1½ feet
Weight:	Up to 3½ lb
Habitat/Range:	Shallow reefs in warm waters. Found around Florida and the Gulf of Mexico
Similar species:	The Blue Angelfish (*Holocanthus bermudensis*) is similar in color, but lacks the "crown" of this species

A particularly beautiful species, the Queen Angelfish is a familiar aquarium fish. It occurs naturally however, in the warm waters of tropical reefs where it generally feeds close to the bottom on plankton, algae, sponges, corals and other marine invertebrates. Generally solitary, this fish is also frequently found in pairs which are thought to form a long-term monogamous bond. Spawning involves the release of several thousand eggs at a time, which hatch in a matter of hours. The young develop rapidly, initially feeding on plankton in the water column, before settling near the bottom after a month or so. Here they reside amongst sponges, sometimes acting as "cleaner fish" for larger, often predatory species, removing parasites from their bodies, gills and mouths.

BLUE TANG ▲

Scientific name:	*Acanthurus coeruleus*
Identification:	Disk-shaped, with a continuous dorsal fin, high-set eyes and a small mouth. Juveniles are bright yellow, becoming increasingly blue or purple with age. Gray stripes may be present on flanks
Length:	Up to 14 inches
Habitat/Range:	Found around shallow reefs in the Atlantic Ocean, from New York to the Gulf of Mexico and south to Brazil
Similar species:	The Blue Tang is closely related to the Ocean Surgeon (*Acanthurus bahianus*) but may be distinguished by its coloration

The Blue Tang is a common herbivorous species which grazes on algae around reefs and rocks in weedy shallows. It may be found on its own or in pairs, but also often occurs in larger groups with other surgeonfish such as the Doctorfish (*Acanthurus chirurgus*) and Ocean Surgeon. These names are derived from the characteristic, scalpel-like spines which are located on either side of the tail. These are usually folded into a groove on the caudal peduncle, but are extended when the fish is threatened, and are able to inflict quite deep wounds. For this reason the Blue Tang should always be handled with care.

BLUEBANDED GOBY

Scientific name:	*Lythrypnus dalli*
Identification:	Small, bright orange body with up to 9 vertical, electric-blue stripes. Two dorsal fins are present, and the dorsal spines of males are longer
Length:	Up to $2\frac{1}{2}$ inches
Habitat/Range:	Rocky shallows and reefs in the Pacific Ocean around southern California
Similar species:	The Zebra Goby (*Lythrypnus zebra*) has more numerous stripes

The Bluebanded Goby belongs to the family *Gobiidae*, which is amongst the largest groups of fish in the world, containing perhaps two thousand species which occur in both fresh and saltwater habitats. Most are small, and this species is no exception. It is found in warm coastal waters, particularly around reefs and islands, and it is sometimes also known as the "Catalina Goby" due to its abundance off Santa Catalina Island. It spends most of its time on or amongst rocks which it clings to with a suction-like disc, formed by the connection of its pelvic fins. Rarely venturing far from its rocky habitat, the Bluebanded Goby darts in and out of crevices in order to feed on tiny plankton or to defend its territory. Nests are established in such locations, and following spawning the male will guard the eggs until hatching takes place.

SERGEANT MAJOR

Scientific name:	*Abudefduf saxatilis*
Identification:	Laterally compressed with a greenish-yellow back, continuous dorsal fin and white or silvery sides marked with 5 vertical, black stripes. A dark spot is present at the base of each pectoral fin
Length:	Up to 7 inches
Habitat/Range:	Coral reefs or rocky areas from Rhode Island, south beyond the Gulf of Mexico. Most abundant in the tropical and subtropical shallows of Florida and the Caribbean
Similar species:	The Night Sergeant (*Abudefduf taurus*) is darker overall with wider vertical bars

The Sergeant Major belongs to the Damselfish family, most of which are inhabitants of coral reefs. Damselfish are unusual in that almost all members of this group have a single pair of nostrils (most fish have two), and many undergo a transition from being male to female as they grow. This can sometimes make it difficult to distinguish between the sexes. However, as the Sergeant Major approaches spawning, the male adopts a deep blue coloring and becomes highly territorial, even chasing larger fish. This species is found around reefs, jetties and wrecks, and is omnivorous, feeding on plankton, small invertebrates and algae. Although it may be found quite far north, it is far more numerous in warm waters. Its name is taken from the five black bars on the flanks, reminiscent of military insignia.

DOLPHINFISH

▼

SHARKSUCKER

Scientific name:	*Coryphaena hippurus*
Identification:	Iridescent blue, green and yellow, with black and gold spots. The body is elongated, with a continuous dorsal fin, and tapers from the large mouth to a deeply forked tail. Males have a highly domed forehead
Length:	Up to 6½ feet
Weight:	Up to 87lb
Habitat/Range:	Pelagic, most common in tropical and sub-tropical waters of both oceans, but found as far north as Nova Scotia and Washington
Similar species:	The Pompano Dolphinfish (*Coryphaena equiselis*) is smaller and deeper-bodied

Scientific name:	*Echeneis naucrates*
Identification:	Slender, gray or brown with paler sides and belly. A black stripe runs from the tip of the protruding lower jaw, through the eye to the end of the tail. The leading dorsal fin is formed into a sucking disk
Length:	Up to 3 feet
Habitat/Range:	Inshore or at sea, south along the Atlantic from Nova Scotia, and in the Pacific from California
Similar species:	The Whale Sucker (*Remora australis*) and Marlin Sucker (*Remora osteochir*) tend to be more discriminating in their choice of host

A fast-swimming, schooling species, the Dolphinfish is found mainly in the open ocean, near to the surface, and is thought to travel long distances, migrating in accordance with fluctuations of temperature and the availability of food. It is a voracious predator, hunting around rafts of Sargassum weed or other floating objects where its prey may congregate for shelter. It feeds on numerous surface-dwelling fish, particularly flyingfish, but is also known to consume squid and other invertebrates. The Dolphinfish has a high metabolism and rapid growth rate, growing perhaps twelve inches or more in a year, and it is widely harvested for human consumption.

Most members of the *Remora* family, or *Echeneida*, are characterized by a highly modified dorsal fin which forms a sucker on the top of the head. They use this disk to attach themselves to large fish, marine mammals, turtles and floating objects, but they are also free-swimming. Remoras are not parasitic on their hosts, instead feeding on parasites and scraps of discarded food. Despite its name, the Sharksucker does not attach itself exclusively to sharks, but may cling to various large fish, dolphins, turtles and boats. It may at times even attempt to hitch a ride on scuba divers.

STOPLIGHT PARROTFISH ▼ CALIFORNIA SHEEPHEAD

Scientific name:	*Sparisoma rubripinne*
Identification:	Oblong and moderately compressed with a bluntly rounded head, continuous dorsal fin and beak-like mouth
Length:	Up to 2 feet
Weight:	Up to 3½ lb
Habitat/Range:	Found in shallow, tropical, Atlantic waters around southern Florida, the Gulf of Mexico, and throughout the Caribbean Sea
Similar species:	This species may be distinguished from other parrotfish by its color and patterns

Scientific name:	*Semicossyphus pulcher*
Identification:	Robust, compressed body. Females are reddish brown whilst males have a black head, rear and tail, with a red midsection. Both sexes have white chins. Head becomes domed in large individuals
Length:	Up to 3 feet
Weight:	Up to 36lb
Habitat/Range:	Rocky areas and kelp beds in shallow, inshore waters from Baja California to Monterey Bay
Similar species:	The adult California Sheephead is unlikely to be confused with other species

Stoplight Parrotfish exhibit sexual diamorphism, with some females becoming male in later life. The females and "primary" males share similar coloration, being mainly brown with rows of white spots and a bright red underside. However, those males which began life as females (referred to as terminal males) are mostly green, with orange markings on the head and edge of gill covers. They spawn throughout the year in the deeper parts of coral reefs. Stoplight Parrotfish are a herbivorous grazing species which generally inhabit shallow parts of reefs and rocky areas. They consume algae growing on rocks and the polyps which grow on calcified corals using their fused, beak-like teeth. Pharyngeal teeth in the throat are used in breaking down the hard skeletal coral that is ingested as the fish feed.

The California Sheephead is a protogynous hermaphrodite. All individuals of this species begin life as females, and undergo a dramatic transformation, becoming male at about seven or eight years of age, when they are typically around twelve inches long. During this sex change, the appearance of the Sheephead alters from a uniform red, as the rear third of the body and the head become black. The middle of the body remains red however, and the lower jaw white. Like many other wrasses, this species has enlarged canine teeth which it uses to dislodge shellfish from rocks, but it also feeds on crustaceans and soft-bodied invertebrates.

RED SNAPPER

Scientific name:	*Lutjanus campechanus*
Identification:	Deep-bodied, with a large head, small red eyes and a pointed snout. The body and fins are pinkish red, shading to a paler belly
Length:	Up to 3 feet
Weight:	Up to 20lb
Habitat/Range:	Over rocks and reefs in the Atlantic Ocean, from North Carolina south to the Gulf of Mexico and Brazil. Sometimes found further north
Similar species:	The Blackfin Snapper (*Lutjanus bucanella*) closely resembles this species but has a distinctive black spot on the pectoral fins

A popular food and sport fish, the red snapper supports a large commercial fishery, particularly on the Gulf coast. It is a carnivorous reef species, which feeds in part on small, herbivorous fish, but unlike the closely related Dog Snapper (*Lutjanus jocu*), it has not been implicated in ciguatera poisoning. The juveniles are usually found in shallows, over mud or sand, initially feeding on planktonic crustaceans. As they mature, the young begin to consume larger invertebrates such as shrimps, squid, and octopus, and they seek shelter and prey in deeper waters. The adult Red Snapper tends to occur offshore around deep reefs and wrecks. Here they feed on small fishes, mollusks and crustaceans. The Red Snapper also seeks deeper, warmer water in winter, with the peak spawning period generally being from summer through to fall.

GIANT SEA BASS ▲

Scientific name:	*Stereolepis gigas*
Identification:	Heavy-bodied, slate-gray, with black spots, though individual adults may exhibit various color patterns. Juveniles are red with black spots
Length:	Up to 7½ feet
Weight:	Up to 560lb
Habitat/Range:	Rocky reefs and inshore kelp beds, occasionally open waters. Found from Humboldt Bay to the Gulf of California
Similar species:	The Wreckfish (*Polyprion americanus*) attains a comparable size, but may be distinguished by rough, bony protuberances on its head

At one time the Giant Sea Bass was far more common in the waters of southern California; however for many years this species supported a large commercial fishery, and was subjected to further pressure by sport angling and spear fishing by divers. This species suffered particularly as it was often sought in shallow inshore waters during the summer spawning season. Just twenty years ago, the Giant Sea Bass faced the threat of extinction off the California coast, but it is currently increasing in numbers due to protective measures, including a ban on commercial and sport fishing.

OCEAN SUNFISH

Scientific name:	*Mola mola*
Identification:	Large, deep and highly compressed with extremely long dorsal and anal fins which are set well back. The tail fin is short and scalloped. Typically silvery in color
Length:	Up to 14 feet
Weight:	Up to 3300lb+
Habitat/Range:	Mainly pelagic, found in the Atlantic south of Newfoundland, and in the Pacific from British Columbia
Similar species:	The Sharp-Tailed Mola (*Masturus lanceolatu*) has a more obvious caudal fin, whilst the Slender Mola (*Ranzania laevis*) has a much narrower body

The Ocean Sunfish is the most common of the three mola species, and shares a characteristically truncated appearance, with a very blunt head and relatively small mouth. It feeds on a range of food however, from tiny planktonic organisms to larger invertebrates such as squid, jellyfish, sponges, and crustaceans. Small fish are also consumed. This species is thought to feed at a variety of depths, but it is most often encountered close to the surface, and its common name comes from its apparent sunbathing. Whilst the large size of adults precludes a great deal of predation, both Killer Whales and Sea Lions are known to attack them, and the young may be eaten by numerous carnivorous fish and mammals. The female Ocean Sunfish is incredibly fertile and produces several million eggs at a time.

QUEEN TRIGGERFISH

Scientific name:	*Balistes vetula*
Identification:	Roughly oval in shape, with a large head. Green or bluish-gray back, yellow below. Blue markings are present on the face and fins, and there is a patch of enlarged scales above each pectoral fin
Length:	Up to 2 feet
Habitat/Range:	Coral reefs, and rocky areas from Massachusetts, south to Florida, the Gulf of Mexico and beyond to Brazil. Uncommon beyond North Carolina however
Similar species:	Most other triggerfish lack enlarged pectoral scales

The Queen Triggerfish is usually found around reefs, rocks or other submerged structures, but it is also encountered in nearby sand and weed beds, foraging for food. It mainly feeds close to the bottom on invertebrates, including mollusks and sea-urchins, which are a favorite prey. In order to avoid their spines and feed on the less protected underside, the Queen Triggerfish overturns urchins by blowing water under them. Triggerfish are able to change their color in response to their surroundings, or perhaps when threatened, but their characteristic defense mechanism involves erecting three strong dorsal spines which normally lie flat on the back.

SCRAWLED COWFISH

Scientific name:	*Acanthostracion quadricornis*
Identification:	Deep, wide and box-like. Gray-green or yellowish with bright blue markings. A spine is present above each eye and at each side of the lower rear
Length:	Up to 1½ feet
Habitat/Range:	Shallow, densely vegetated coastal waters. Occurs along the Atlantic from Massachusetts to the Gulf of Mexico
Similar species:	The Honeycomb Cowfish (*Acanthostracion polygonia*) is olive colored with a dark, web-like pattern on its head

The Scrawled Cowfish is a member of the Boxfish family, *Ostraciidae*, and possesses a hard, bony carapace from its head to the base of the tail. The name "cowfish" is derived from the cow-like horns above each eye, and this species is unusual amongst Atlantic boxfish in also having projections on the rear corners of its carapace. These probably serve as a deterrent to many would-be predators. Some species are also highly poisonous, but the Scrawled Cowfish is widely caught for human consumption in the Caribbean. It feeds in weedy shallows, preying on crustaceans and soft-bodied marine invertebrates.

PORCUPINEFISH

Scientific name:	*Diodon hystrix*
Identification:	Back is gray or tan with small black spots which extend onto the fins, the underside is white. Body is covered in numerous spines. Beak-like mouth and large eyes
Length:	Up to 3 feet
Habitat/Range:	Shallow inshore waters, south from California in the Pacific, and in the Atlantic from Massachusetts to northern parts of the Gulf of Mexico, beyond to Brazil
Similar species:	The Closely related Balloonfish (*Diodon holocanthus*) is somewhat smaller and has large dark blotches only on the body

The Porcupinefish's name is derived from the presence of long spines located on the head and body. These normally lie flat, but when threatened the Porcupinefish inflates its body by taking in water, and as it expands, the spines become erect. This species is a predatory fish which feeds mainly on invertebrates, using its strong jaws to crack open the hard shells of crabs, mollusks and sea urchins. Adults are usually solitary, and are found in sheltered inshore areas, hiding amongst caves and crevices in reefs and wrecks. The young hatch in the open ocean and remain pelagic until they are about eight inches in length, often sheltering amongst floating Sargassum weed. These fish secrete toxins from their skin and are not widely caught for human consumption.

LINED SEAHORSE ▼

Scientific name:	*Hippocampus erectus*
Identification:	The vertically held body is ringed with bony plates and the head is horse-like. The tail is prehensile and normally coiled forwards. Fan-like dorsal fin
Length:	Up to 6 inches
Habitat/Range:	Occurs on shallow reefs and amongst seaweed from Nova Scotia, south along the Atlantic coast to the Gulf of Mexico and South America
Similar species:	As its name suggests, the Longsnout Seahorse (*Hippocampus reidi*) has a longer nose

The Lined Seahorse is amongst the most unusual of all fish, not only in terms of appearance, but particularly with regard to its reproductive behavior. Seahorses practice monogamy, usually pairing for life, and although males of other fish species sometimes care for their young, the male Lined Seahorse is actually equipped with a pouch into which the female deposits her eggs. They hatch after about three weeks and the young are carried until they are able to swim freely. Seahorses swim slowly, moving about and latching onto vegetation with their prehensile tails. They feed on tiny crustaceans, sucking them in with their vacuum-like snouts.

ATLANTIC NEEDLEFISH

Scientific name:	*Strongylura marina*
Identification:	Cylindrical and elongated. Blue-green back, silver underside. The jaws are very long and contain many needle-like teeth
Length:	Up to 2 feet
Habitat/Range:	Coastal shallows from New England to the Gulf of Mexico, also enters freshwater
Similar species:	The Timucu (*Strongylura timucu*) was long believed to be the same species, but is not found in freshwater

The Atlantic Needlefish belongs to the family *Belonidae,* and is closely related to the flyingfishes. It often exhibits similar behavior when swimming at speed in open waters, rising onto its tail at the surface of the water. The Atlantic Needlefish is a mainly nocturnal predatory species, equipped with a slender, toothy bill, and it preys on fry and small schooling fish as they come into inshore waters. It may be solitary or occur in small groups, and though generally found close to the shoreline, it may also be found further out and at greater depths, particularly in colder conditions. This species is known to enter streams and rivers, and is thought to spawn in both marine and freshwater habitats.

Marine Invertebrates

Above: The Giant Pacific Octopus (*Octopus dofleini*)

MOLLUSKS

Mollusks form a huge group of invertebrates, comprised of perhaps 100,000 individual species, most of which are found in marine habitats. Some are rather like the familiar, terrestrial slugs and snails, or gastropods, whilst others, such as clams and oysters, have hinged shells, and are known as bivalves. The most advanced are the cephalopods, including various species of squid, cuttlefish and octopus, which have well-developed nervous systems and brains. Mollusks are generally characterized by having soft, muscular bodies and hard protective shells (or the vestigial remnants of shells). Amongst the most primitive forms of marine mollusks are the chitons, or polyplacophora, a group which has remained largely unchanged for millions of years. They are oval in shape, with a shell composed of eight overlapping plates, and are often sedentary, found clinging to rocks and coral where they graze on algae. The **Pacific Giant Chiton** (*Cryptochiton stelleri*), also known as the **Giant Gumshoe Chiton** or **Gumboot Chiton**, is the largest species of its kind, reaching up to twelve inches in length. It feeds primarily on red algae, and is found from Alaska to California. Somewhat

more advanced, are the marine gastropods, such as abalone, limpets and nudibranchs, or sea slugs. The **Red Abalone** (*Haliotis rufescens*) also grows to around twelve inches long, but has a flattened, slightly coiled shell with a series of holes, which are used to expel water as the animal breathes. It too, grazes on algae, and it is found off the coast of California. This species is widely consumed by man, and the iridescent mother-of-pearl that lines its shell is often used in jewelry. The **Red-Gilled Nudibranch** (*Coryphella verrucosa*) is a true sea slug, and lacks a shell and gill chambers, breathing through the long, red papilla on its back. True sea slugs also have fairly advanced jaws, consisting of bony plates that are rubbed together to crush their food, and many have a nervous system which is concentrated in one place, rather like a simple brain. This species is found from Canada to New England.

After the gastropods, the largest group of marine mollusks is the bivalves, characterized by having hinged, flattened shells which enable them to filter-feed whilst being burrowed into the sediment of the seabed, and many species possess two elongated siphons with which they suck in plankton and other microscopic particles. The **Blue Mussel** (*Mytilis edulis*) is native to the Atlantic, but has been introduced to the Pacific coast, and is probably one of the most familiar bivalves, widely consumed by man. It is a sedentary creature, and at low-tide it is often found clinging to rocks or piers and jetties in large numbers. It can survive being exposed to the air for long periods of time, even when it is hot, by sealing itself tightly within its shell with a small amount of water. It secures itself to rocks and other surfaces by secreting sticky threads, which harden upon contact with the surrounding water. The **Giant Pacific Oyster** (*Crassostrea gigas*) is another edible species, and can be distinguished from other oysters by its size and shape; it has a highly elongated shell, and can grow to up to twelve inches in length. Its shell is typically grayish-white, and its exterior surface is ridged with the concentric growth rings common to most bivalves. It is found on the Pacific coast, from Canada to California. The **Soft-shelled Clam** (*Mya arenaria*), is another important commercial species, and one which has been widely introduced outside of its natural range for the purpose of human consumption. It is generally oval and grows to around four or five inches across.

Of all the mollusks, the class *Cephalopoda*, which contains squids, cuttlefishes and octopuses, is composed of the most advanced species. All are marine, and predatory, and they share such characteristics as highly developed eyes and advanced nervous systems. Unlike many mollusks, most Cephalopods lack a shell, although species such as the **Pearly Nautilus** (*Nautilus pompilius*) have a spiraling shell reminiscent of fossilized ammonites. In other species the shell has become softer and has been internalized. Members of this group may also be recognized by having grasping tentacles rather than a muscular foot. Octopuses possess eight tentacles or arms, equipped with sucker-like disks, whilst cuttlefishes and squids usually also bear an additional pair of elongated tentacles used in hunting. The **Long-finned Squid** (*Loligo pealei*) also known as the Square-toothed Squid, is a common species occurring off the eastern US, and it is one that is harvested commercially. It grows to around two feet in length and is often reddish, but its color is highly variable. Many cephalopods are able to change color in order to blend into their surroundings, or as part of their courtship and threat displays, and some are also capable of producing a cloud of "ink" to confuse or otherwise deter potential predators. Squids, cuttlefish and octopuses are able to swim freely, but many octopuses spend much of their time walking over the seabed on their tentacles. The **Pacific Giant Octopus** (*Octopus dofleini*), is amongst the largest and most highly evolved of all mollusks, and is also thought to be the most intelligent. It has been observed solving problems, such as learning how to remove prey from lobster pots for example. It may exceed 10 feet in length, and is an efficient predator of other mollusks, crustaceans and fish, but it has also been known to attack people, and large specimens should be regarded as potentially dangerous. This species is usually reddish, purple or brown, and is found along the length of the Pacific coast. The **Common Atlantic Octopus** (*Octopus vulgaris*) meanwhile is a large species which occurs from New England, south to the West Indies.

Opposite: The Pacific Oyster (*Crassostrea gigas*)
Above: The California Spiny Lobster (*Panulirus interruptus*)

CRUSTACEANS

The crustaceans are a large group which range in form from tiny planktonic shrimps to large crabs and lobsters, but all members of this group share certain distinctive characteristics. Their bodies are segmented, and contained within a chitinous exoskeleton, which in larger species acts as a protective armor, and they have two pairs of antennae, a feature which distinguishes them from all other arthropods. Almost all crustaceans are aquatic, with the exception of woodlouse species. The smallest marine crustaceans are highly important as a food source for other marine animals, including some of the largest creatures in the sea, the plankton-feeding whales, whilst many crabs and lobsters are consumed in large numbers by man. The **Spiny Lobster** (*Panulirus argus*) is a familiar and commercially important species which occurs in the Atlantic Ocean, but it has become less abundant through being caught for food in large numbers. It grows to around twelve inches long and is red and white in color, with small spines. Unlike the larger **Northern Lobster** (*Homarus americanus*) which is a more active predator, it lacks large, powerful claws, and feeds on small mollusks and carrion. The crabs are closely related to lobsters, but are somewhat more advanced, with a centralized nervous system, which enabled the development of a more compact body shape. The **Blue Crab** (*Cancer sapidus*) is a common and easily recognizable species found in the Atlantic, and is also widely eaten. It is blue or greenish, around eight or nine inches long, with an oval carapace that becomes pointed at its widest extremes. Often found walking in the shallows, the last pair of legs of this species are flattened, enabling it to swim well. Far more unusual is the **Atlantic Horseshoe Crab** (*Limulus polyphemus*) which is actually more closely related to the spiders than it is to other crabs. It is regarded as something of a relic, having changed very little from fossilized species known to date from up to 400 million years ago. This species is unmistakable, growing up to two feet in length, with a domed, leathery carapace and long tail. It is found in shallow coastal waters from Canada to the Gulf of Mexico, where it scavenges for mollusks, other invertebrates and small fish.

Above: The Giant Green Sea Anemone (*Anthopleura xanthogrammica*)

Sponges, corals and anemones are often mistaken for plants, but they are in fact amongst the most simple of multicellular animals. The sponges belong to the phylum Porifera, meaning "pore-bearing", and their interiors, which are composed of a skeletal framework of tissues and canals, open onto pore-covered surfaces. Sponges constantly circulate water through the chambers of their bodies in order to breathe and to take in plank-tonic food, and the dried, spongy skeletons of some species are familiar as bath sponges, used by man for centuries for their capacity to hold water. Sponges are found throughout the world, and most dwell in shallow coastal waters where they attach themselves to rocks and reefs. The **Boring Sponge** (*Cliona celata*), found along both North American coasts, not only attaches itself to rocks and corals, but actually bores into them by means of chemical secretions, excavating a cavity in which to live. Much of its body may then be hidden in a crevice, but this species can grow to around twelve inches in diameter. Like sponges, anemones secure themselves to rocks and other surfaces, and suck in water

to feed and respire, but they are somewhat more complex, and are characterized, as are the closely related jellyfish, by having radial symmetry, with many tentacles positioned around a central mouth. All are carnivorous, and their tentacles are typically armed with stinging cells, used both for protection, and in order to subdue their prey. Many common anemones are quite small, but the **Giant Green Anemone** (*Anthopleura xanthogrammica*), is a large species found along the Pacific Coast. It may grow to around twelve inches across, and takes its color from algae that live inside its body. Jellyfish belong to the same group of animals, known as the coelenterates or cnidaria, but differ in being free-swimming, with their tentacles hanging downwards, as opposed to projecting upwards, as in the anemones. The **Lion's Mane Jellyfish** (*Cyanea capillata*), is a large species growing up to $1\frac{1}{2}$ feet across, and its tentacles may extend to over thirty feet in length. It is often encountered close to the surface where it consumes prey as large as fish, and its sting can be dangerous to people. It is found on both coasts of North America.

ECHINODERMS

Many echinoderms exhibit a radial symmetry similar to that of anemones or jellyfish, but in starfish, for example, the body is divided into separate arms, whilst sea cucumbers are elongated. Most species also have a separate mouth and anus, rather than a single opening leading to a digestive cavity. Echinoderms typically have spiny skin and tubercles or tube feet which may be used for locomotion, manipulating food or for defense. Starfish, or sea stars are probably the most well known examples of this group, and they demonstrate considerable variation, from the more robust, heavy-bodied individuals, to feathery, fragile-looking species. **Forbes' Sea Star** (*Asterias forbesi*), is a medium-size specimen, common along Atlantic shorelines from New England to the Gulf of Mexico. It grows to about 10 inches in diameter, and like most starfish, usually has five arms. It is highly variable in color, ranging from brown or green, through various reds to orange or purple, and is covered in small spines. It moves quickly on its tube feet, searching for prey on rocks or on the seabed, feeding on small mollusks such as snails, clams, mussels and oysters. Sea Urchins are also familiar and common echinoderms, and although many species are spherical and spiky, the sand dollars are flattened and usually covered with very short spines. The **Common Sand Dollar** (*Echinarachinius parma*), is an abundant species found along the Atlantic coast around Canada and the northern US, and is frequently washed up on beaches or buried in sandy shallows. It is usually brownish or purple in color, and has radial, petal-like markings on its topside. A more characteristic urchin is the **Green Sea Urchin** (*Strongylocentrotus droebachiensis*), which is spherical, around 3 inches in diameter, and covered in spines up to $\frac{1}{2}$ an inch long. It inhabits colder waters along both North American coasts, feeding on algae which it grazes from rocks. The sea cucumbers are elongated, but also display the characteristic five-pointed symmetry. They usually have tube feet on their undersides, which they use to move about on the ocean floor, and numerous spines or tentacles on their uppermost side. They vary greatly in size and color, but the **California Sea Cucumber** (*Stichopus californicus*), is a typical example, around twelve inches long and two inches in diameter. Like many sea cucumbers it is often quite brightly colored, probably as a defense mechanism, and some species are able to envelop and immobilize potential predators with a web of threadlike tubes which they eject from the anus.

Below: The California Sea Cucumber

Index to Common Names

Picture Credits

Abert's Squirrel Mickey Gibson/AA   Alligator Stan Osolinski   Alligator (pages 154/1550) Philippe Henry   Alligator Gar Wolfgang Polzer/Okapia   Alligator snapping turtle OSF   American Black Duck Leonard Lee Rue III   American bumblebee Breck P. Kent/AA   American cockroach OSF   American Coot Stan Osolinski   American crocodile Stan Osolinski   American Crow Breck P Kent   American Dipper James H Robinson   American eel J&F Burek/AA   American Kestrel Lon E Lauber   American Redstart Richard Day   American Robin Richard Day   American toads Zig Leszczynski/AA   American White Pelican Bob Bennett   Anhinga John Netherton   Apis mellifera Satoshi Kuribayashi   Arctic fox Tony Martin   Arizona scorpion John Mitchell   Atlantic cod Doug Allan   Atlantic salmon Andreas Hartl/Okapia   Backswimmer James H. Robinson   Badger Michael Cox   Bald eagle flying (inside and front cover) Lon E. Lauber   Bald eagles (in tree) W. Shattil & Bob Rozinski   Banded gecko Zig Leszczynski/AA   Bank swallow G A Maclean   Barn owl (inside and back cover) Bill Paton   Barn swallow Terry Andrewartha   Barrows Goldeneye Chris Sharp   Beaver Stan Osolinski   Bee assassin Brian Kenney   Belted Kingfisher Richard Day   Beluga whale Bruce Macdonald/AA   Big brown bat Fred Whitehead/AA   Bighorn sheep Ray Richardson/AA   Bison C.C. Lockwood/AA   Bison in the sunset (pages 78/9) Alan & Sandy Carey   Black & White warbler Robert Lubeck   Black bear (eating berries) Daniel Cox   Black bear Judd Cooney   Black billed magpie Mark Hamblin   Black Capped Chickadee Ken Cole   Black carpenter ants Donald specker   Black rat Bert and Babs Wells   Black Skimmer Frank Schneidermeyer   Black swallowtail Brian Kenney   Black Tern Dennis Green   Black widow John Cooke   Black widow Scott Camazine   Black-and-yellow argiope Prof Jack Dermid   Black-footed ferret Richard Kolar/AA   Black-tailed jackrabbit (inside and back cover) Stan Osolinski   Blanding's turtle Stan Osolinski   Blotched porcupinefish Karen Glowett-Holmes   Blue grouse Matthias Breiter   Blue Jay Mike Price   Blue shark Tobias Bernhard   Blue tang Laurence Gould   Blue-Gray gnatcatcher Richard Day   Blue-spotted salamander (front cover) Breck P. Kent   Bobcat (inside and front cover) Daniel Cox   Boblink John Gerlack   Bohemian waxwing Mark Hamblin   Boreal red-backed vole Tom Ulrich   Bottle nosed dolphins (jumping) Konrad Wothe   Bottle-nosed dolphin Howard Hall   Broad-headed skink Zig Leszczynski/AA   Brook lamprey Andreas Hartl/Okapia   Brook trout W. Gregory Brown/AA   Brown bear (front cover) Daniel Cox   Brown bear resting Mattias Breiter   Brown bear pages 8/9 Daniel Cox   Brown headed cowbird Richard Packwood   Brown pelican Marie Read   Brown thresher Tom Ulrich   Brown trout OSF   Bufflehead Mark Hamblin   Bull frog Joe McDonald/AA   Bull snake OSF   Burbot Dr F. Ehrenstrom & L Beyer   Burrowing owl Stan Osolinski   Bushtit John Anderson   California legless lizard Zig Leszczynski/AA   California sea cucumber Richard Herrmann   California spiny lobster Howard Hall   Californian sea lions Frank Schneidermeyer   Canada geese (pages 182/3) Daniel Cox   Canada Goose Henry R. Fox/AA   Canada lynx Daniel Cox   Caribou Bennett Productions/SAL   Carolina locust Brian Kenney   Carp Rudie Kuiter   Catfish AA   Cedar waxwing Tom Ulrich   Chimney Swift Richard Day   Chipping Sparrow Tom Ulrich   Chuckwalla D.& J.Bartlett/SAL   Clarkes Nutcracker Tom Ulrich   Cloudless sulphur Brian Kenney   Coast horned lizard Zig Leszczynski/AA   Coati Daniel Cox   Collared lizard John Gerlach/AA   Collared peccary D& M Zimmerman   Common Merganser Konrad Wothe   Common goldeneye Mark Hamblin   Common Grackle Richard Day   Common loon Daniel Cox   Common Moorhen Geoff Kidd   Common nighthawk Richard Day   Common rat Mark Hamblin   Common raven Richard Packwood   Common Snipe Bob Rozinski   Common tern Manfred Pfefferle   Common toad Paulo de Oliveira   Copperhead Tom Ulrich   Corn snake Prof Jack Dermid   Cottnmouth Zig Leszczynski   Coyote Victoria McCormick/AA   Desert iguana Zig Leszczynski/AA   Desert tortoise Stan Osolinski   Differential grasshopper E. R. Degginger/AA   Dolphinfish Richard Hippurus   Double Crested Cormorant William Gray   Downy Woodpecker Richard Day   Dunlin Tony Tilford   E. bluebird Tom Ulrich   E. box turtle Zig Leszczynski/AA   E. chipmunk Mark Hamblin   E. coral snake Zig Leszczynski/AA   E. cottontail Stan Osolinski   E. diamond back rattlesnake AA   E. fence lizard David M Dennis   E. Fox Squirrel Tom Ulrich   E. hog nose snake Zig Leszczynski   E. indigo snake Brian Kenney   E. king snake Zig Leszczynski   E. Kingbird Joe McDonald   E. Meadowlark John Harris   E. milk snake David M Dennis   E. Mole Brian Kennedy   E. ribbon snake Breck P.Kent/AA   E. Screech Owl John Netheron   E. slender grass lizard Zig Leszczynski/AA   E. spadefoot toads Zig Leszczynski/AA   E.-tailed blue butterfly Daybreak imagery   Ebony jewelwing Tom Leach   Elephant seal B.C. Harrison   Elk Tom Ulrich   Epallipes John Mitchell   Evening Grosbeak John Gerlack Fisher Daybreak Imagery   Florida chicken turtle David M. Dennis   Forficula auricularia OSF   Fork-tailed katytid OSF   Fox Sparrow Michael Habicht   Giant black seabass Richard Herrmann   Giant green sea anenome Anne Wertheim/AA   Giant Ichneumon wasp J.H. Robinson   Giant pacific octopus Rodger Jackman   Gila monster Claude Steelman/SAL   Golden Crowned Kinglet T C Nature   Golden Eagle Konrad Wothe   Golden-mantled squirrel Stan Osolinski   Gopher tortoise Prof Jack Dermid   Gray Catbird Stan Osolinski   Gray hairstreak butterfly Patti Murray/AA   Gray wolf Lon E. Lauber   Gray wolf (in snow) Steve Turner   Great Barracuda Tobias Bernhard   Great Black-Backed Gull Richard Packwood   Great Blue Heron Frank Huber   Great egret Stan Osolinski   Great horned owl Mike Hill   Great plains toad Michael Fogden   Great Roadrunner James Robinson   Great spangled fritillary (pages 276/7) Daybreak imagery   Great white shark Tobias Bernhard   Greater Yellowlegs Tom Leach   Green anole James H. Robinson   Green bottle fly James H. Robinson   Green darner Scott Camazine   Green frog Zig Leszczynski/AA   Green lacewing Harry Fox   Green moray Thomas Haider   Green sea turtle David Fleetham (inside and front cover)   Green stink bug Bill Beaty/AA   Green tree frog Brian Kenney   Grey squirrel Mike Birkhead   Grey whale Scott Winer   *Gryllus pennsylvanicus* James E. Lloyd/AA   Gypsy moth Harry Fox   Hairy Woodpecker Alan G Nelson   Halloween pennant Brian Kenney   Harbor seal Joe McDonald/OPAKIA   Harlequin bug nymphs Bill Beaty/AA   Harp seal Doug Allan   Hawksbill turtle David Fleetham   Hellbender salamander David M. Dennis   *Hemaris thysbe* Brian Kenney   Hermit thrush Tom Ulrich   Herring gull Mark Hamblin   Hoary marmot Jack Wilburn/AA   Hooded Merganser Frank Schneidermeyer   House mouse Roger Jackman   House wren Niall Benvie   Housefly Donald Specker/AA   Humpback whale David Fleetham   Indigo bunting Tony Tilford   Japanese beetle Donald Specker/AA   Killdeer Stan Osolinski   Killer whale Tobias Bernhard   Killer whale (pages 90/91) Jeff Foott/OKAPIA   King mackerel Henry Ausloos   Kit fox Claude Steelman/SAL   Large mouth bass Zig leszczynski/AA   Laughing gull Pattie Murrey   Least chipmunk Stan Osolinski   Least flycatcher Ted Levin Least sandpiper Terry Andrewartha Leatherback turtle Olivier Grunewald Leopard frog OSF Leopard lizard OSF Lesser earless lizard (pages 122/123) Raymond Mendez/AA Lesser gray treefrog Joe McDonald/AA Little brown bat Joe McDonald/AA Loggerhead Shrike Charles Palek Loggerhead turtle Howard Hall Longlure frog fish Mark Webster Long-tailed weasel Judd Cooney Luna moth John Mitchell Magnolia warbler Robert Lubeck Mallard Richard Packwood Manatee Herb Segars/AA Manta ray Howard Hall Manta Ray Richard Hall Marbled salamander Zig Leszczynski/AA Meadow vole Breck P. Kent Mexican bats at sunset Mary Plage Mink Tom Ulrich Mink frog Chris Sharp Minke whale Sylvia Stevens/OPAKIA Monarch butterfly Dennis Green/SAL Moose Harry engels/AA Mosquito fish Kathie Atkinson Mountain goat David C. Firtts/AA Mountain lion (in snow) Ronald Toms Mourning dove Jack Dermid Mudpuppy Prof Jack Dermid Mule deer Stan Osolinski Muskox Lon E. Lauber Muskrat Tom Ulrich Mute swan Norbert Rosing Nine banded armadilllo Alan Root/SAL Northern cardinal Tom Ulrich N. cricket frog Zig Leszczynski/AA N. diamondback terrapin Zig Leszczynski/AA N. elephant seal Howard Hall N. Harrier Mark Hamblin N. hog sucker Raymond Mendez/AA N. Mockingbird Stan Osolinski N. pike Dr F Ehrenstrom & L Beyer N. Pintail Eric Woods N. red salamander Zig Leszczynski/AA N. water snake Breck P. Kent/AA Nurse shark OSF Nutria Leonard Lee Rue III/AA Ocean sunfish Richard Herrmann Opposum Tom Ulrich Ord's kangaroo rat W. Shattil & Bob Rozinski Osprey Alain Christof Pacific bluefin tuna Richard Herrmann Pacific oyster Karen Gowlett-Holmes Paddlefish Norbert Wu Painted bunting Tom Ulrich Painted lady Paul Franklin Painted turtles Stan Osolinski Peregrine falcon W. Shattil & Bob Rozinski Pickerel Breck Kent/AA Pickerel frog Zig Leszczynski/AA Pied-Billled grebe Stan Osolinski Pika Tom Ulrich Pilot Black or Black rat snake Zig Leszczynski Pine marten Tom Ulrich Pink salmon (pages 322/323) Victoria McCormick/AA Polar bear Dan Guravich Polar bears fighting Daniel Cox Polar bear with cub Daniel Cox Polyphemus moth David M. Dennis Porcupine Ronald Toms Prairie dog Zig Leszczynski Prairie Falcon Steve Turner Praying mantis Daniel Cox Praying mantis (landscape) Manfred Pfefferie Pronghorn Tom Ulrich Puffins Mark Hamblin Pumkinseed Paul Kay Queen angelfish Zig Leszczynski/AA Queen butterfly Daybreak imagery Queen trigger fish Zig Leszczynski/AA Racoon (inside and front cover) Daniel Cox Rainbow darter Raymond Mendez/AA Rainbow trout Rudie Kuiter Red admiral D J. Saunders Red banded leafhopper Kjell Sandved Red bat Prof Jack Dermid Red breasted nuthatch John Gerlach Red Crossbill Hans Reinhard Red fox W. Shantil & B. Rozinski Red fox Breck P. Kent/AA Red sockeye salmon Richard Herrmann Red squirrel Niall Benvie Red winged blackbird Frank Schneidermeyer Red wolf Robert Winslow/AA Red-headed Woodpecker Richard Day Red-shouldered hawk David Tipling Red-Tailed Hawk Tom Ulrich Regal moth Prof Jack Dermid Ring Billed Gull Joe McDonald Ring neck snake OSF Ring-Necked Pheasant Richard Packwood Ring-tailed cat W. Shattil & B. Rozinski River otter Tom Ulrich Robber fly wasp James H. Robinson Rock Dove Stan Osolinski Rock Squirrel Stan Osolinski Rosy boa Mike Linley/SAL Rough green snake Joe McDonald/AA Rough-skinned newt David M. Dennis Rubber boa David M Dennis Ruby Crowned Kinglet Michael Habicht Ruby-Thoroated Hummingbird Richard Day Ruffed Grouse Stan Osolinski Rufous hummingbird Robert Tyrell Sagebrush lizard John Gerlach/AA Savannah Sparrow Tom Ulrich Sawfish Norbert Wu Scalloped hammerhead shark Gerard Soury Scarlett Tanager Tom Edwards Sea lamprey Breck P. Kent/AA Sea otter Howard Hall Seahorse OSF Seargent major Laurence Gould Semipalmated Plover Tom Ulrich Sharp-Shinned

Hawk Alan G Nelson Shiner perch Rodger Jackman Short-tailed shrew Breck P. Kent/AA Short-tailed weasel Tom Ulrich Silver argiope Prof Jack Dermid Six-lined racerunner Prof Jack Dermid Small copper butterfly John Woolmer Small white butterfly Gordon Mclean Snapping turtle Leonard Lee Rue III/AA Snow bunting Tom Leach Snow Goose John Gerlach Snowshoe hair A&S Carey Snowy owl Konrad Wothe Sockeye salmon (page 378) Daniel Cox Song Sparrow Chris Sharp South-eastern 5-lined skink Zig Leszczynski/AA Southern flying squirrel Maresa Pryor/AA Southern stingray Norbert Wu Spangled fritillary Richard Kolar/AA Spectacled caiman Richard Packwood Spectacled caiman Michael fogden Sperm whale Howard Hall Spiny softshell David M. Dennis Spotlight parrotfish Paul Kay Spotted salamander Zig Leszczynski/AA Spring peeper Zig Leszczynski/AA Star-nosed mole Mike and Elvan Habicht/AA Starry flounder Joanne Huemoellar Stellers Jay Len Rue Jnr Striped hawk moth Irvine Cushing Summer Tanager Lon Lauber Swordfish Norbert Wu Tarantula Marty Cordano Ten-lined June beetle Marty Cordano Termites James H. Robinson Thirteen-lined squirrel John Gerlach/AA Tiger salamander Marty Cordano Tiger swallowtail John Mitchell Timber rattlesnake Frank Schneidermeyer Timber rattlesnake Tom Ulrich Tree Swallow Ken Cole *Triatoma protracta* Richard Sheill/AA Trumpeter swan Stan Osolinski Tufted Titmouse N V Howell Tundra Swan John Downer Turkey vulture Ben Osborne Two-spotted ladybird Harold Taylor Varied thrush Michael Habicht Viceroy butterfly (inside and back cover) PJ DeVries Walrus Leonard Lee Rue III/AA Western box turtle OSF W. Grebe Don Enger W. harvest mouse W. Shattil and B Rozinski W. Meadowlark Frank Schneidermeyer W. nosed shovel snake Marty Cordano W. rattlesnake Tom Ulrich W. swallowtail butterfly Kjell Sandved W. Tanager James H Robinson Whale shark (pages 346/7) Tammy Peluso White Crowned Sparrow Daniel J Cox White Throated Sparrow Daniel J Cox White whale Jeff Foott/OKAPIA White-tailed deer Zig Leszczynski Willet Stan Osolinski Wolverine Michael Cox Wood frog Richard Kolar/AA Wood nymph John Gerlach/AA Wood turtle Breck P. Kent/AA Woodchuck Mark Hamblin Woodhouse's toad W. Shattil & B. Rozinski Worm snake Michael Fogden Yellow Billed Cuckoo Richard Day Yellow-eyed junco Joe McDonald Yellow jacket Breck P. Kent/AA Yellow perch Breck Kent/AA Yellow rumped warbler Richard Day Yellow Warbler Kenneth Day Yellow-bellied marmot W. Shattil and Bob Rozinski Zebra longwing butterfly Brian Kenney

Bibliography

National Audibon Society Field Guide to Mammals Revised Edition John O. Whittaker, Knopf, New York, 1986

Princeton Field Guides Mammals of North America Ronald W. Kays and Don E. Wilson, Princeton University Press, Princeton, 2002

The Encylopedia of North American Birds Michael Vanner, Parragon, Bath, UK, 2002

The Golden Field Guide: Reptiles of North America Hobart M. Smith and Edmund D. Brodie Jnr., St Martin's Press, New York, 1982

The National Audibon Society Guide to Familiar Reptiles and Amphibians of North America, John L. Behler, Alfred A. Knopf, New York, 1988

North American Wildlife: Mammals, Reptiles and Amphibians, Reader's Digest, 1998

National Audubon Society Field Guide to Fishes Carter R. Gilbert and James D. Williams, Alfred A. Knofp, New York, 2002

Peterson Field Guide to Reptiles and Amphibians Rober Conant and Joseph T. Collins, Houghton Mifflin Company, New York, 1998

National Audubon Society Pocket Guide: Familiar Mammals of North America, Alfred A. Knopf, New York, 1988

National Audubon Society Pocket Guide: Insects and Spiders, Alfred A. Knopf, New York, 1988

National Audubon Society First Field Guide: Insects, Christina Wilsdon, Scholastic, New York, 1 998

Peterson First Guides:Butterflies and Moths, Paul A. Opler, Houghton Mifflin, New York, 1994

Peterson First Guides: Fishes, Michael Filisky, Houghton Mifflin, New York, 1989

An Instant Guide to Mammals, Pamela Forey and Cecilia Fitzsimons, Gramercy, New York, 2001

Simon & Schusters Guide to Insects, Dr Ross H. Arnett, Jr., & Dr Richard L. Jacques, Jr., Simon & Schuster, New York, 1981

Harper Collins Complete North American Wildlife: A Photo Field Guide, Gerard A. Bertrand, John A. Burton & Paul Sterry, Harper Collins, New York, 2003

North American Wildlife, Susan J. Wernert, Reader's Digest, New York, 1982

Nature in America, Reader's Digest, New York, 1991

Acknowledgements

Thank you to Ruth Blair and all the research staff at Oxford Scientific Films and Animals Animals in New York. Thanks also to Judy Linard, Simon Pittaway, Kate Truman, Vickie Harris and Graeme Whitfield, Jill Dormon and Paul Pang.